A Most Perilous World

A Most Perilous World

The True Story of the Young Abolitionists and Their Crusade Against Slavery

Kristina R. Gaddy

Kristina R. Gaddy

DUTTON BOOKS

DUTTON BOOKS

An imprint of Penguin Random House LLC

1745 Broadway, New York, New York 10019

First published in the United States of America by Dutton Books,
an imprint of Penguin Random House LLC, 2025

Visit us online at PenguinRandomHouse.com.

Library of Congress Cataloging-in-Publication Data is available.

ISBN 9780593855522

1   3   5   7   9   10   8   6   4   2

Printed in the United States of America

BVG

Design by Anna Booth
Text set in MillerText

The authorized representative in the EU for product safety and compliance is
Penguin Random House Ireland, Morrison Chambers, 32 Nassau Street,
Dublin D02 YH68, Ireland, https://eu-contact.penguin.ie.

For Sidney, Ellis, and Bo

TABLE OF CONTENTS

Kristina R. Gaddy

BALTIMORE, MARYLAND
2025

"How lukewarm we have been!"** Lucy McKim's words made my arms prickle with goose bumps. "Lukewarm"? Could she really think that? I was reading a biography of McKim because she went on to be the driving force behind the 1867 book *Slave Songs of the United States*, the first collection of Black American music ever published, a work I was briefly featuring in my last book, *Well of Souls: Uncovering the Banjo's Hidden History*.

Lucy grew up in the years before the Civil War, daughter of the president of the Pennsylvania Anti-Slavery Society in a household that took in people who escaped slavery on the Underground Railroad. And yet her family was "lukewarm." When she saw the aftermath of slavery firsthand in 1862 in Union-occupied South Carolina, she thought the abolitionists hadn't done enough. I fell a little bit in love with Lucy, to be honest. She was smart, passionate, artistic, and at times, a little depressed and lost. She was also unmistakably a young adult coming of age during the bloodiest conflict her nation had ever known. Months before the outbreak of the Civil War, she mused to her best friend about her favorite pastimes, including novels, poetry, music, and watching sunsets from the shore "alone." Less than two years later, she told that same friend, "We shall dance at funerals next year & flirt across corpses."

Her story was too far removed from the banjo's story in South Carolina, so most of what I wrote about her got cut from *Well of Souls*, but I couldn't stop thinking about Lucy McKim.

I had never imagined what it would be like growing up in a household where everything was singularly focused on the anti-slavery cause. I knew about Lucy's parents' generation of abolitionists—many of us do. While Lucy's father, Miller McKim, might be less well-known today, he was good friends with figurehead of the movement William Lloyd Garrison, who had mentored Frederick Douglass, before an ideological split in the movement turned them into rivals. In reading Lucy's biography, I learned how unconventional her life was. Everything from her bedtime stories to her playmates to her schooling instilled in her the ideas that no person should be held in bondage and that no person had more rights than another. She also lived with violence and chaos, not knowing if her parents would die or be arrested for what they believed in. And this was before the Civil War began and her peers started dying.

There were others who lived this life, too. Garrison, Douglass, and their friends had children around Lucy's age—kids born in the late 1830s and early 1840s, who grew up in high-achieving families with expectations of dedicating their own lives to the unpopular and often dangerous anti-slavery cause.

What was more amazing to me was that no one had written about the lives of these young people from their perspective. William Lloyd Garrison spent his career writing and speaking about anti-slavery and raising money for the cause. A week after Garrison's son George was born in 1836, Garrison wrote in his newspaper *The Liberator* that his son was to "abhor oppression [and] cling to liberty" and dedicate himself to bringing "freedom for all and servile chains undone." Yet even from childhood, George didn't fit his father's version of what it meant to be an abolitionist. He didn't like reading, and he couldn't ever seem to sit still.

When Frederick Douglass's oldest son, Lewis, was born, the most important thing to Douglass was that Lewis was born free. "There are no slaveholders here to rend my heart by snatching [my children] from my arms, or blast a mother's dearest hopes by tearing them from her bosom," Douglass wrote in a public letter to his former enslaver in Maryland. Douglass had escaped enslavement and gone on to become one of the most prominent anti-slavery speakers in the world. Lewis came to understand that freedom and equal rights were paramount, yet he didn't know how those would come to a young Black man like him.

Charlotte Forten faced similar crises of faith, compounded by the fact that she was a Black woman. Her grandfather was a free Black man several generations removed from slavery. He was also a successful business owner and gave Garrison money to support the first issue of *The Liberator*, and her aunts Harriet and Margaretta Forten founded the Philadelphia Female Anti-Slavery Society when they, as women, were not allowed in the Pennsylvania Anti-Slavery Society. Being a Forten meant being politically active, socially minded, and proud of being Black. Charlotte wanted all of those things, but she struggled because sometimes the burden was too heavy.

The shadows that William Lloyd Garrison, Frederick Douglass, Miller McKim, and Harriet and Margaretta Forten cast were long, their expectations of the next generation great. Could George, Lewis, Charlotte, and Lucy really step out from those shadows *and* meet their parents' expectations? Could they do that while being their own people? And by the way, did they even always agree with the older generation? Was that generation actually radical enough when it came to something as important as liberty and justice for all?

I learned George, Lewis, Charlotte, and Lucy couldn't just do what their parents did. They had to try to become their own version of young abolitionists.

"The Resurrection of Henry Box Brown at Philadelphia." On Friday, March 30, 1849, Henry Brown arrived at the Pennsylvania Anti-Slavery Society's offices in Philadelphia, where Lucy McKim's father, Miller, worked.

Lucy McKim

**PHILADELPHIA, PENNSYLVANIA
1849**

L ucy McKim's father stepped inside the door of their Philadelphia home together with a Black man Lucy didn't recognize. The man seemed hungry and tired. It was Friday, March 30, 1849, and for six-year-old Lucy, it wasn't unusual that her father came home with a man she didn't know and that the man took a bath and ate breakfast here. People always came and went from their house. Her father would go to his office and come home for supper with a colleague from work. They'd go back out for a lecture, and maybe an out-of-town visitor would come back to spend the night. Her father trusted the people who he invited in; it was too dangerous not to.

This guest was special, and her father had anxiously awaited his arrival. His name was Henry Brown, and he had shipped himself in a box from Richmond, Virginia, to Lucy's father's office. Her father was Miller McKim, the president of the Pennsylvania Anti-Slavery Society, and he sold anti-slavery books, tried to get people to buy sugar and fabric that wasn't made by enslaved people, and helped run a newspaper that advocated for the abolition of slavery.

Henry Brown arrived in a box because he was enslaved—another man owned him—and Brown wanted to escape. Running away from Virginia to Pennsylvania was dangerous, especially if he had tried to walk or take a carriage or boat. Men hunted runaways for money and returned them to the enslavers. Henry Brown had decided it was better to lock himself in a box with only water and crackers for twenty-seven hours than remain in slavery.

Brown's job in Virginia had been to twist tobacco leaves into knots, which made his hands perpetually sticky and covered in nicotine. He had "escaped the lash almost entirely," but knew that if his owner[1] wanted to beat him, he could. The main reason Brown wanted to escape, though, was because he'd lost what was most important to him: his family. Brown's family was like Lucy's: father, mother, and three children. Only Brown's family were all enslaved, and a year earlier, his wife and children had been sold. Their owner promised Brown he could buy them, but then sold them to another man. With nothing to lose, Brown made his choice to escape.

Soon, people would call him Box Brown, and his tale would become the kind of anti-slavery story Lucy might read in a book. A man hides in a box to escape his evil enslaver. He gets turned upside down and right side up until finally he arrives and is freed from his box to a land of promise. Only Brown's story was true, and everyone was amazed by it.

Lucy's parents used books to teach her and her siblings about the anti-slavery cause. Three years earlier, *The Anti-Slavery Alphabet* appeared at the Philadelphia Female Anti-Slavery Society's Christmas fair, which her mother helped organize. The first page read:

A is for Abolitionist—
A man who wants to free

---

1. In my book *Well of Souls*, I wrote my about my choice to use the words *slave owner* over *enslaver*: "The word enslave is a verb meaning to subjugate into slavery, and so the noun enslaver is someone who makes someone a slave. . . . [people mentioned] in this book are the owners of enslaved men, women, and children and responsible for their continued enslavement." In the years since I've written that, I sometimes question it. If an enslaver is someone who makes a person a slave, isn't the continued enslavement continuing to make a person a slave? However, I also find it important to remember that the enslaver/slave owner did, as far as the law was concerned, *own* a person in the same way he owned land or livestock, and that *enslaver* can diminish that very harsh reality. I have used the two interchangeably in this text.

The wretched slave—and give all
An equal liberty.

Lucy knew she was an abolitionist, a girl who wanted all enslaved people to be free with equal liberty.

The Young Abolitionists, or Conversations on Slavery was a novel for young readers published just a year before Henry Brown's escape. In the book, Jenie and Charlie's mother tells them about the realities of slavery.

"Charlie says that in this country there are slave men and slave women; they don't make slaves of little children, do they, and burn *their* faces, and whip *them* till the blood runs?" Jenie asks her mother.

"Yes, my daughter, the slaveholders make slaves of just such little girls as you are."

A girl younger than Lucy could be enslaved, but Lucy also knew that she wouldn't be a slave. In the alphabet, *B* was for "a Brother with a skin / Of somewhat darker hue." Slaves were Black. Henry Brown was Black. Lucy had brown hair, gray eyes, and pale skin. She was white, and in this country, it was Black people—people who had an ancestor who had been taken from Africa—who could be enslaved. For hundreds of years, people had used religion and bad science to justify the myth of the inferiority of Black people and slavery.

What happened to Henry Brown wasn't a story, though, and Lucy and the children of abolitionists also didn't need made-up stories to teach them the realities of slavery.

A man—or a woman or a child—took desperate measures to escape. Abolitionists who were willing to risk their own safety took these escapees in. They also did more; they dedicated their whole lives—from what they wore and ate to what they said and did—to the anti-slavery cause.

On the last page of the alphabet, Lucy read that this was her calling, too.

Y is for Youth—the time for all
Bravely to war with sin;
And think not it can ever be
Too early to begin.

Freedom and Bondage

"May he be trained up in the way he should go—for he has been brought into a most perilous world."

—WILLIAM LLOYD GARRISON

CHAPTER 1

Lewis Douglass

ROCHESTER, NEW YORK
1854

O ut the window of their home on a hill, thirteen-year-old Lewis Douglass could see who was coming. The rain would fall on the wagon pulling up the private drive a few miles outside the center of Rochester, New York. The moonlight would glow on the strange lady coming through his mother's garden. The snow would cover the footsteps of the family walking to the door.

When the visitors reached the house, they didn't need to say who they were or why they were there. Lewis and his family knew. His father might open the door. His father was, people said, handsome, with light brown skin and his wavy hair parted to one side, although his brow seemed to naturally furrow, making him look more serious than he always was. His father was the famous anti-slavery activist Frederick Douglass, and white people seemed to appreciate his speeches more because he was handsome, lighter-skinned, and serious. The Black people who turned up at their house appreciated a friendly face that looked like them.

They were welcomed by Lewis's mother, Anna, whose eyes were larger and more welcoming than his father's, although she could be stern, too. Lewis looked more like his mother, with big eyes, a long face, and darker skin.

The visitors would smell the food Lewis's mother had been cooking. She would want to make sure the guests had something to eat. They might not have eaten in days.

Lewis and his brothers, Charles and Fred, made a fire and a bed and conveyed the people to a room when they were ready. To smell the newly cooked meal, to feel the warmth of the fire, to relax in a bed and think that they were safe tonight, and would soon be safe forever, were such welcome experiences. The Douglass home was less than fifteen miles away from Lake Ontario, from boats that could take the people to freedom in Canada.

When the visitors were ready, they might share how they had come to be here. A woman from Kentucky might tell Lewis how, in Ohio, she had picked up her disguise of a Quaker with a black dress and large bonnet. A father from farther south might inform Lewis and his family that his own wife had been sold, and he'd escaped with their three-week-old daughter so she wouldn't be taken from him, too. A man might tell Lewis he had slipped onto a ship in Virginia, hidden in a space that wasn't larger than a coffin, and disembarked in Boston before crossing Massachusetts and New York in a carriage. Lewis's own father had escaped enslavement in Maryland by sneaking out of Baltimore on a ship.

These people had traveled through a land of shadows, and of dreams, and Lewis's home shone a light for such travelers, held ground for such travelers. Although Lewis had been born free, he knew of the held breaths, the fear of watchmen at the gates and slave patrollers in the forest. Behind their visitors was slavery, "already crimsoned with the blood of millions," as Lewis's father wrote, and in front of them, "the flickering lights of the North Star" and freedom.

As Lewis and his family took in the visitors' stories, they knew to still hold their breaths. Lewis's family may have made their home comfortable, but in New York, someone could still arrest a runaway. The new Fugitive Slave Law of 1850 said a man could come to Lewis's house and arrest these people and take them back to the South. Four years ago, just after the law had passed, a "party of manhunters" came to Rochester looking for Lewis's father. His father didn't know whether the documents saying he was a free man mattered, whether these men cared that he was free. His father hid in the house and told his friends to keep an eye out for suspicious-looking white men. They had moved to this country house to be farther from the city, to create a place of safety. But could one be sure the hunters would not come another night? A night when fugitives might be hiding inside?

When the people were safely hidden in the house, Lewis and his brothers passed notes to family friends about the activities of the Underground Railroad and asked for donations so they could purchase a ticket for a boat trip across Lake Ontario.

Lewis might shuffle them into a carriage or hide them under a blanket in the wagon and then follow the Genesee River north to where it emptied into the lake at the Charlotte lighthouse. The people would board a steamboat or schooner that Lewis trusted.

They vanished across the lake like the morning fog, never to return to Rochester, and one supposed they'd finally be able to take a breath. They would no longer be *runaway slaves* or *fugitives*, but free people.

Four years had passed since the Fugitive Slave Law went into effect, and Lewis had seen hundreds of people come through Rochester on their way to freedom. His mother made sure their home was always open, even if that invited danger in. For every person they opened the door to, Lewis's mother and father could face six months in jail or a thousand-dollar fine. Lewis would not exist if his father had not escaped, and their family would not be here if not for those who had helped his father. So what was six months in jail or a fine if they could give one person freedom, one family a chance?

CHAPTER 2

George Garrison

BOSTON, MASSACHUSETTS
MAY 1854

Just like he did most mornings, eighteen-year-old George Garrison left his family's home on Dix Place and walked to his job at G.P. Reed's music store in central Boston. Along the winding streets in the city center, horses pulled carriages past shops that were opening, banks got ready for the day, and newspaper offices eagerly awaited messages on the telegraph wire. A few blocks from the music store was the office of *The Liberator*, the abolitionist newspaper George's father, William Lloyd Garrison, had founded and edited. This Wednesday, May 24, 1854, everyone was especially eager for information. On Monday, the US House of Representatives had passed the Kansas-Nebraska Act—"Another Triumph of the Slave Power," as his father's headline read—and soon it would be signed into law by President Franklin Pierce.

At the store, George was supposed to be learning bookkeeping, but when he arrived at six o'clock in the morning, he would sweep and tidy before they opened. During the day, he would go pick up sheet music from publishers around the corner or tickets from the New Theater, Music Hall, or Melodeon that they could sell at the shop. Sometimes, he'd stay as late as eight o'clock in the evening to lock up.

George was a good worker, but he was much more interested in politics and political happenings than the music business. When he went on his errands, he could hear the murmuring of reactions to the Kansas-Nebraska Act. The two new states were supposed to be free from slavery, but this bill said that people in the territories could vote on whether they wanted slavery—what was called *popular sovereignty*. To pass the bill in the United States Congress, the Southern pro-slavery states needed support from some Northern politicians. From the music store, George would hear the 113-gun salute fired to celebrate the 113 House votes for the bill. Those people firing the guns, they were in essence celebrating slavery. Since the bill had already passed the Senate, when President Pierce signed the bill into law, he would complete the orderly constitutional process that would allow slavery to spread westward into new states.

Even though they were a political family, George's father did not believe in voting, "as a matter of moral consistency." If his father voted, it meant he believed in the Constitution, which did not outlaw slavery. For him and those with similar beliefs, voting—even for anti-slavery candidates—meant supporting slavery until the Constitution was amended. Abolitionists like George's father who did not believe in voting or violence were called nonresistants or nonresisters.

George felt stubborn and independent, something he got from his father, and although he and his father looked more alike than ever—with their pale skin; long faces, and long noses; and deep-set, serious eyes—they did not think alike. George wanted to learn by doing, not by reading books. He was not going to be an editor, a writer, or an anti-slavery speaker. Those jobs did not appeal to him. George was supposed to be a nonresister, but he was not sure it was the best way to achieve their abolitionist aims. People made laws like the Fugitive Slave Act and Kansas-Nebraska Act by voting. Even if the Constitution did not allow everyone an equal vote, nonresisters were turning their backs on a key part of the democratic process. "No union with slaveholders," his father said. States without slavery should not be made to be part of a country with slaveholders.

As George went about his work on Thursday, May 25, the Kansas-Nebraska Act should still have been what everyone was talking about, but the evening before, as Democrats had celebrated their legislative victory, a Black man named Anthony Burns left his job at a clothing store around the corner from the music store. A police officer named Asa Butman arrested Burns because Butman suspected Burns was a runaway. The abolitionists did not consider Butman a regular police officer, though; he was a constable who was known to pursue bounties on runaway slaves. The *Boston Daily Evening Transcript* reported that Butman arrested Burns under the orders of a United States Marshal by a warrant issued by United States commissioner Edward G. Loring. If George's father ever needed evidence that the government supported enslavers, this was it.

The news of a man hunted down and arrested under the Fugitive Slave Law quickly spread to the Black community and white abolitionists. George often went to *The Liberator*'s offices at the New England Anti-Slavery Society, which it turned out was where all the excitement seemed to be stemming from now.

The Boston Vigilance Committee, another anti-slavery organization, met to figure out a plan to free Burns. Three years earlier, Butman and another police officer had arrested a Black man named Thomas Sims under the same law, and the commissioner of the US Circuit Court in Boston sent him to Georgia to be enslaved. Unitarian minister and abolitionist Thomas Wentworth Higginson was on the Vigilance Committee and blamed his fellow committee members for not doing enough to free Sims. Unlike George's father, Higginson thought the use of violence acceptable if he used it to free an enslaved person.

Now, with Anthony Burns's case, the Vigilance Committee needed to let people know what was happening. Theodore Parker, another Unitarian minister who George loved hearing preach about anti-slavery on Sunday mornings, wanted the message from the Vigilance Committee to be clear.

On Friday morning, posters and fliers proclaimed the message across the city. Parker had made it plain and fiery. That night, thousands of people gathered at Faneuil Hall to hear speeches and discuss what to do.

CHAPTER 3

Charlotte Forten

SALEM, MASSACHUSETTS
MAY 1854

Thenews made Charlotte angry and sad all at once. The story of Anthony Burns's arrest in Boston on May 24 had traveled quickly to Salem, Massachusetts, where sixteen-year-old Charlotte lived. She had a new journal, and although she wasn't planning to write anything on the evening after Burns's arrest, this was too important not to make note of. For any "true friend of liberty and humanity," anyone who had the slightest inclination toward the abolitionist cause, his arrest had to arouse "feelings of the deepest indignation and sorrow," she wrote.

Burns wanted to be free—he wanted to walk the ground and breathe the air of the "Old Bay State," Charlotte's adopted home. She had never been in chains like Burns or like the more than three million people enslaved in the Southern and western states, but she believed that every human being deserved freedom. Massachusetts was supposed to be a place of freedom for people who looked like Charlotte and Anthony Burns.

Slavery had effectively ended in Massachusetts in the 1780s, and with William Lloyd Garrison and his American Anti-Slavery Society in Boston, the whole state should have been firmly in the anti-slavery camp. The city was supposed to be much less prejudiced than a place like Philadelphia, where Charlotte had grown up.

In Philadelphia, the government didn't allow Black and white students in the same schools. It didn't matter if Charlotte's grandfather James had made a small fortune in his business making sails for boats and that generations of her family had been born free. Men had taken Charlotte's great-great-great-grandfather from his family and life in Africa, placed him on a ship, and sold him into slavery in Pennsylvania more than 150 years before Charlotte was born, and that was why she would have to go to a segregated school. Charlotte's father did not think those schools were good enough for her, so she'd only ever had private tutors. She received an education, but it wasn't the same as being in a classroom, learning from other students, and feeling as though she had a right to be there, regardless of where her family came from.

Charlotte's family friend Charles Lenox Remond had offered Charlotte a place to live in Salem so she could attend public school. Charlotte loved it, even though she knew her ancestry still mattered to some of the other students. In truth, the fact that Charlotte had light brown skin still mattered to many people, especially those who were willing to aid in the arrest and imprisonment of a Black person simply because someone thought they looked like a fugitive slave.

Burns's arrest hardly made sense to Charlotte. He "was arrested like a criminal in the streets," she thought, even though he should have been free. Taking back his freedom—"freedom which, he, in common with every other human being, is endowed"—shouldn't have been a crime. It was *Burns's* body, *Burns's* life, *Burns's* freedom. No other man should be able to take that from him. And no other state should tell Massachusetts how to enforce its laws. Would the people of Boston uphold the state constitution that had effectively banned slavery almost seventy-five years earlier in Massachusetts? Or would they capitulate to the federal Fugitive Slave Law of 1850 and Southern Slave Power, disgracing themselves by sending Anthony Burns back to slavery?

"I can only hope and pray most earnestly that Boston will not again disgrace herself by sending him back to a bondage worse than death," Charlotte thought.

That everyone wasn't an abolitionist sometimes frustrated Charlotte, even made her angry. Everything in Charlotte's life had been tied to the anti-slavery cause. Charlotte sometimes thought of the Bible verse: "Remember them that are in bonds as bound with them." For her, this meant to "Remember the poor slave as [though you are] bound [enslaved] with him." She knew she wasn't a slave, and that her experience of the world differed from that of Anthony Burns or her ancestors who had been enslaved.

Charlotte thought of Anthony Burns and hoped the city would redeem itself and release him.

Abolitionists called a meeting after the arrest of Anthony Burns to decide what they should do. This meeting led to a faction of abolitionists storming the courthouse in an attempt to free Burns.

New-York Daily Tribune

MAY 1854

BOSTON FUGITIVE SLAVE CASE. GREAT MEETING AT FANUEIL HALL[2]. ATTACK ON THE COURT-HOUSE

BOSTON, FRIDAY, MAY 26, 1854.

Immense excitement prevailed in this city this evening on account of the arrest of Burns, the alleged fugitive Slave. The call for a meeting in Fanueil Hall attracted hundreds more than could get inside the building. The principal speakers were Wendell Phillips, Theodore Parker, and Francis W. Bird. The tenor of the speeches was highly inflammatory—denouncing the Fugitive Slave Law as one which should not be obeyed, and counseling open resistance.

At about 9 o'clock a motion to adjourn to the Court-House at 9 o'clock to-morrow morning, when the examination of Burns takes place, was carried by acclamation.

Immediately thereafter a person rushed into the Hall, exclaiming "There's a crowd of negroes[3] in Court-square attacking the Court-House where Burns is confined." This announcement caused the immediate rush of 2,000 to 3,000 excited people to the Court-House Square. An attempt was at once made to break open the Court-House door on the east side, which, owing to the strong fastenings, failed.

The leading rioters then went to the west entrance, and with a heavy plank, used as a battering engine, stove through the pannels of the door, and broke some windows.

Numerous pistols were fired, and the mob became formidable. The Center Watchouse being in the immediate vicinity, a posse of determined watchmen dashed in, and succeeded in arresting eight or ten of the leading rioters after a desperate conflict.

The prompt arrest of the ringleaders suppressed further violence, and an increased police force, who were soon after on the ground, and stationed at the several entrances to the Court-House, will probably preserve quiet for the night. Burns is confined in an upper room of the Court-House. The officials having charge of him are well armed, and had the mob gained an entrance, it is doubtful if they could have carried him off.

Col. Suttle, who claims Burns as his property, was arrested to-day on a charge of attempting to kidnap a citizen of Massachusetts, and is held under bail.

The examination of Burns takes places at 9 A. M. tomorrow. It is openly asserted that if the decision is against freedom, he will be forcibly rescued.

Eleven o'clock.-From 500 to 800 persons remained in Court Square, but no further violence is anticipated to-night.

---

2. The *New-York Daily Tribune* repeatedly misspelled "Faneuil" in the original newspaper.
3. The use of the word "negro" at this time was not considered offensive by white people but was still not as politically correct a term as "colored." Both are now considered dated, and if used today, offensive.

CHAPTER 4

Charlotte Forten

BOSTON
MAY 1854

A **week after Anthony Burns's arrest, on Wednesday, May** 31, Charlotte stepped off the train in Boston. Usually, she loved coming to the city. She would people-watch at the Common or listen to lectures at Faneuil Hall or Tremont Temple, to "the burning and eloquent words of those who plead for the oppressed, whose pure and elevated character, daunt-less courage and lofty purpose ennoble New England, and alone redeem our degenerate land."

She thought today would be different because she'd heard that "the excite-ment in Boston is very great" after Theodore Parker had put out his fliers about Anthony Burns's arrest and people attacked the courthouse. But as Charlotte walked through the city three days into Burns's trial, she was surprised that Boston wasn't like the newspapers described. Everyone thought the excite-ment from the previous Friday and Saturday would continue into this week, with the Anti-Slavery Convention coinciding with the trial and people coming from out of town and getting riled up by speeches.

Now that she was here, Charlotte didn't see mobs on the street or peo-ple gathering and making noise, but she still felt "much real indignation and excitement" as she walked from the train station through the twisted streets of Boston's center.

The courthouse was so spare, it almost looked like a tomb, with its narrow, rectangular facade, portico with Roman columns, and heavy door at least as tall as three men. On this day, even calling it a courthouse was generous. It was "now lawlessly converted into a prison, and filled with soldiers," Charlotte thought, and she could feel the anger bubbling inside her. The soldiers guarding Burns were cowards, she thought, misguided by a desire to serve authority and not guided by morality.

Charlotte continued around the corner to a concert hall called the Melodeon, where the anti-slavery meetings were being held. Charlotte yearned to hear Theodore Parker, but he was not there. For members of the Vigilance Committee who believed in "deeds," as Parker said, they could no longer just talk about the case. People said the Committee had been meeting at the office of *The Liberator* and at Tremont Temple, continuing their plans to make sure that the court did not send Burns back to slavery in Virginia.

At the Melodeon, the audience was primed to hear the latest on the Burns case. Charlotte's family had been attending anti-slavery meetings her whole life. Sometimes, the meetings were large, with thousands of people coming from all over the country to hear Charles Lenox Remond, William Lloyd Garrison, or Frederick Douglass speak. Other times, the meetings were small, held in a community building or church in a town where people didn't talk of abolition. Often, many things were the same. The speakers had to rouse the emotions of the crowd while balancing the facts of why slavery was detrimental, and they had to speak confidently.

That confidence was one reason that Charlotte thought she could never be an anti-slavery lecturer, even if she sometimes said that was what she wanted to do. "I do think reading one's composition before strangers is a trying task," she wrote in her journal.

The lectures at the anti-slavery meetings were not exactly like reading something before a crowd, though. The audience did not always sit quietly and contemplate what the speaker said. If you felt compelled, you could cheer or yell your approval. If you didn't like what the speaker had to say, you could boo. And if they asked you a question, you could answer. The energy would be palpable.

At the Melodeon awaiting Burns's verdict, the crowd stood for a cause greater than themselves, and when they were together in a room like this, all those emotions coursing through their bodies, they knew that they could end slavery and injustice. It wasn't surprising that good speakers could get a crowd riled up and have them take to the streets.

The meeting Charlotte attended on Wednesday, May 31, was on the second day of the annual New England Anti-Slavery Convention. The speakers had planned to talk about the Kansas-Nebraska Act, but instead they had to address what was happening to Anthony Burns mere blocks away. For the abolitionists, his case highlighted the fact that the North couldn't follow their own state laws if those laws went against federal laws.

For abolitionists, the Fugitive Slave Law also felt like it went against the Constitution. Under the law, there was no way for someone like Burns to contest his freedom. A person accused of being a fugitive slave could not testify on their own behalf. The law said Burns could not present a defense in his own words to the judge, could not say, "No, I am not a slave," even if it were true. The local governments were also supposed to help federal marshals return people to slavery, even if those people were now in a state where slavery was illegal. Some free Black families were scared and chose to move to Canada.

At the Anti-Slavery Convention, people felt upset and outraged, and the speakers spoke of a moral, a lesson about the state of the nation and what they, as anti-slavery activists, still needed to do.

"The North has no union with the South," abolitionist and women's rights advocate Lucy Stone told the crowd at the anti-slavery convention. The federal government was saying that in Massachusetts, they had to give in to laws the South had enacted.

Stone asserted that before long, there would be "a war, which is destined to wage hotter, and to grow more intense, until, in the end, Liberty shall be triumphant." There might be bloodshed along the way, but that would lead to liberty and peace, she said, and the crowd cheered. Stone didn't care if the United States dissolved to bring about this liberty.

Stone told the crowd, "I do not know what bloody tragedies are between us and that hour; I only know that in the end, there *must* come Liberty, and there must come Peace." *Liberty*, that was what this was always about for Charlotte.

During a break between the morning and afternoon speeches, Charlotte was invited to the Garrison family home at Dix Place. This visit provided a balm to the upset of the day—to seeing Burns guarded, as Parker had said, "in Boston" by "Bostonians," who were now nothing more than "minions of the South." Charlotte knew that at the Garrison home, they shared her values and she would be welcome. She longed for the togetherness of her own family, but they were in Philadelphia.

Outside of his home, William Lloyd Garrison ("Lloyd" to his friends and family) might have been a firebrand who frightened slaveholders with his words. But here, he would get down on the floor and play with Frank, who was five, and let Fanny, who was nine and a half, kiss his bald head. Garrison's oldest son, George, was Charlotte's age, and like all the Garrison children, could join in the conversations, although he was rather quiet. Helen Garrison was lovely, Charlotte thought, a perfect wife for Lloyd, the great abolitionist. For one, she looked like the Quaker abolitionist woman she was, with her black dress and lace collar, and dark hair parted in the center and pinned at the back in a simple bun. The look was out of style, but Helen Garrison wasn't concerned with modern fashions. Her concern was being a wife and mother who advanced the cause of abolition through her womanly duties. Helen didn't want to speak in public like Lucy Stone but was content to raise their children as abolitionists and share her opinions on abolition and nonresistance at gatherings in her home. This was what an abolitionist wife should be like, at least according to the older generation, and Charlotte felt a kinship with the desire to support the cause without being in the spotlight.

———

Charlotte left the Garrisons' home and walked back toward the train station. Burns was still at the courthouse, awaiting the judge's verdict. They saw militiamen, marines, and regular troops everywhere, trying to keep people off the street, trying to keep people from freeing Burns. The soldiers made Charlotte's heart sick.

Later, Charlotte wrote about what had happened that day and spending time with the Garrisons. William Lloyd Garrison himself, Charlotte thought, "is indeed the very highest Christian spirit." She thought him and his non-resistant principles good, moral, and Christian. She could never be like him, though. She understood those principles, but she admitted, "I cannot hope to reach [that highest Christian spirit . . .] for I believe in resistance to tyrants, and would fight for liberty until death."

CHAPTER 5

George Garrison

BOSTON
JUNE 1854

Geeorge and his family could guess the verdict the judge would deliver on Friday, June 2, in Anthony Burns's case. State militiamen and marines appeared on the streets not long after dawn. They guarded the courthouse and the large cannon that sat in Court Square. By seven o'clock in the morning, people heard the shouts that guided the soldiers' marching, the brass bands that accompanied the troops, and the loading of weapons. The mayor did not want another uprising against the jailers. Many of the shops in the center of Boston, especially the businesses owned by abolitionists, had decided to stay closed for just this reason.

Around nine o'clock, the judge ended any remaining suspense and said the Fugitive Slave Law was constitutional and that Anthony Burns was not a free man just because he was in Massachusetts. Burns would walk in chains through a free city.

George did not want a riot, but destruction could be fascinating. He made note of train crashes, boat wrecks, and even murders in his diary. His parents thought he should not dwell on violence, but violence might free Burns. Thomas Wentworth Higginson and Theodore Parker of the Vigilance

Committee believed this. If enough people pressed in close, if they attacked the men guarding Anthony Burns—if they caused an uprising—then maybe Burns could slip away down some narrow alley and run and hide and run and hide until he got to Canada.

For now, Burns's only route was out the courthouse door, down the steps, down State Street, past the Customs House, to T-Wharf. A lot of people wanted to witness it—both those who agreed with the decision and those who were incensed. George would have wanted to be there.

Along the route, people leaned out of windows covered in black bunting, a sign of their mourning. People were pushed back by firemen and police.

Men in uniform marched on State Street, getting ready for the escort. Burns had more protection than the president would have. He'd be accompanied by a guard of both state and federal troops: the cavalry detachment of Boston Lancers, US infantry, and more marines and troops manning guns and cannons.

At two o'clock, when Burns stepped out of the courthouse, the bells of Black churches started ringing across the city. Along the route, the bells mixed with horse hooves stamping, boots beating against cobblestones, hisses and cries of "Shame! Shame!" and the clink and clunk of pieces of brick hitting soldiers and the street.

Someone brought a black coffin with the word *Liberty* painted in white across the top. Someone else threw a bottle of sulfuric acid at the troops. Someone splashed homemade pepper spray on the soldiers. Someone tried to drive a carriage through the procession. The tension built and built, and it nearly was a riot. But somehow Burns and his guards made it to the docks.

Had the citizens of Boston really done everything they could to free him?

George's father was passionately against what had hap-pened to Burns, and George knew it. When they were younger, George and his siblings would play with the type at *The Liberator* office. Now that they were older, they helped their father proofread the paper before publication, and William Lloyd Garrison was never afraid of letting his children read newspapers and magazines he brought home, or stare at photos of enslaved people who had been brutally beaten. This was the real world, and they all needed to be prepared for it.

George's father thought that the judge's decision made Burns an object rather than a man, the Declaration of Independence a lie, "the Golden Rule an absurdity," a line he may have spoken at home before he wrote it in *The Liberator*. George's father may have been indignant, but in the end, he had only words. Forceful words, but words nonetheless.

George's father wasn't as radical as Higginson or Lewis Hayden—the men who had tried to free Burns from the courthouse on Friday, May 26. George knew some white and Black men wanted to fight for freedom, and maybe fighting would bring freedom to all of the enslaved.

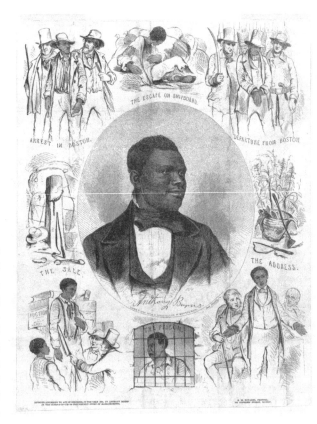

Anthony Burns was arrested on May 24, 1854 in Boston, accused of escaping enslavement in Virginia. His arrest and trial infuriated abolitionists in Massachusetts. This illustration shows his portrait with scenes from his life.

CHAPTER 6

Charlotte Forten

SALEM
JUNE 1854

When Charlotte heard the news of Anthony Burns, she knew Massachusetts had submitted to Slave Power. She knew that if the abolitionists in Massachusetts tried to free him again, soldiers would shoot them, an order that came from "a government which proudly boasts being the freest in the world," but was really just a government of tyranny and oppression.

CHAPTER 7

George Garrison

BOSTON
FALL 1854

A party from the New England Emigrant Aid Company would leave Boston for Kansas on September 26, 1854. Since the passage of the Kansas-Nebraska Act earlier that year, George had been keeping track of the settlers moving from Massachusetts to the Kansas Territory. The first group had left in July with only twenty-nine people, but now groups left at a steady pace. Sometimes, he went to watch them leave from the Worcester Depot, the crowd sending them off with cheers. Now these abolitionists and free soilers—people who might not have been abolitionists but just wanted an opportunity to own land and farm it themselves—were the hope for making Kansas a free state. These emigrants planned to settle in the territory on land not already owned by the Shawnee, Delaware, and Pottawatomie Native Americans. The Emigrant Aid Society helped them move to sway the politics in favor of free labor, with the idea that they would eventually vote for an anti-slavery state constitution and elect anti-slavery senators and representatives to the US Congress.

George wanted to be on one of those trains leaving. He would need money to get to Kansas; his friend had told him it would be at least thirty-seven dollars in train fare. And he would need his parents' permission. Even though he was eighteen, his parents did not consider him an adult who could make a decision like that.

On Sunday, September 24—two days before the September company was going to leave—George sat with his father and mother after their dinner guests left and told them he wanted to go to Kansas. "They are very much opposed to my going there," George confided in his diary, and their attitude should not have surprised him. First, his father did not like the idea of the emigrants in general. While other abolitionist papers wrote positively about the groups leaving, his father hardly mentioned it at all. His father did not believe that these emigrants would do anything for the abolition movement at home. George's mother was always worried about her children and would rather have George stay at home. They thought he simply needed a new job that he liked better than the music store.

———————

Two months later, in November 1854, George received a letter from Samuel Tappan, a member of the first group from the Emigrant Aid Company. Tappan wanted them to write letters to each other every week, with George providing news clippings about what the press was saying about Kansas and Tappan offering accounts of what was happening on the ground.

George could not stop asking people whether it was practical for him to go to Kansas, and Tappan, he thought, could offer him advice. Tappan told George he could come to Kansas and get a job in a printing office or at a newspaper, both jobs George knew well from his father's work.

George's father had not changed his mind, though, and was even more firm in George not going after the reports of violence began between the free soilers and slavers. Tappan told George that the people of Kansas had been wronged by the "ruffians" coming across the border from Missouri, attacking them and destroying their property.

"Our forefathers left us the accursed system of slavery," Tappan wrote George, "and as a matter of course we their children must suffer the consequences, which I had much rather do than leave it for those who come after us." Tappan was five years older than George and said slavery had to end in their generation, by the hand of their generation.

George knew going to Kansas was not practical and that his parents were against it, but he could not get the idea of going out of his head and was beginning to get "Kansas fever."

CHAPTER 8

Lewis Douglass

ROCHESTER
JUNE 1855

L ewis's days at the offices of *Frederick Douglass' Paper* were filled with reading newspapers from across the country and picking out the most interesting news to print; running to the telegraph office to see if any important news had come in; and assisting the printer in picking out the metal letters from the wooden type trays and placing those letters carefully into words and sentences and paragraphs backward so that when they finally rolled ink over the letters and pressed paper on top, they'd have a newspaper. The printer would press a test of the four pages of the newspaper they'd print that week. For the last six years, Lewis's father or the paper's co-editor, Julia Griffiths, would review it. When they'd fixed any mistakes, the press started humming, the ink rolled across the letters, and soon, they'd have "another arrow sent on its way to do the work of puncturing the veil" of slavery and racism in this country, as Lewis's mother, Anna Douglass, said.

Lewis looked at the Friday, June 22, 1855, issue. Could one say it was extraordinary that they'd gotten it printed? This was the first week in years that Julia Griffiths had not helped them. Last week, she returned to England. For almost half of Lewis's life, she had been ever-present. First as governess to him and his siblings, then as boarder in their home, then as co-editor of the newspaper and Lewis's boss when his father was on speaking tours, and perhaps most importantly, as a confidant to Lewis's father. The rumors about the relationship between Griffiths and Lewis's father had caused strife between Lewis's parents and between Lewis's father and his former mentor, William Lloyd Garrison.

And perhaps that was one of the reasons why Lewis's father was so protective of their family's private life, and Lewis and his siblings knew that they should be protective of their family, too. There were too many people who wanted to discredit his father and his beliefs, and they'd use personal attacks to get there, if they must.

In the summer of 1855, there was too much happening to look backward, though.

In the June 22 issue of the paper, they reprinted news about the ongoing violence in Kansas, a story of a gang of pro-slavery men firing on an anti-slavery man who refused to leave his home. The political parties also had to contend with how they should view this violence and if they supported popular sovereignty, and they reported on that as well.

There was also an amazing coincidence. The week before, Anthony Burns— who had been sent back to slavery from Boston in 1854—passed through Rochester on his way to Oberlin College, where Lewis's sister Rosetta had just returned from studying for a year. They'd made a note of it in the weekly happenings. After Burns had been returned to Virginia, an abolitionist bought Burns and freed him, and then an anonymous donor gave him a scholarship to Oberlin. Lewis knew he'd never go to college; his father believed the world needed Black doctors and lawyers, but they also needed Black men who could be mechanics, carpenters, engineers, and printers.

In the latest issue of the paper, Lewis's father was also trying to promote the Convention of Radical Political Abolitionists, which would begin on June 26 in Syracuse, New York. "Come up, friends, body to the work.—We have no time to lose. The battle rages," his father wrote.

In Syracuse, they could say the convention was a success.
By the afternoon of the first day, on June 26, 1855, four hundred people
crowded into the upstairs meeting room of the rather small Syracuse City Hall.
A handbill for the meeting declared, "The object of this Convention is to re-
organize the Great Army of Freedom on radical and permanent grounds, and
to raise men and 'material aid' to push on the great cause."

Most of the men and women gathered thought "human Slavery unconstitutional, illegal and wicked," which went beyond just the idea that slavery was
morally wrong and contradicted William Lloyd Garrison's view that the Constitution supported slavery. Being political was radical, but maybe not radical
enough.

On the third day of the convention, John Brown spoke about the situation
in Kansas. Lewis's father first met Brown in 1847 and thought Brown "well
known as an active and self-sacrificing abolitionist." Brown was white, tall, and
imposing—and a forceful speaker. For years, Brown had been thinking of ways
to liberate enslaved people, and told people about how Toussaint L'Ouverture
started the revolution in Haiti and freed people there, or how people liberated
themselves from plantations in Jamaica, hid in the mountain jungle, and then
attacked plantations to liberate more people. Brown thought the Allegheny
Mountains in Virginia and Pennsylvania could be used to lead people from the
South to Canada.

One of the members at the convention read letters from Brown's sons in
Kansas about how pro-slavery men "burn their houses and barns, destroy their
crops, maim their cattle, and otherwise annoy them." Worse, these slaveholders
were "well armed and thoroughly organized, while the friends of Freedom have
no arms and are without organization."

Brown told the crowd he was going to Kansas. He wanted men to come to
the territory, and for "means to aid himself and friends in sustaining the cause
of Freedom in Kansas." He wanted money and weapons in the fight against
slavery.

Over the last five years, the Fugitive Slave Act and the conflict in Kansas had consumed Lewis's father's thinking, and the pages of their newspaper. Radical and political abolition seemed the only way forward for a young man like Lewis.

Charlotte Forten's Journal

SEPTEMBER 1855

September 12, 1855

*I wonder that every colored person is not a
misanthrope. Surely we have everything to make us hate
mankind. [. . .] Oh! it is hard to go through life meeting
contempt with contempt, hatred with hatred, fearing, with
too good reason to love and trust hardly any one whose
skin is white, however lovable, attractive and congenial
in seeming. In the bitter, passionate feeling of my soul
again and again there rises the question "When, oh! When
shall this cease?" "Is there no help?" "How long oh! how
long must we continue to suffer—to endure?" Conscience
answers it is wrong, it is ignoble to despair; let us labor
earnestly and faithfully to acquire knowledge, to break
down the barriers of prejudice and oppression. Let us
take courage, never cease to work,—hoping and believing
that if not for us, for another generation there is a better,
brighter day in store, when slavery and prejudice shall
vanish before the glorious light of Liberty and Truth;
when the rights of every colored man shall everywhere be
acknowledged and respected and he shall be treated as a
man and a brother.*

—Charlotte Forten

George Garrison's Diary

Boston, June 4, 1856

Affairs in Kansas look very dark and gloomy for the free state settlers.

Boston, June 6, 1856

The news from Kansas is bad, bloodshed and fighting is the order of the day.

Boston, June 19, 1856

The Republican National Convention nominated yesterday, John C. Frémont, of California for President, and today Wm. L. Dayton, of New Jersey, for Vice President. They were both elected on the first formal ballot.

Letter to George Garrison
from Francis Meriam

JUNE 1856

Paris, June 27, '56

Dear George,

I received your interesting and well written letter of April 13th on the 30th of the same month, for all the trouble which you must have taken, I am very much obliged. [. . .]

I am now well posted up about facts, by the regular receipt of the N.Y. Tribune, but I do not know the philosophy, the truth, of these facts. What does your father think about affairs, particularly Kansas? I think his name will stand far above all others of this age in History. I take more interest in the affairs of America, than ever I did while at home. I am a stronger abolitionist than before.

I am not sure that this letter does not find you gone to Kansas (and then I did not think it sensible) as I know that you thought of going some time ago to work there. If I were in the United States now, and I thought that there was sufficient spirit among the free state men for any body of them to stand up manfully and fight for their rights, I would go with you to Kansas, not to work, but to fight. If I were in your place now [. . .] I would go ask Francis Jackson to provide you with a Sharp's rifle, or better a Greene's rifle which repeats 50 times after once charging and a Colts revolver and sufficient money for the journey and to sustain you, and I would go to Kansas and fight. It thoroughly riled me when, I heard that Lawrence had been destroyed, and then I feared that the free state men had submitted. Then I heard that it was so, is it true? [. . . .]

Write long letters soon if you please, Your friend

F.J. Meriam

CHAPTER 9

George Garrison

BOSTON
JUNE 1856

George hated keeping up correspondence. He would rather clean up the cellar than write to friends, but some friends it might be worth hearing from. Francis Meriam was a year and a half younger than George, and while George knew plenty of other abolitionists his age that he didn't get along with, he liked Meriam, and so would write to him, since he'd asked.

George followed the action in Kansas closely, and Meriam was correct: the issue was not simple or being reported on well. The newspapers said Missourians who supported slavery would cross the border and put a few logs and rocks together, claiming they were building homes. Then, they would go back to Missouri in hopes they would be allowed to vote in Kansas elections. There were also reports that men simply crossed into Kansas to vote illegally.

Now it was nearly war in Kansas. Free soilers burned the cabins of slavers, poisoned their livestock and dogs. They helped people escape from enslavement, and one man was reported to have tried to start a revolt among the enslaved in Missouri. Slavers kidnapped and shot free soilers, not all of whom were abolitionists. Newspapers reported that free soilers and abolitionists would be murdered as soon as they entered Kansas.

And, as Meriam heard, Lawerence was in ruins. Slavers burned the Free State Hotel and destroyed the free-soil newspaper offices in Lawrence, and everyone knew the free soilers would retaliate.

None of this had really quelled George's Kansas Fever, though, and Meriam's uncle Francis Jackson would be the perfect person to ask for help getting to Kansas. Jackson had known George since he was little and did not share the nonresistant values of George's mother and father. If George wanted to go against his parents' wishes, he could ask Jackson for help. But he was not ready to do that yet.

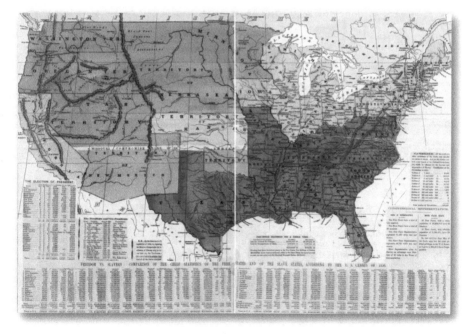

"Political Map of the United States, designed to exhibit the comparative area of the free and slave states." In this 1856 map, the states and territories where slavery is allowed are dark gray and where slavery is illegal are light gray. The territory of Kansas is not shaded because Kansas had yet to vote on whether to allow slavery.

Salem Register

JULY 1856

VALEDICTORY POEM.

The following is the Poem, written and read by Miss CHARLOTTE L. Forten, on the occasion of the Farewell Exercises of the Second Graduating Class of the State Normal School in Salem, on Tuesday afternoon, July 22, as mentioned in the Register of Thursday;

No, naught of good for others can be done,
Till actions spring from principle alone.
In life uphold, is love of God and man.
But selfish motives grow, and, spreading far,
Infect the press, the pulpit and bar.—
E'ev in the Nation's councils, we but see
Of Right and Justice the vain mockery
They boast of Freedom in this land of ours;
Yet every breeze that comes from the Southern bow'rs,
Laden with the rich fragrance of bright flow'rs,
Brings us the captive's cry of deep despair,
His bitter moan, his agonizing prayer.
That beautiful South-land—is freedom there?
Is perfect freedom here, in our own North?
Too few there are who rightly know its worth,
While any can be found who basely kneel,
E'en while the Southron's haughty pow'r they feel,
While he shall dare insult, attack and slay
The noble few who scorn his brutal sway.

CHAPTER 10

Lewis Douglass

ROCHESTER
AUGUST 1856

L ewis's father had spent much of his time over the last year traveling and speaking and selling copies of his new autobiography, *My Bondage and My Freedom*. Sometimes, Lewis or his brother Fred joined their father.

The lectures over the summer of 1856 were about the election—that was all anyone could talk about. At first, his father supported the Radical Abolitionist Party, but in August, he endorsed John C. Frémont, right there in the pages of his newspaper. Voting for the Republican, his father said, would be the "deadliest blow upon slavery" at this particular time. Bringing abolitionists into the now-mainstream party could make the party more radical.

Lewis—too young and not a property owner—could not vote. There was little he could do right now for liberty when he had to stay in Rochester and work for his father's paper.

Drawings by George's brother
Wendell Garrison of the 1856
presidential candidates, Democrat
James Buchanan and Republican
John C. Frémont.

CHAPTER 11

George Garrison

BOSTON
OCTOBER 1856

O n the evening of **October 29, 1856, the streets and** houses in south Boston into downtown glowed, even though a sliver of the waxing moon provided hardly any light. The election was just six days away, and George thought this was "a close and desperate struggle." All around the Garrison home on Dix Place, people lit torches and house lights in support of Frémont, the Republicans, and the marchers in the streets. The lights rose and with it, hope for change.

George's home was in the middle of the parade route, and the sound of men and horses reverberated in the night air.

George estimated that the parade that followed had ten to fifteen thousand men, all of whom snaked their way through city's streets. Homes along the parade route lit their gas lamps, hung out American-flag bunting, American flags, or colorful paper lanterns, and kept shooting off fireworks. The Republican clubs of each city's ward walked together, as did delegations from Providence, Rhode Island, and towns outside of Boston. They carried banners with political messages and even images. Banners with *Weapons furnished by the New*

England Aid Company and an illustration of a sawmill and hotel, or *Gift of Boston to Lawrence* with a school, church, and newspaper office were meant to combat the idea that people from the east were only sending guns and ammunition to Kansas settlers. Other banners told of the violence of the pro-slavery supporters: a painting of the burned and destroyed buildings in Lawerence; a banner with the name of every free soiler who had died in Kansas.

Brass bands from all over New England came to play. George would have hardly stopped hearing one before another appeared, taking over with forceful marching melodies. Along the route, fireworks popped and people cheered. The parade had started at nine and went on for hours. George could not have slept if he had wanted to. The Frémont supporters shot rockets and artillery shells from the hill on the Common around midnight, signaling an end to the night's festivities.

The *Boston Evening Transcript* reporter was convinced this grand display and the support from all the spectators showed how in favor of the Republicans Bostonians were: "all beholders must have been convinced of the prevalence of free sentiments in our community."

To George, the election felt like a turning point. Although for months he had not been writing in his diary regularly, he was keeping track of politics. The Democratic nominee was James Buchanan, who supported the idea that each state should decide if they wanted slavery or not. George's family thought of the Democrats as absolutely pro-slavery. The American Party or Know Nothings supported Millard Fillmore, the former president, and wanted to limit immigration.

Political abolitionists could only support Frémont. His supporters were Frémonters—pronounced "free-monters"—a name that fit nicely with the idea of free soil and freedom for the enslaved. Republicans did not have an anti-slavery platform, but Southerners and Democrats saw them as abolitionists in disguise.

George's father did not approve of the Frémonters or the Republican Party, believing that the Republicans would bring complacency and simply limit the spread of slavery, rather than abolishing it. If the Republican Party allowed slavery to continue in Southern states, then they could not be supported.

George knew the Republicans were the only ones moving in the proper direction, though. "God spread the right," George thought when he saw the Frémont supporters, his words a play on the Bible verse "God spread the light." They must spread the information about and free states—spread the morally right thing.

An undated photo of Lucy McKim, probably from the time she was at the Eagleswood School.

CHAPTER 12

Lucy McKim

EAGLESWOOD, NEW JERSEY
OCTOBER–NOVEMBER 1856

The setting autumn light cast a glow on the persimmon and apple trees heavy with fruit and the blooming goldenrod and purple aster flowers. Lucy loved autumn. She had turned fourteen on October 30, 1856, and that school year brought her from her family's home in Philadelphia to Eagleswood in New Jersey, a boarding school run by her father's mentor, Theodore Dwight Weld; his wife, Angelina Grimké Weld; and her sister, Sarah Grimké.

Sometimes, Eagleswood felt a world away from Philadelphia, even though it was only a few hours by train. Here, she could spend almost as much time as she wanted with her best friend, Ellen Wright; go on long walks in next to the marshes; or even go swimming in the bay next to the school. As far from Philadelphia as she might have been, Lucy's attendance at the school was because of the segregated public schools at home where only "bigoted and narrow" people sent their children, according to Ellen's aunt, and her family was most certainly not that. Eagleswood accepted Black and white students, and boys and girls for "intellectual and moral training" in service of the abolitionist cause.

As head of the school, Weld was rather strict with his rules of no tea or coffee and modest dress for everyone, but every Saturday, they did have a dance in the school's main hall. Lucy loved music and dancing, and this November 1, 1856, might have been a celebration of her birthday just two days before, too.

Weld and his assistant danced with the students, but Angelina and Sarah did not. The sisters had been Quakers, like Lucy's mother, and Quaker values still influenced the school. Lucy's mother had not been allowed to sing or dance growing up, a life Lucy couldn't imagine.

At school, Lucy played piano and violin, loved going to concerts, and wrote music. Lucy, her music teacher, and the other music students would provide the band for the Saturday dances.

Guests would come to the dances, too. For the past week, one of the guests at Eagleswood was the writer Henry David Thoreau. In such a communal place as Eagleswood, it was strange that he always wanted to be by himself, but on the other hand, he had written *Walden, or Life in the Woods* all about being alone. Thoreau did come to the dance but did not enjoy himself or "society" that evening.

The next evening, on Sunday, November 2, Lucy and the other students gathered to hear Thoreau lecture in the same hall.

"I wish to speak a word for Nature, for absolute freedom and wilderness, as contrasted with a freedom and culture merely civil," Thoreau said, "to regard man as an inhabitant, or a part and parcel of Nature, rather than a member of society."

Thoreau realized his view was "an extreme statement . . . for there are enough champions of civilization: the minister and the school-committee," he said, perhaps raising his eyes to Weld at that moment.

Thoreau was going to talk to them about walking and the wild. He had already given one lecture the previous Sunday at Eagleswood, and as Lucy sat and listened, Thoreau combined the literal idea of walking and being wild with political ideas of abolition. The students were quiet and attentive.

Eagleswood was much more a part of nature than Lucy's home in

Philadelphia, and Lucy loved being here. She and Ellen loved to sit on the steps of the bathhouse and watch the sun set over the salt grass marsh and the water of the bay. Lucy could feel a part of nature and a part of the society at Eagleswood.

Thoreau spoke literally: walking into the woods and marshes would deliver you from a village and "man and his affairs, church and state and school, trade and commerce, and manufacturers and agriculture, even politics, the most alarming of them all." But walking would also give you freedom from old ways of thinking and old habits, would give you a "roughness of character" and an "intellectual and moral growth," which was exactly what Weld wanted for his students.

At Eagleswood, Lucy might be removed from the everyday action of her father's work in Philadelphia, but here she could gain the freedom to think and do as she wanted. On the surface, she didn't want to be a dour Quaker like the Grimké sisters, and instead put braids and ribbons in her hair and wore patterned and frilly dresses. She also thought she could be more than a supportive mother and wife. Perhaps she could be a musician.

"We go westward as into the future, with a spirit of enterprise and adventure," Thoreau said. "For every walk is a sort of crusade . . . to go forth and reconquer this Holy Land from the Hands of the Infidels."

The presidential election was days away on Tuesday, November 4, and Thoreau mentioned reconquering land from infidels. He hated the Fugitive Slave Law and was incensed when Anthony Burns was taken back to Virginia. The government as it was now was allowing slavery to spread. Even if Lucy's father, Miller McKim, didn't believe in voting, nonresistants believed John C. Frémont winning the presidency might tip the balance in favor of a federal government opposed to slavery.

"Give me for my friends and neighbors wild men, not tame ones," Thoreau went on. It was the wild men in Kansas who seemed to be doing the most visible anti-slavery work in recent months, even if they were breaking the law. Thoreau didn't believe in laws for laws' sake. "We may study the laws of matter at and for our convenience, but a successful life knows no law," he said.

"So we saunter toward the Holy Land, till one day the sun shall shine more brightly than ever he has done, shall perchance shine into our minds and hearts, and light up our whole lives with a great awakening light, as warm and serene and golden as on a bank-side in autumn," Thoreau finished.

Yes, autumn always made everything look "perfectly lovely and fresh" in Lucy's mind, and hopefully the election would do the same.

George Garrison's Diary

NOVEMBER 1856

*Buchanan was elected the 4th of [November], having
carried all the slave States but one, and five free states.
Fremont carried eleven free states. Fillmore carried
one state, vis., Maryland. The Republicans though
disappointed at the result, are not disheartened at all; they
mean to fight on till they triumph, cost what it may.*

Charlotte Forten's Journal

NOVEMBER 1856

Saturday, November 8, 1856

*Alas! for the hope of the people! Again has Might
triumphed over Right; Falsehood over Truth, Slavery over
Freedom. But these things cannot last much longer. Surely
a just God will not permit them.*

CHAPTER 13

Charlotte Forten

BOSTON
DECEMBER 1856

Outside the Music Hall in central Boston, horses pulled sleighs over the snow-covered ground, and the air nipped at Charlotte's cheeks. Charlotte loved Christmas, and since she was living and working as a teacher in Salem and her father had moved to Canada, she decided to go to Boston on Christmas Day 1856 for the annual Anti-Slavery Bazaar that would wrap up the bloody and depressing year that was 1856.

Inside, the women of the Boston Female Anti-Slavery Society had draped garlands of pine, rhododendron branches, and holly. Charlotte drifted about the neatly decorated tables, thinking the women organizing the fair managed to find many beautiful things to sell. Set upon the tables in front of Charlotte were porcelain vases and cups; jewelry and watch boxes; carved wooden chairs and music stools from France; inkstands and candlesticks in iron and bronze; and fans, slippers, embroidered handkerchiefs. These goods were beautiful, to be sure, but more importantly, none had been made by enslaved people. At the fair and in free labor stores, women sewed clothing made of linen and wool instead of cotton, and they made cakes and candies with molasses instead of sugar.

They also sold books and anti-slavery publications. Ten years earlier, the children's book *The Abolitionist Alphabet* had been published for the fair.

Some people Charlotte's age went to the fair in hopes of getting to flirt. William Garrison Jr. came to the fair and talked with young women he knew, but Charlotte already felt too old for all that, even though she was just nineteen and didn't have a romantic interest.

Charlotte was happy to talk to the adults she admired, including Maria Weston Chapman, who organized the fair. She was one of "the noblest and best women," in Charlotte's mind. Chapman slipped her arm through Charlotte's, and they walked around the fair together, stopping to talk to friends and acquaintances, including William Lloyd and Helen Garrison. Charlotte only wished that she could accept the invitations to stay in Boston for a few days.

How far they had come. At the close of the fair, the Massachusetts Anti-Slavery Society would celebrate its twenty-fifth anniversary. When Charlotte was young, the women hosted the fair in someone's home and resold donated items. Now, they rented this hall and managed to get friends from Europe to send these treasures.

And yet, as far as they had come, their goals remained the same. In Weston Chapman's announcement of the bazaar, she wrote their goal was "to look far ahead in moral enterprises" and the money would be spent "awakening that high, right feeling in the hearts of men." While some money would go to help people escaping from slavery, much more would go to publications, the free pamphlets they gave out, and paying anti-slavery lecturers. To the American Anti-Slavery Society and those who supported Garrison, the abolition fight was still a moral one. They needed to convince the majority of Americans of the moral wrong of slavery, to move them from apathetic to abolitionist. That was how this fight would be won.

As Charlotte walked through the fair, she wondered how Weston Chapman could be so sweet and kind and pay *her* any attention. Charlotte couldn't help but think of herself as a nobody. She couldn't see herself as these women saw her: the daughter of a prominent abolitionist family who, although not a lecturer, wrote stunning poetry for the cause. Just a few months earlier, Garrison had published one of Charlotte's poems in *The Liberator*.

Another one of the organizers, Lydia Maria Child, told Charlotte she'd visited their home in Philadelphia once, when Charlotte was nothing more than a "wee toddling," but Charlotte didn't remember that. Child was an author and had been editor of the *National Anti-Slavery Standard* and was an inspiration for Charlotte. Educating others and writing could be tools of anti-slavery work, tools Charlotte would be happy employing.

Everyone gathered here would continue "demanding the immediate abolition of slavery," but the election and the free-soil debate would make that even harder. There might have been a glimmer of hope, however. The day after Christmas, *The Liberator* reported that the question of the 1820 Missouri Compromise (federal legislation that was supposed to limit the expansion of slavery), the Kansas-Nebraska Act, and popular sovereignty would come before the Supreme Court in a case involving a Black man named Dred Scott.

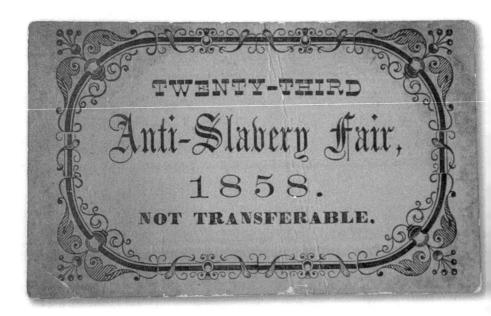

PART 2
1857–1859

An Unknown Darkness

"How strange it is that in a world so beautiful,
there can be so much wickedness."

—CHARLOTTE FORTEN

CHAPTER 14

Lewis Douglass

ROCHESTER
SPRING 1857

loomy. Lewis returned to this word often, a word his father liked to use in his speeches and writings, too. This spring, *gloomy* felt an especially appropriate adjective.

Just a few days after President Buchanan's inauguration in March 1857, Lewis heard the news of the Supreme Court's decision in the *Dred Scott v. Sanford* case. Dred Scott had sued for his freedom after his enslaver took Scott; his wife, Harriet; and their two daughters to a free state. If they were on free soil, he should be free, Scott argued. The defense argued that Scott could not sue at all because he wasn't a United States citizen.

"The question was simply this," the *New-York Tribune* reported: Can a person like Scott—*or Lewis*—"whose ancestors were imported and sold as slaves, become a member of the political community formed and brought into existence by the Constitution of the United States, and, as such, become entitled to all the rights and immunities of a citizen"?

On March 6, 1857, the Supreme Court said no.

According to seven of the nine justices of the Supreme Court of the United States, Scott could not bring this suit. According to the majority opinion written by Chief Justice Roger Taney, neither Dred Scott nor Lewis Douglass were citizens, regardless of whether they were enslaved or free. Taney's decision effectively said that "colored men of African descent are not and cannot be citizens of the United States," as Lewis's father put it.

In Rochester, Lewis was now the foreman at his father's newspaper office. In the months following the decision, as they continued to report on the implication of the court case, Lewis would have to read Justice Taney's words, print his words, be oppressed by his words.

What was Lewis if not a citizen? If this country didn't care for him, should he care for it?

In his speeches that spring and summer, Lewis's father said he had hope: hope for the end of slavery, hope for liberty, hope for the rights of all people in the United States. His father spoke of the future, but what was the future? Lewis couldn't see "the white flag of freedom"; couldn't see an end to the bondage of millions; wouldn't even be considered a citizen of these United States. Lewis couldn't attend any school he wanted, couldn't get any job he wanted, couldn't marry anyone he wanted. Where was his hope amidst so much discrimination and hate?

The front page of *Frank Leslie's Illustrated Newspaper* on June 27, 1857 had drawings of Dred Scott; his wife, Harriet; and their children, Eliza and Lizzie, with the story of Dred Scott's case in the Supreme Court.

Note that the N-word appeared in the article (third column, final paragraph), but it is redacted here.

throat with his sharp knife.

George Thompson Garrison.

Compo. No. 1.

Disobedience.

Once upon a time a boy name Robert, wished to go to the river to sail in a boat. This was soon after a freshet, and his mother thought he had better not go, but he was determined to go and so he went away before she knew it. He went down to the river got into the boat, and pushed out into the stream. Now there was a very strong current in the middle of this stream, which ran over a high dam. He got drawn into the current and began to go down. He tried all he to get back, but his oars suddenly broke, and he could do nothing. The people on the shore saw him, but could do nothing to save him from going over the dam. The boat went over the dam, and was broken to pieces Robert's body was found the next day, about a mile from the dam, and was buried. M

George Garrison's composition warning boys to not be disobedient, which he wrote while at the Hopedale School in Northampton, Massachusetts.

Composition at the Hopedale School by George T. Garrison, Age Fifteen

1851

Disobedience.

Once upon a time a boy name Robert wished to go to the river to sail in a boat. This was soon after a freshet [a flood], and his mother thought he had better not go, but he was determined to go and so he went away before she knew it. He went down to the river, got into the boat, and pushed out into the stream. Now there was a very strong current in the middle of this stream, which ran over a high dam. He got drawn into the current and began to go down. He tried all he could to get back, but his oars suddenly broke, and he could do nothing. The people on the shore saw him, but could do nothing to stop him from going over the dam. The boat went over the dam, and was broken to pieces. Robert's body was found the next day, about a mile from the dam, and was buried. May this be a warning to all disobedient boys.

George T. Garrison

CHAPTER 15

George Garrison

**BOSTON
SPRING 1857**

Once upon a time, a young man named George wished to go west. This was during a time of great strife, and his mother and father thought he had better not go. But on February 13, 1857, George turned twenty-one, and his parents could no longer keep him at home. He was free. "Hip! Hip! Hurrah!" George wrote in his diary.

Going to Kansas still flew in the face of his father's nonviolent principles. But George's friend had written to him about the possibility of moving to Nininger, Minnesota, another territory that also needed free-state settlers. The West "seemed to be the best opening for the young, the enterprising, and the industrious," George told a friend.

———

George left home on April 28, 1857, with regret and excitement both swirling around his head. He would miss his family. His father and mother gave him their blessing in the end, but they were not pleased and wished he would stay. But George wanted to labor as a pioneer and hoped that this change would bring him a new advantage in life. Money, a career, a purpose.

A family friend explained how George should get to Battle Creek, Michigan through Albany, Rochester, and Detroit by train. George spent three days in Battle Creek with other family friends, and while there, he met the remarkable Sojourner Truth. She had such an interesting life, George thought. She had been born enslaved in New York and freed by the New York state emancipation law in 1827. The Lord had given her the name Sojourner Truth, she said, because she traveled to tell people the truth of God.

Truth traveled and spoke about abolition and equal rights for Black people. A formerly enslaved woman speaking up against injustice was rare, and it "gave me a great deal of pleasure at seeing her," George wrote.

From Battle Creek, George took the train to Chicago, then took the night train for Dunleith, Illinois. From there, he got on the steamboat *City Belle* and chugged up the Mississippi River for two days and two nights.

Finally, on May 8, George stepped off the boat in Minnesota. His friend William Reed met him at the landing. Reed had grown a great deal larger since the last time George had seen him and sported a thick beard and mustache. He looked like a man of the West, George thought.

All in all, it had been a very pleasant journey. George had crossed the suspension bridge above the Niagara Falls, stood on the shores of Lake Michigan, and seen the cliffs that rose above the Mississippi River. Now, a new chapter could begin.

CHAPTER 16

Charlotte Forten

PHILADELPHIA
SUMMER 1857

The boat pulled out of the docks in Philadelphia and began to move up the Delaware River on a June morning in 1857. Charlotte had made the trip many times out to Byberry and was delighted to be on the water when the sun shone and the farm beckoned. She was on her way to visit her aunt Harriet and uncle Robert Purvis, who worked at the Pennsylvania Anti-Slavery Society with Miller McKim and had founded the Philadelphia Vigilance Committee.

Charlotte loved the water, and the fresh air might do her well, too. All winter and spring in Salem, she'd felt tired, sick, and lonely. When her students didn't do well in class, she worried she wasn't doing a good job, which made her too depressed to do anything in the evenings, which made her feel more lonely—even worthless. The doctor told her she shouldn't teach over the summer, and friends said that coming back to Philadelphia would be good for her.

Good weather and flower picking, visits from friends, and good books did make Charlotte feel better. That spring, she'd enjoyed *Autobiography of a Female Slave*, a novel by a white woman named Martha Griffith about a beautiful and light-skinned enslaved woman in Kentucky. The book had come out in 1856. As fortune would have it, Griffith—Mattie to her friends—was on the boat going to Byberry.[4]

On the boat, Charlotte and Griffith, who was nine years older, talked at length about what they were writing and reading. While many people had compared Griffith's book to Harriet Beecher Stowe's *Uncle Tom's Cabin*, released four years earlier, Griffith actually thought that Stowe hadn't portrayed the reality of slavery well enough. Charlotte had enjoyed *Uncle Tom's Cabin*, although "everything which is written in opposition to this iniquitous system" of slavery, Charlotte admitted, she read "with pleasure."

Griffith felt as though *Uncle Tom's Cabin* made cruelty an exception rather than the norm that upheld slavery. Charlotte thought parts of Griffith's book "almost too horrible to be believed," but Griffith said she saw each of the horrible things she wrote about in the book herself. She had not grown up with or even heard abolitionist teachings as Charlotte had, but she saw the cruelty and the suffering and knew it was wrong. Even though Griffith's book was fiction, Charlotte thought the novel showed a "terrible reality" and found Mattie pleasant, but "plain and unpretending."

After a day in Byberry, Charlotte took the boat back to Philadelphia, where Charlotte and her friend Jane Putnam decided they wanted ice cream. They walked into one ice cream parlor, and whoever was working refused to serve the two Black women. They left and went to another. There, too, the person working refused to sell them ice cream.

Charlotte felt so terrible, she could hardly say anything. Putnam gave them some choice words Charlotte didn't think they would forget.

Charlotte and Griffith had spoken about prejudice earlier that day, but Charlotte knew that her white friends would never know how she felt. White abolitionists didn't understand that terrible feeling of being refused service. They didn't feel the burning red of embarrassment on their cheeks. They didn't

---

4. Martha "Mattie" Griffith later married Albert Gallatin Browne Jr. Contemporary editions of her novel are sometimes attributed to Martha Griffith Browne.

feel like they were less than, simply for being. Now the Supreme Court and federal government said that Charlotte wasn't a citizen, wasn't protected by the Constitution because she was Black.

"None but those who experience it can know what it is—this constant, galling sense of cruel injustice and wrong," Charlotte wrote in her journal. "I cannot help feeling it very often, it intrudes upon my happiest moments, and spreads a dark, deep gloom over everything." When she thought of summer nights listening to music with friends, walks along the shore or the winding streets of Salem, she tried to push those feelings of darkness down, put them away, but they always came rushing back.

In July 1863, George's brother Wendell Garrison traveled through Philadelphia and sketched in his diary a sign "conspicuously posted" in a horse-drawn street car. He wrote that he believed that "such contemptible signs will not remain up forever."

CHAPTER 17

George Garrison

**MINNESOTA
SUMMER 1857**

The West really was the debauched place that George's father imagined, and George didn't try to hide that in his letters home.

On July 4, 1857, George did not listen intently to anti-slavery speeches like he would have at home. In Nininger, someone read the Declaration of Independence (which his father called a lie after the Anthony Burns trial) while most people were doing "a great deal of drinking during the day, and several [people] got dead drunk," George reported to his father.

George noticed men did not really shave here, so that summer, he grew a beard, too, despite his father's "strong aversion to the hair epidemic which has so strangely swept over the country during the last four years." To grow a beard was to be associated with gamblers, highwaymen, and pirates, according to William Lloyd Garrison.

George's father told him not to "make worldly success, or the accumulation of property" his chief goal, and yet in almost every letter home, George tried to prove that he was making a success of himself in Minnesota. In the summer of 1857, George got a job at the *Emigrant Aid Journal* newspaper, he was loaning out money to earn interest, and he was even thinking of buying property in town.

His father still thought George should return home, work at *The Liberator*, and enjoy what Boston had to offer. Luckily, George's brother Wendell defended him. Wendell reported that he told their father "that you were getting what you needed more than money, just now, and that was experience and self reliance."

George knew that if he worked hard, saved money, and perhaps even bought a piece of land to resell later, when more people arrived in Nininger, he could make something of himself. He felt that he could not do that in Boston.

George liked Minnesota very much, and he had "not the slightest idea of returning home," he wrote his mother.

New lyrics to "The Star-Spangled Banner" in the student newspaper *The Diamond*, edited by George Garrison

1851

Oh, say, can you see, by Freedom's clear light,
A stain on the Banner that's over you flying;
Which enshrouds the bright starts in the blackness of night,
And proclaims to the world that your liberty's dying?
Hear its victims despair,
How it bursts on the air,
And proclaims to the world that your flag is still there;
For the Star-Spangled Banner in TRIUMPH now waves,
O'er a land where one-sixth of people are slaves.

Oh weep! All ye lovers of liberty's name;
Oh! Weep for the utter disgrace of your nation;
And pray that her Banner be cleansed for the stain
That has worked thus her sad desolation!
With power and with might,
Strive, pray, that the night,
Of oppression be pierced by the Gospel's pure light—
That the Star-Spangled Banner in triumph may wave,
O'er a land unpolluted by the toil of the slave.

Charlotte Forten's Journal

JULY 1857

Saturday, July 4, 1857

*The celebration of this day! What a mockery it is! My soul
sickens of it. Am glad to see that the people are much less
demonstrative in their mock patriotism than of old.*

CHAPTER 18

Charlotte Forten

PHILADELPHIA
JULY 1857

A few days after July 4, 1857, Charlotte and her aunt stepped out of the Forten family home on Lombard Street. The three-and-a-half-story brick house was grander than others on the block, and it was one place Charlotte felt at home in Philadelphia. As a child, Charlotte had spent Christmases and Easters here with her extended family, and now, when she came to Philadelphia from Massachusetts, it was where she stayed.

The weather was lovely, and good weather always improved Charlotte's mood. Charlotte and her aunt planned to take a long walk, and they found themselves heading north, past churches, cemeteries, and historic sites, including Independence Square and Benjamin Franklin's grave.

Soon, they were at the Pennsylvania Anti-Slavery Society office. Miller McKim welcomed them in, as gracious and pleasant as ever. William Still was there, too; he worked closely with Charlotte's uncle Robert Purvis on the Vigilance Committee and as a conductor on the Underground Railroad. He'd also been at the office when Henry "Box" Brown arrived from Richmond in 1849.

William Still smiled, looked at Charlotte, and asked, "Have you written any poetry lately?"

Charlotte's eyes must have gone wide, and maybe some color came to her cheeks. She didn't know what to say and just stood there blankly. How did he know she was a poet? Had he read her "doggerel," as she called it, that William Lloyd Garrison published?

"No, sir, I never wrote any," Charlotte lied. She quickly turned away and started talking to someone else.

Charlotte knew that must have appeared rude, but she was so embarrassed when anyone brought up her poetry. She enjoyed writing, but she didn't take the time to be proud of her writing. Even when Garrison published her recent poem, Charlotte didn't make a note of it in her journal and hardly wanted anyone to know she'd written it. She could never see herself as others saw her.

An undated photo of Charlotte Forten,
probably taken around the time she
attended the Salem Normal School.

CHAPTER 19

George Garrison

NININGER, MINNESOTA
DECEMBER 1857

O n December 31, 1857, George walked from his lodgings through the thick snow to the second floor of Wheeler & Kemp's hardware store, to the new hall where they would dance all night. Not much happened in Nininger, Minnesota, so George decided to go even though he thought he was not "able to dance."

George was not impressed with the women who attended the dance. "Most of them were country girls, and were not dressed in the very latest styles," he wrote his mother. Though, if he was honest, he was always "bashful when with women," and he felt they did not know what to make of him. He danced the cotillions, which were not too intimidating, and reported that he enjoyed himself and stayed until five o'clock the next morning.

———————

On New Year's Day, George felt homesick. He did not often get letters from his father, and when he did, his father was never supportive of George's decision and kept telling him to come home. "Your 'great West' will be soon reeling beneath the blow [of the current economic difficulties], and multitudes among you will find that their golden dreams of wealth are nothing but frightful mockeries," he had written to George in October 1857.

Despite the fun at the ball, that New Year's Day—the coldest, harshest George had experienced—George was beginning to have doubts himself.

"Have I to be a confounded printer all long life?" George wondered in his diary. He enjoyed the work but did not think it would bring him success. "If I am to lead a worthless life, or to have to continue like what it has been to some extent, may I find an early grave."

He knew that at any time, he could go back home to Boston. But George felt that if he was not able to succeed in the West, with all the opportunity there, "I shall never be able to [be successful] anywhere."

Back east, his family said the economic downturn was affecting young men especially. His friend Francis Meriam returned from France in the fall and was not able to find a job. George's father said Meriam still was "burning to go to Kansas" to fight with the free soilers, "but his mother and grandfather forbid such a step, very wisely."

George wanted to see "great changes" for abolition in 1858, but Minnesota did not seem to be the center of anything. Back in Boston, Massachusetts senator Charles Sumner visited his family's house many times and was still recovering from injuries sustained when South Carolina congressman and enslaver Preston Brooks attacked him more than a year earlier for simply speaking about the situation in Kansas. At Tremont Temple, the great orators spoke of fugitive slaves and the Haitian Revolution and Toussaint L'Ouverture. George's brother William had gone to a lecture in Salem where he met "some very handsome young ladies [including] the prettiest one, Miss Forten."

George's father thought that "animal appetites and passions are far more developed than intellectual or moral cultures" in Minnesota, but George did have the pleasure of seeing Asa B. Hutchinson of the Hutchinson Family Singers, and "it seemed like old times to hear him," George thought. The

Hutchinsons performed at anti-slavery meetings back east and sang popular songs with new anti-slavery lyrics. "My country 'tis of thee, Stronghold of Slavery" was a favorite.

Some of the prominent men in Nininger started a lyceum, where they posed a question and expected every member to contribute to the discussion. One evening in January, they discussed if voters should decide whether slavery should be legal. Voting allowed citizens to voice what they wanted for their own state, but this democracy nearly caused a war in Kansas. The men concluded that citizens deciding the slavery question did not work.

George was hesitant to speak during these meetings, despite his father's encouragement. "You are in an excellent position to let your light shine on the subject of temperance, anti-slavery, and the other reforms of the age," his father told him. George was not afraid to use his voice, "but the trouble with me is that I have not got the ideas," he thought, and he would not make a fool of himself by getting up and speaking about something he did not know.

George felt debating a question required studying. And if there was anything in this world that George hated, it was studying. He disliked it when he was in school and he disliked it now. He saw the necessity of it, but that would not make him want to do it. He was content to listen to the others.

CHAPTER 20

Charlotte Forten

SALEM
JANUARY 1858

The new year came and went for Charlotte. She had returned to Massachusetts in August 1857 and gone back to teaching, but
she wasn't happy in Salem, either.

"I cannot bear to think how I have misspent and lost the precious, precious
hours that can return no more," she wrote in her journal. She made resolutions
for the new year but buried them in the depths of her heart rather than writing
them down.

On January 1, 1858, she wrote to her father. He'd moved with her stepmother and brothers to England. Once upon a time, she would have longed
to go with them. She'd wanted to live in a quiet English home, perhaps one
reminiscent of the windswept landscape of a Brontë sister's novel. That wish
came from a different time, before Charlotte had begun a career as a teacher
and before she felt so sick all the time. Her father also said he was "utterly
unable" to help her financially, a rather strange statement. Her stepmother
was a free Black woman from South Carolina who had inherited money
from her first husband's estate, which included the sale of the people they'd
owned. Charlotte didn't want to be dependent on anyone—she'd "rather die

ten thousand times than that"—and might have felt particularly strange about where her stepmother's money came from. Charlotte would need to work to support herself.

"I wonder why it is that I have this strange feeling of not *living out myself*," Charlotte wrote in her midwinter reflection. Her existence of teaching, sewing, and reading in Salem "seems not *full* not expansive enough." She yearned for more.

"I must need some great emotion to arouse the dormant energies of my nature," she thought.

CHAPTER 21

Lewis Douglass

ROCHESTER
JANUARY 1858

I n winter, snow would pile outside the Douglass home in Rochester, and by late afternoon, the sky darkened. Lewis walked the thirty minutes home from the office where he'd worked on the newspaper all day. That winter, they'd published articles on fugitive slave cases and what was happening in Kansas, as well as the usual poems, recipes, and advertisements for hotels, fabric sellers, and pharmacists.

In late January 1858, darkness and cold covered the landscape outside, but Lewis's house filled with light and energy. That month, his father's friend John Brown had appeared on their doorstep looking for a place to retreat and work on his grand liberation scheme.

Brown looked like an old-fashioned preacher. He'd grown a large white beard since his speech at the Convention of Radical Political Abolitionists in Rochester and wore a starched collar, cravat, vest, and coat. One couldn't help but feel his religious presence. At the Douglass house, he would stand up and lean on a chair, as if it were a lectern and the dining room his pulpit. Brown would recite scripture or begin speaking as if giving a sermon off the cuff, and one might not know the difference if one did not know the Bible.

"God has given the strength of the hills to freedom."

"Thou shalt not deliver unto his master the servant which is escaped."

Brown had also laid out a map on two boards in the house, where forts connected secret passages in the Allegheny Mountains of western Virginia, Maryland, and Pennsylvania. Take the people from the plantations of Maryland and Virginia, hide them here, he said, ferry them north to Canada, and cause fear and panic among the enslavers in the South. That was the essence of the plan; a *grand exodus*, to use a biblical phrase. If given the chance, the enslaved would participate in their own liberation. Lewis's father believed this—it was what enslaved Frederick Bailey had done before he'd become the free man Frederick Douglass.

Lewis and his brothers sat enraptured by the drawings, diagrams, and wooden blocks Brown laid out. Here was a battle to come, and Brown was the general, planning his troops' movements. Even Lewis's little sister, Annie, who was about to turn nine, listened to Brown and thought him a good friend.

Lewis's father, on the other hand, saw flaws in the plan and asked Brown about the logistics. Were these forts real? Where would his men get food and supplies in the mountains? What would they do when the slave catchers and police came after them? Brown might counter with moral arguments or examples of other uprisings by enslaved people in Jamaica or Haiti, but he didn't always have an answer to specific challenges, and Lewis's father grew more skeptical.

Most days, Lewis didn't see Brown. Lewis worked from morning to night, and Brown was upstairs, turning his ideas into words and sentences scrawled on sheet after sheet of paper. Brown wrote letters to his sons in Kansas, to his wife and daughters in New York, and to friends who might be interested in helping him and asked Lewis's brother Charles to walk two miles into town twice a day to drop them off and pick up new mail. Everything was about the plan he'd laid out on the boards and what he called his "Provisional Constitution," something he'd been working on for more than a decade. When his invasion and overthrow of Slave Power succeeded in Virginia, this would be the interim government he'd establish, Brown said. He thought that slavery was in "utter disregard and violation of those eternal and self-evident truths set forth in our Declaration of Independence" and of his own morals.

He talked of his constitution all day, every day. Lewis wanted to hear these plans, but they began to bore his father.

And yet, his father still helped John Brown, letting Brown into their home and introducing him to other Black abolitionists. Lewis's father did believe in struggle and agitation. That could bring progress. He'd said it so eloquently a year earlier:

> If there is no struggle, there is no progress. Those who profess to favor freedom and yet deprecate agitation, are men who want crops without plowing up the ground, they want rain without thunder and lightening. This struggle may be a moral one, or it may be a physical one, and it may be both moral and physical, but it must be a struggle. Power concedes nothing without a demand. It never did and it never will.

CHAPTER 22

Charlotte Forten

**PHILADELPHIA
JUNE 1858**

C harlotte returned to Philadelphia in March 1858. Her depression had not let up since January, and she felt too sick and weak to
continue teaching in Salem.

In Philadelphia, she had time to think about her life in "the so-called City
of Brotherly Love, where, strange to say, the doctrine of love to all mankind is
quite out of fashioned," especially when it came to people who looked like her.
She had time to think about Salem and Boston and her time in New England.
She had time to write.

Charlotte wrote a piece that in essence did what she respected so many
writers for: used words to make a difference. And on June 19, 1858, her essay
"Glimpses of New England" appeared in the *National Anti-Slavery Standard*,
and although it was mostly a love letter to New England, she managed to
weave in anecdotes about the people who didn't support anti-slavery and her
distaste for them.

Yet her depression couldn't let her see what she'd accomplished. She admitted in her journal that she had "a mingling feeling of sorrow, shame and

self-contempt" and didn't think that she had "wit, beauty and talent" or intelligence, when everyone around her told her that she did.

Worse yet, her family friend—the smart, beautiful, talented anti-slavery orator Sarah Parker Remond—accused the article of having a pro-slavery stance, according to another friend. The essay was certainly not pro-slavery. Like Martha Griffith had done in *Autobiography of a Female Slave*, Charlotte recounted what she saw and experienced in New England, even if that meant pointing out prejudice from abolitionists.

If Remond thought that telling the truth about New Englanders made the essay pro-slavery, she was misguided. Charlotte pitied Remond. But those kinds of remarks were exactly why Charlotte wanted to keep her writing to herself.

CHAPTER 23

Lewis Douglass

MCGRAWVILLE, NEW YORK
JUNE 1858

Most days passed the same at the newspaper office, but sometimes, Lewis would travel with his father to lectures or conventions. In June 1858, his father had been invited to New York Central College in McGrawville to give a commencement speech.

Lewis went with his father and saw that the college's classrooms were unlike almost every college in the country, with white, Black, and Native American men and women sitting and learning together. His father would speak about the "self-made man" and how genius alone would not bring a man or woman success. It took hard work, too. This was a new speech his father was working on, but the ideas were ones he was thinking about all the time at home.

The speech wasn't what would stick in Lewis's mind. Instead, all he could think of was a student: beautiful, with big brown eyes and light brown skin. He'd seen her before. She was Amelia Loguen, and her father, Jermain Wesley Loguen, was a friend of Lewis's father and a daring conductor on the Underground Railroad in Syracuse. Two years ago, the Loguens came to Rochester, but Lewis had no chance to speak to Amelia then because his younger brother had stolen all her attention, even staying home from work to entertain her.

Lewis noticed her outfit, too. Amelia wore "that near-masculine approach to men's unmentionables"—bloomers. The loose pants and tunic freed women from tight corsets and massive hoopskirts, but also made a statement that like the garment's inventor, Amelia Bloomer, they believed in women's equality and rights.

The outfit didn't detract from Lewis's attraction to Amelia. She also sang "I'll never see my darling any more," and Lewis wished he could be her darling, or at least have someone introduce him to her so he could say something—anything—to her.

Eaglewood. Nov. 12th. 1858.

So you thought you were a fool for writing to me! Well, we were wont to differ sometimes on certain subjects! Dear Nell, neither have you written to me during these long months, longer to me than to you, who were able to read, write, and sew. Yes, here I am again at Eaglewood, with only two studies, Latin and Music, and yet so busy that I can hardly get time to turn around; Industry is indigenous to this place! I have ten scholars, take lessons on the violin, practice an hour every day on the piano, perform Gamma Sigma duties, Sadma, Mermaid, & Eaglewood band ditto, write compositions & speak, and do a variety of other things too innumerable to mention. This sketch of my daily life may not be uninteresting to you, and if you please we will resume our intercourse just where we left off, and not count the many

Lucy McKim's November 12, 1858, letter to her friend Ellen Wright.
Lucy and Ellen corresponded frequently, and Lucy would often
squeeze in as much writing as she could on a single sheet.

Letter from Lucy McKim to Ellen Wright

NOVEMBER 1858

Eagleswood Nov. 12th 1858

So you thought you were a fool for writing to me! Well, we were wont to differ sometimes on certain subjects. [. . .] Yes, here I am again at Eagleswood, with only two studies, Latin and Music, and yet so busy that I can hardly get time to turn around. Industry is indigenous to this place! I have ten scholars, take lessons on the violin, practise an hour every day on the piano, perform [. . .] Eagleswood band [duties . . .] write compositions & speak, and do a variety of other things too innumerable to mention. This sketch of my daily life may not be uninteresting to you, and if you please, we will resume our [exchange of letters] just where we left off, and not count the many stitches that have been dropped in our separate histories. Yet our relations will be somewhat changed, the office of Mentor which I so unworthily filled, I will resign with pleasure. You are now 18, and with the wisdom acquired in the partial retirement of the last year, can easily dispense with the mock-heroic advice of a girl just launched into all the follies and sentimentalities of sweet sixteen! Don't imagine me satirical, I assure you that folly I have renounced long since, now I am only humble.

    [. . .]

    Farewell darling, if I had more time I could not say anything else worth your personal (I don't mean to convey the idea that what I have written is) so until we meet,

                    Your affect[ionate] friend
                        Lucy Mc.

CHAPTER 24

George Garrison

A **year and a half into his Minnesota sojourn, George did** not think this town as great as advertised. George was sick of the people, of his job at the newspaper, and of the town as a whole, and he wanted to leave for good. If only his father would have let him go to Kansas a year and a half ago, how different things would be now, George thought. It was never too late, though.

His family wanted him to return home, but they didn't understand that "to go back and work in the [*Liberator*] office would settle" his fate forever and he'd never make anything of himself. George would never make anything of himself at all if he returned to Boston.

"Everything is dead, dead, dead" in Nininger, George wrote his brother William.

In his letter to William, George parroted the questions he knew his family would ask: "Have I not decided to come home? Am I not foolish remaining West any longer? Have I not had Western experience enough yet?"

"No! No! No!" he countered the hypothetical question. He was not going home. He was going to Kansas. Only he needed at least thirty dollars to get there.

George asked William for the money, since he had not been paid for his work at the newspaper. George knew William was always willing to help him, but he feared that if William consulted their parents, they would say George needed to come home. Regardless of what his parents said, "you may remain assured I have made up my mind," George wrote his brother. He would get to Kansas one way or another.

———

On October 18, fifty dollars arrived from William. After four years of Kansas fever and nearly a year and a half in Minnesota, George would finally be on his way to Kansas.

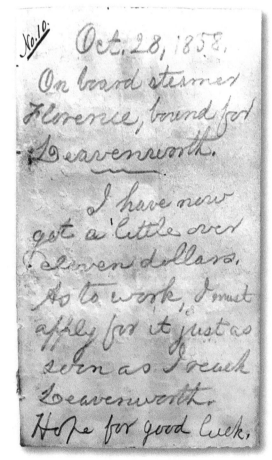

George Garrison recorded in his diary that he was finally on his way to Kansas in late October 1858.

George Garrison Poem

Nov. 13th 1858

I move on Fortune's rapid wheel:
my lot
Forever changing, like the
changeful moon
That each night varies;
hardly new perceived;
And less she shows her
bright horn by degrees
She fills her crib with light,
but when she reigns
In all her pride, she then
begins once more
To waste her glories, till
dissolved and lost
She sinks again to darkness.

Charlotte Forten's Journal

I am lonely tonight. I long for one earnest sympathizing soul to be in close communion with my own. I long for the pressure of a loving hand in mine, the touch of living lips upon my aching brow. I long to lay my weary head upon an earnest heart, which beats for me,—to which I am dearer far than all the world beside. There is none, for me, and never will be. I could only love one whom I could look up to, and reverence and that one would never think of such a poor little ignoramus as I.

CHAPTER 25

George Garrison

LAWRENCE, KANSAS
JANUARY 1859

Kansas was almost as wild as George's father feared. A newcomer could be shot outside the hotel, or a building might be set on fire by a pro-slavery mob. Even the editor of the *Herald of Freedom* newspaper was charged with assault and battery. George also quickly learned to avoid the literal rats "both alive and dead" that crowded the streets of Lawrence.

None of this made George want to go home, even though that was still the constant refrain from his parents. His father said he appreciated George's "high sense of independence" but warned George that he should not be so independent as to "subject himself to perennial suffering." George had suffered, but he also knew that if he had followed his father's advice two years ago, he would never have left Boston and would never have gained as much knowledge about the world as he had.

Lawrence did have more "anti-slavery feeling" than Nininger. George got a job at the *Lawrence Republican* because of his father's name, but found many people were still ignorant of his father's principles. George regretted that he had not taken one of his father's books with him.

"I am sure if I had it could have done a great deal of good by lending it to my friends and those who are anxious to know your principles," George wrote his father. While people supported the ideas of free labor and states without slavery, they were not necessarily abolitionists, George explained.

There was abolitionist activity, though. In December 1858, John Brown returned to Kansas from New York and escaped with eleven enslaved people from Missouri with a plan to bring them to Iowa. George heard from people in Lawrence and from the newspapers about Brown's plans. To head north through a treacherous western winter seemed unwise, but John Brown had proven himself as a brave, if reckless, man.

On Sunday, January 23, 1859, George came home to his lodgings and found that his landlord was hiding a man. George understood the man to be a fugitive from enslavement, and the pro-slavery newspapers reported that more than one man had been "stolen" from Missouri and transported to Kansas. The man was supposed to travel with John Doy to Iowa, but by the evening, kidnappers found out the man was at George's. Soon, a dozen men had come to defend the house and the man. George knew that Missouri ruffians would set a house on fire if they wanted to. George's father would hate to see him pick up a gun, even in self-defense, but what would be the other option?

George and the others brought the fugitives to a safe place by morning, where they waited until Tuesday.

Later, George heard John Doy's whole party was betrayed for money by a man thought to be reliable. George thought it even worse that this man had also betrayed John Brown and his party, who were still on the way to Iowa. George was anxious to hear news of Brown's party, worrying they would be overtaken and killed, although knowing Brown's reputation, it would not be without a fight.

On his birthday—February 13—George heard that "Old John Brown has arrived safely in Iowa with the fugitive slaves he rescued from Missouri." From there, they would travel on to Canada.

CHAPTER 26

Lewis Douglass

ROCHESTER
APRIL 1859

I n April 1859, John Brown stepped into the printing office in Rochester, New York. Lewis and his family had been keeping up with Brown's whereabouts since he'd left their house the year before. They had followed the harrowing story of his escape from Missouri with eleven people, first to Iowa, then to Detroit, where they finally crossed into Canada in March. Now Brown could regale them with the story of the fight and the flight.

Brown was a hero, but he had also drawn attention to himself. Lewis's sister Rosetta thought Brown needed to lie low, since there was now a three-thousand-dollar reward for his capture.

But here he was, trying to get support from Lewis's father for the plan he'd laid out at their house and his Provisional Constitution again. Lewis's father was supportive—he even started penning a note about Brown's visit. But when Brown asked if Lewis's father would join in his next action, Frederick Douglass could not say yes.

CHAPTER 27

Charlotte Forten

PHILADELPHIA
APRIL 1859

"**Heard to-day that there has been another fugitive** arrested," Charlotte wrote in her journal on April 4, 1859. It had been five years since the day she heard about Anthony Burns's arrest in Boston. Now she was outside Philadelphia, staying with her aunt Harriet and uncle Robert Purvis, when she heard a Black man named Daniel Webster had been arrested by a US Marshal. Webster lived in Harrisburg, Pennsylvania, with his family and had been arrested "on pretense he had committed some crime." The US Marshal, working in essence on behalf of a Virginia slave owner, said Webster was Daniel Dangerfield, who had escaped about six years ago. The marshal brought Webster to Philadelphia for a hearing before the US commissioner's court.

Her uncle went into Philadelphia for the trial, and Charlotte anxiously waited for news.

"How long, oh, how long shall such a state of things as this last?" she wondered in her journal. Were things ever going to change?

Charlotte's uncle waited with Miller McKim and others out-side the proceedings in support of Daniel Webster.

On Wednesday morning, Charlotte was "gladdened" to receive the news that Webster had been released. Unlike in Anthony Burns's case, the commissioner said the evidence of Daniel Webster's identity as the fugitive didn't add up.

"The Commissioner *said* that he released him [Webster] because he was not satisfied of his identity," Charlotte wrote. Daniel Dangerfield escaped in November 1854, "while it was proven [during the trial] that Daniel [Webster] was in Harrisburg at least in the Winter of 1853 or the Spring of 1854."

"Others are inclined to believe that the pressures of public sentiment—which was, strange to say, almost universally on the right side—was too overwhelming" for even the commissioner to resist releasing Webster, Charlotte added.

Five years ago, Boston—that city so full of abolitionists—had marched Anthony Burns back to enslavement. Today, Philadelphia, the city Charlotte thought so full of prejudice, thrust Daniel Webster onto the shoulders of a man and paraded him down the street, cheering.

As evening settled on Philadelphia on Friday, April 8, Char-lotte made her way to a street off Independence Square that didn't feel like more than an alley. Tucked around the corner from the supposed birthplace of American freedom, Sansom Street Hall was a plain-looking four-story building. Here, Philadelphians attended concerts, political conventions, dances, religious gatherings, and, tonight, a large anti-slavery meeting.

For almost ten years, the Fugitive Slave Law had made a mockery of the anti-slavery laws in the North. Tonight, they would celebrate a victory against "Slave Power" with Daniel Webster's freedom.

Charlotte packed into the room with so many familiar faces, the energy palpable. But at the back of the hall, she heard "stamping, hallooing, groaning." Charlotte and the others could barely hear what the speakers at the front were saying. The speakers, including her uncle, had only their voices to amplify across the crowd. With all the noise, they couldn't be heard.

"A crowd of Southerners was present, and ere the meeting had progressed far they created a great disturbance," Charlotte wrote in her journal that night. Whether they were actually from the South was unclear, but they had pro-slavery sympathies.

The president of the meeting tried to calm everyone down and bring it back to order, but there was almost no use. If the speakers couldn't be heard and the intruders wouldn't settle, this could only escalate. The excited energy turned into tumult surging from the back of the hall. Charlotte and the others stood crowded together and without knowing how it happened, people began moving forward in a crush of people. Charlotte should have felt frightened, but she was too excited, too full of that positive energy still, to think of fear.

Then the police arrived.

In the past, the police allowed mobs to burn buildings and houses and even threaten Charlotte's family. Her uncle and Miller McKim had been in Philadelphia in 1838 when a pro-slavery mob had attacked the African American community and burned the new anti-slavery meeting hall to the ground. "The veterans in the cause," as Charlotte thought of them, murmured that today at Sansom Hall reminded them of that day. But times had changed. Today, the police arrested some of the people making the disturbance and calmed the situation.

Charlotte's uncle was able to speak again in celebration of Webster's release.

Charlotte knew she would remember that night at Sansom Hall like those veterans remembered the night in 1838.

"It gives one some hope for Philadelphia," Charlotte thought.

Maybe it was bigger than Philadelphia, though. Maybe more people were becoming more willing to see that enslavement was morally wrong. Maybe they would actually do something about it.

PART 3
1859–1861

Glimmers of Light

"He who looks upon a conflict between right and wrong, and does not help the right against the wrong, despises and insults his own nature, and invites the contempt of mankind. [. . .] In such a contest there is no neutrality for any man. You are either for the Government or against the Government. Manhood requires you to take sides, and you are mean or noble according to how you choose between action and inaction."

—FREDERICK DOUGLASS, 1863

CHAPTER 28

Lewis Douglass

ROCHESTER
OCTOBER 17, 1859

On Monday, October 17, 1859, the telegraph machine clicked and clicked, transmitting harrowing news to Rochester, New York. Lewis heard something happened in Harpers Ferry, Virginia—Harpers Ferry in the Allegheny Mountains, the place John Brown spoke of for his grand exodus of enslaved people from the South; Harpers Ferry, the town just fifty miles south of where Lewis's father went to meet with Brown earlier that year. The news had to be about Brown.[5]

Every new telegraph seemed to say something different about what was happening. First, two hundred fifty white people and a few Black people attacked the town. Then, a report that the prior reports of an insurrection had been false. Later, the reports were deemed true, with five hundred to seven hundred white and Black insurrectionists involved. Those numbers would have seemed doubtful, though, given how desperate John Brown was for support every time he'd asked Lewis's father for help.

Then another telegraph: abolitionists had "attempted to seize the Arsenal

---
5. Today, Harpers Ferry is part of West Virginia. The state was created in 1863 when the pro-Union Virginia government voted to make West Virginia a separate state, to be admitted to the Union. At the time, it was also often written as Harper's Ferry.

[at Harpers Ferry] and hold the place." Maybe Brown found his army after leaving the Douglass home.

By Tuesday, October 18, newspapers reprinted the news, although *news* seemed too generous for what was reported in the newspapers. When one heard the word *news*, one supposed that meant *truth*. No one knew the truth yet.

Lewis might have known more than what the newspapers printed and authorities knew, since he had sat around a table with Brown, seen his drawings and maps, and heard him talk of his plans.

The next dispatch came through: "Capt. Brown and his son were both shot. The latter is dead, and the former is in a dying state. He lies in the Armory enclosure, talking freely. He says he is old Ossawatomie [sic] Brown, whose tests in Kansas have had such wide notoriety; that his whole object was to free the slaves, and justifies his action."

What did "talking freely" mean? Would Brown name his supporters? Would the name Frederick Douglass cross his lips?

Lewis's father wasn't home. He was in Philadelphia on a speaking tour, but Lewis knew his father had good friends there, friends who could protect him.

Lewis and his brother would need to update this week's edition of *Frederick Douglass' Paper*.

DOCUMENT

Frederick Douglass' Paper

OCTOBER 21, 1859

THE INSURRECTION!

ROCHESTER, OCT. 21, 1859

We call attention to the highly exciting news concerning the insurrection at Harper's Ferry, which we print in full in our present issue. We have, of course, but one side of the picture given, and that is furnished by the oppressor. Acting upon the motto, 'Resistance to tyrants is obedience to God,' and with the illustrious example of the heroes of '76 before them, a good number of men, with the fire of Liberty burning upon the altar of their hearts, have 'STRUCK FOR FREEDOM!'—With what success the effort has been crowned, our readers are ere this probably aware.

But as the Editor is absent on a lecturing tour, we refrain from further comments. We will merely say that we may expect a series of similar tragedies while the monstrous crime of turning men into chattels, robbing them of every right, and subjecting them to every wrong, is encouraged by this Republican nation.

CHAPTER 29

Lewis Douglass

ROCHESTER
OCTOBER 20, 1859

With the morning of October 20 came a telegram to Rochester:

"Tell Lewis (my oldest son) to secure all the important papers in my high desk."

The telegraph operator was a friend of the Douglass family and would know how to get in touch with Lewis.

Lewis knew what his father meant. His father had letters from John Brown and the Provisional Constitution locked in his desk.

The irony of the telegram was that the papers were secure; they were already locked inside the desk. But someone could get into that desk and implicate Lewis's father in John Brown's crimes. So Lewis grabbed a chisel and forced the desk open. Lewis destroyed the papers, making sure that the police or marshals or whoever arrived would have a harder time incriminating his father.

The next day, Lewis's father showed up at the house. He had traveled from Philadelphia to New Jersey then through Pennsylvania to their home. He'd almost been arrested, and being in their home was too dangerous. Lewis's father had to get to Canada, maybe even England. Lewis was used to his father leaving—he did that all the time. He also always came back. One could only imagine how long he would need to be gone for now. The neighbors took Lewis's father to the ferry to cross Lake Ontario.

Six hours later, the federal marshals knocked on the door, asking for Mr. Frederick Douglass. Lewis could honestly say his father was gone.

Death and Burial of F. J. Merriam.
Special Dispatch to The N. Y. Tribune.

PHILADELPHIA, Wednesday, Oct. 26, 1859.

F. J. Merriam of Boston, who had some connection with the affair at Harper's Ferry, but who escaped before the taking of the Arsenal, has since died of his wounds. He was hurriedly buried in this State by fugitive slaves.

The report of Francis Meriam's death and burial appeared in newspapers across the country. Newspapers often misspelled Meriam's name with two *r*s.

CHAPTER 30

George Garrison

ON BOARD STEAMER *ANGLO-SAXON*, BOUND FOR CINCINNATI
NOVEMBER 1, 1859

The *Anglo-Saxon* chugged up the Ohio River, puffs of gray-black clouds billowing from the smokestacks at the front of the boat, the paddle wheel smacking the water at the back. George could have taken an overland route on a train, but he preferred traveling by riverboat—that was one thing he had learned about himself in the West. He left Lawrence, Kansas, on October 20 after two and a half years away and would be back in Boston by Thanksgiving.

Somewhere in the middle of the river—where George could see the free state of Ohio to his left and the slave state of Kentucky to his right—he read the news that John Brown had started an insurrection at Harpers Ferry, Virginia. Then, he saw even stranger news: "the death of Francis J. Meriam announced in the *Louisville Daily Democrat*," he noted in his diary. From the newspaper report, George learned that Meriam was involved in the action at Harpers Ferry, "died at some place in Pennsylvania of the wounds" he received, and "was hurriedly buried by fugitive slaves."

George had thought Meriam would be in Boston when he arrived. In January 1859, George's brother William wrote that Meriam had been at the Garrison house looking for George. Meriam was not getting along with his family and had decided "his life would be shortly finished." Meriam had a Black lawyer in Boston draw up his will, which would give his large inheritance to the Anti-Slavery Society. He also wanted his body burned after death, which George's brother knew was not something a sane person would do.

"I hoped to get George for my executor, for he is a fellow of pluck and would not be afraid to follow out my instructions," Meriam told William.

William was worried Meriam meant to kill himself, but instead, in early 1859, Meriam went to Haiti with James Redpath, a British man who had reported on John Brown's activities in Kansas and wanted to start his own slave revolt in Missouri.

Meriam, newly back from Haiti, came to the Garrison house again on October 7, 1859, telling George's brothers about his travels in Haiti and his observations there. Redpath had been interested in the possibility of Black Americans emigrating to Haiti if abolition would not come to the United States.

Meriam heard about Brown's plans after he left the Garrison house on October 7, and he went to Baltimore. Meriam was "just reckless enough to engage in such a desperate undertaking" as joining Brown, according to William.

George looked at the notice in the newspaper. "The news of his fate has made me feel quite sad," George confided in his diary. "I was calculating to take him by the hand in Boston when I reached there. Fate has decreed otherwise."

The news of the insurrection and Meriam's death changed George's plan. He planned to get off in Wheeling, Virginia[6], take the Baltimore and Ohio Railroad to Washington, DC, and then continue north to Philadelphia to visit Miller McKim. That train would roll right past Harpers Ferry. Before October 1859, there would have been no reason for him to stop in such a small town.

Now no one could talk of anything else, and every newspaper George picked up, regardless of political leaning, wrote of Brown, trying to uncover

6. Today, Wheeling is part of West Virginia.

what had really happened and what Brown's goal really had been. Was Brown trying to take a group of fugitives from Virginia north through Pennsylvania to New York, and then to freedom in Canada, in a mission similar to what he had done in Missouri the fall before? Or was he trying to lead a massive uprising of hundreds of enslaved people and spur a revolution like what had transpired in Haiti more than fifty years earlier?

George could not simply look out the window when the train rolled past this now-historic city.

When George stepped off the train, the cliffs on the Mary-land side of the Potomac River loomed overhead while the bridge Brown's men had taken over during the raid stretched before him. The town was just a half a day away from Baltimore and Washington, DC, by train, a day away by carriage. The troops arrived too quickly once Brown's men shut down the railroad, and any action was doomed.

The mood in Harpers Ferry was still tense. Since Brown's arrest, newspapers reported that some of Brown's men still hid in the mountains. People sounded alarms, and the government handed out weapons to citizens. Rumors circled that Northern friends of John Brown might try to rescue him from the jail in Charles Town, just seven miles away. If someone had recognized George as the great abolitionist agitator's son, they might not have let him pass so easily and quietly through town.

George had been in Kansas too late to make money or join in the free-state fight. Now he was in Harpers Ferry, two weeks after the insurrection, in which his friend had played a part. Would he ever be in the right place at the right time?

George did not stay long; he needed to continue his journey home.

CHAPTER 31

Lucy McKim

EAGLESWOOD
NOVEMBER 1859

B y mid-November 1859, fall was creeping toward winter at the Eagleswood School in New Jersey. Lucy had just turned seventeen and was back studying Latin and music and teaching music lessons to younger students.

Lucy could always expect visitors to turn up at Eagleswood to lecture or stay for a few days. This November, John Brown's wife, Mary Brown, arrived unexpectedly. Mary Brown was waiting for news of her husband, and Lucy's father and his friend Thomas Wentworth Higginson thought that peaceful, out-of-the-way Eagleswood would be a safe place for Mary Brown to wait.

Mary Brown looked exactly as you might expect John Brown's wife to look: sturdy, large, plain. Pleasant-looking, in a way. "A good head," according to Lucy's sister, Annie. She was quiet, though. Her husband's trial was over; the government of Virginia found him guilty of treason, insurrection, and murder. He would hang; the question was when.

Lucy's father arrived at Eagleswood soon after Mary Brown and was thinking about the thing that no one wanted to talk about—that someone would need to help Mary Brown take John Brown's body back to New York. Through friends, Lucy's father had also managed to bring a letter from John Brown.

Mary Brown wasn't confident in her reading and writing and asked Rebecca Spring to read the letter. Rebecca Spring was one of the Quaker founders of the community next to Eagleswood and had gone to see John Brown in jail a few weeks earlier.

"I will begin by saying that I have in some degree recovered from my wounds," Brown's letter began, "but that I am quite weak in my back and sore about my left kidney."

John Brown's tone seemed calm, understanding, and accepting of his fate. He also felt that what he was trying to do had been supported by God. So many of Jesus's supporters and disciples had once suffered, too.

"Think, too, of the crushed millions who have no comforter," John Brown wrote. "I charge you all never (in your trials) to forget the griefs of the poor that cry, and of those that have none to help them." Remember the enslaved, and do something to stop their oppression. What was most important was that the fight was not over.

After Spring finished reading the letter aloud, Lucy's sister, Annie, thought it was so beautifully written and that John Brown was a man to be proud of: "May we not feel that such worth will find its way to the heart of everyone and work a change in this sad state of affairs?" Lucy and Annie were proud to be abolitionists.

Lucy's father hadn't supported Brown when he had come to Philadelphia looking for people to back up his plan earlier that year. Like William Lloyd Garrison, Lucy's father didn't believe in violence as a solution to the evil of slavery. Garrison called the attack "misguided, wild, and apparently insane" in his newspaper and thought that Brown "was crazy, and has long been so."

Lucy's father didn't agree that Brown was crazy. Brown was a hero, her father thought, who was "making tyrants tremble."

Mary Brown wanted to see her husband, even though he'd told her not to come. He thought it would all be too upsetting for her. The governor of Virginia was also unsure if he should allow Mary Brown or any other abolitionists into the state. Lucy's father would bring Mary Brown to Philadelphia and wait to see if she could travel to Virginia to see her husband.

CHAPTER 32

George Garrison

BOSTON
NOVEMBER–DECEMBER 1859

George walked in the door at 14 Dix Place in the evening of the day before Thanksgiving. His family was overjoyed. His brothers William and Wendell had not changed that much in the almost three years since George had been gone, but his sister, Fanny, and baby brother, Frank, had grown considerably. Fanny was almost fifteen and a young lady, and eleven-year-old Frank did not seem like so much of a little boy. George had his beard, but otherwise, he had not changed much in his physical appearance since he left, his brother William thought. They all sat down for supper, and George shared stories of his western life, and they shared news about friends.

John Brown—and his imminent death—was still on everyone's minds. William thought Brown a martyr, but their father thought that even martyrs should "resort to no weapons of death, even in self-defense." Brown had "a noble purpose," their father said, and he should be celebrated. But his method was wrong; Brown had resorted to weapons and murder.

During Brown's trial, George's father asserted in his newspaper that "all bloody and violent methods of opposition to slavery have been uniformly discouraged by the Abolitionists, in general, on the ground of policy, prudence, and probability of success, and, by those of their number who are non-resistants, on the ground of principle." George knew not all abolitionists felt that way.

What if, as William thought, Brown's death would be the point "from which American Slavery dates its violent & bloody annihilation?"

George had never been as nonresistant as his father. He was almost twenty-four years old, and for longer than that, his father had tried to use "moral suasion" to convince white people that slavery was immoral. More people than ever were aware of and in support of the anti-slavery cause, but was slavery not still in place? Was slavery not still expanding? Was slavery not still what the country's economy relied upon?

George's father also wrote during Brown's trial:

"BUT LET NO ONE WHO GLORIES IN THE REVOLUTIONARY STRUGGLE OF 1776 DENY THE RIGHT OF THE SLAVES TO IMITATE THE EXAMPLE OF OUR FATHERS."

If tyrannical, violent power is the oppressor, could nonviolence really overthrow that power?

———

The city of Boston woke on Friday, December 2, 1859, to the sound of bells tolling for John Brown. Today, he would be executed in Charles Town, Virginia[7] .

A few hours later, George received a message from his brother William: Francis Meriam wanted to see George. The Garrisons had heard rumors that Meriam was not dead but in Canada, but now Meriam was in Boston. William told George to go to a friend's house, where they could talk.

This was why people questioned Meriam's sanity: he was making his whereabouts known while the governor of Virginia still had a five-hundred-dollar bounty on his head. If the wrong person heard of Meriam's whereabouts, he might end up on the gallows just like Brown.

When George arrived, there was the same Francis Meriam he had known: his somewhat wild brown hair and beard, his face a little blotchy, his one glass

---

7. Today, Charles Town is part of West Virginia.

eye a little cloudy. George could finally clasp his friend's hand, both in awe of what Meriam did with Brown and grateful that he was alive.

Meriam confided that he was in Boston to avenge Brown's death. Meriam had not known Brown long but admired him tremendously. Meriam's time from October 7 at the Garrison house to now was a fantastic story. In the fall, Meriam heard from Lewis Hayden (one of the heroes of the attempted rescue of Anthony Burns in 1854) Brown's "general purpose and plan." Brown needed money to execute his plan, and Meriam had his inheritance that he wanted to donate to the abolitionist cause. Less than a week before the insurrection, Meriam met Brown in Philadelphia, and Brown told Meriam to go to Baltimore to buy ammunition and then bring it to the farm in Maryland where Brown and his men had been staying. When Meriam arrived, he also had six hundred dollars in cash, which Brown thought they could use to buy food and provisions after the attack. Meriam's arrival with ammunition and cash was what allowed the raid to start on October 16.

Meriam was short, thin, and had poor vision, so during the attack, Brown told him to guard the farm rather than go into Harpers Ferry. When the attack failed, Meriam escaped to Pennsylvania, and playing dead was a good way to get the authorities to leave him alone. Then friends helped him get to Canada.

Now no one wanted Meriam in Boston. It was too dangerous. Meriam's friends had contacted their friend Wendell Phillips and Meriam's grandfather Francis Jackson to figure out what to do with Meriam. They would have to hide Meriam from the authorities until the situation became safer, and they all knew the safest place for him was still Canada.

That evening, most everyone else would be preoccupied with the antislavery meeting at Tremont Temple in honor of Brown and his men. Meriam's grandfather and Phillips would get Meriam to another friend in Concord, Massachusetts. That friend would take Meriam to the writer-abolitionist Henry David Thoreau, who would force Meriam onto a Canadian-bound train.

CHAPTER 33

Lucy McKim

EAGLESWOOD
DECEMBER 1859

L ucy's father left Eagleswood with Mary Brown. She stayed with the McKims until they received permission from the governor of Virginia to travel to Charles Town. It would have been improper for Mary to travel alone with men, so Lucy's mother accompanied them to Harpers Ferry.

Lucy could be proud of her parents, supporting Mary on what would be the worst days of her life and offering emotional support that she desperately needed. As strong as Brown looked, she had also been shaky and withdrawn at Eagleswood.

The McKims and Brown would take the train from Philadelphia to Baltimore and Baltimore to Harpers Ferry. They would take John Brown's body back to his home in North Elba, New York, where he would be buried.

It would all be too horrible to think about. But Lucy could follow her father's movements in the newspapers.

The Journey of John Brown's Body

DECEMBER 1859

THE NEW YORK HERALD

DECEMBER 2, 1859: ARRIVAL OF THE REMAINS IN PHILADELPHIA—The mortal remains of John Brown passed through this city this afternoon, on their way from Charlestown [sic], Va. to Essex county, New York, where they will be interred, as we understand.

The remains were in charge of the widow of Brown, who was accompanied by Messrs. Hector Tindall and Miller McKim, of this city, who had gone south with Mrs. Brown.

The train by which the body arrived came in from Baltimore at Broad and Prime streets at twenty minutes of one o'clock. For half an hour previous there had been quite a crowd of colored persons and a few white sympathizers in waiting, who, mingling with the usual crowd of carriage and omnibus drivers, baggage smashers, &c., who collect about the station at Broad and Prime streets, made quite a concourse of people.

A reception committee, headed by Rev. Dr. Furness, was in attendance, to receive Mrs. Brown and party, at the station.

A large police force was also detailed for service, and the Mayor and Chief of Police were present on the arrival of the train.

NEW-YORK DAILY TRIBUNE

DEC. 5, 1859.

On Thursday the body of John Brown will be buried at North Elba, according to his direction.

[Signed,]

WENDELL PHILLIPS

J. MILLER McKIM

THE LIBERATOR

DEC. 16, 1859

—THE BURIAL OF JOHN BROWN—

The carriage which bore Mrs. Brown stopped at the door. She alighted with difficulty, being much agitated. Instantly there was a sharp, low cry of 'Mother!' And, in answer, another in the same tone of mingled agony and tenderness, 'O! Anna!' And the mother and daughter were locked in a long, convulsed embrace. Then followed the same scene with the next daughter, Sarah; and then Ellen, the little girl of five, was brought, and another burst of anguish and love ensued. Then came the daughter-in-law, Oliver's widow, and there went up a low wail, before which flint itself would have softened. It was a scene entirely beyond description.

But soon all was composed [. . .] In a few moments, Mrs. Brown announced to Mr. McKim and Mr. Phillips, that the family were all gathered in another room, waiting anxiously to hear a recital of what had happened; and the rest were invited to join them. [. . .]

Mr. McKim, at Mrs. Brown's request, began, and related, as well as he could in so short a space as was allowed, all that had happened of particular interest to them from the time of their mother's arrival in Philadelphia, on the 12th of Nov. up to that moment. [. . .]

The funeral was to take place at 1 o'clock from the house; by that time the neighbors were gathered, and all were ready. [. . .]

Mr. J. Miller McKim, of Philadelphia, then made some very feeling, pertinent and impressive remarks.

DEAR CHILDREN, said Mr. McKim, my heart bleeds for you; but your father,

your husband, your brothers, not only died bravely, but they died usefully; they were all benefactors; they were all martyrs in a holy cause. Not only had he heard testimony borne at the South to the bravery and uprightness of the leader in the extraordinary undertaking, but similar testimony, only in a less degree, to the same qualities on the part of his sons. Oliver Brown, Watson Brown, Dauphin Thompson, William Thompson, all were attested to be—with the exception of this one act, the assault on Harper's Ferry—without reproach, as well as without fear. Don't weep for them, then, as though their lives had been spent in vain, and their death would prove of no effect. The world will yet acknowledge itself debtor to them, and history will embalm their memory. And it is due to those who are in prison to say that they, too, are not unworthy of tribute on this occasion. Some of Capt. Brown's friends, said Mr. McKim, speak as though they regarded the result at Harper's Ferry as a disaster. Disastrous in some respects it was, but in no respect a failure. Mr. Brown said, in one of his last letters, "The Captain of my salvation, who is also a Captain of Liberty, has taken away my sword of steel, and put into my hands the sword of the spirit." This is well said, like all his utterances. With his sword of steel he struck to hollow shell of Southern society, political and social, and revealed its emptiness. [. . .] He did much better than if he had established, as it would appear was his purpose, an armed exodus of fugitive slaves. He did infinitely better than if he had organized—which certainly was not his purpose—an insurrection. [. . .] His utterances were in the demonstration of the spirit, and with power. They have gone out into the world and are doing their work.

The John Brown Song

1861

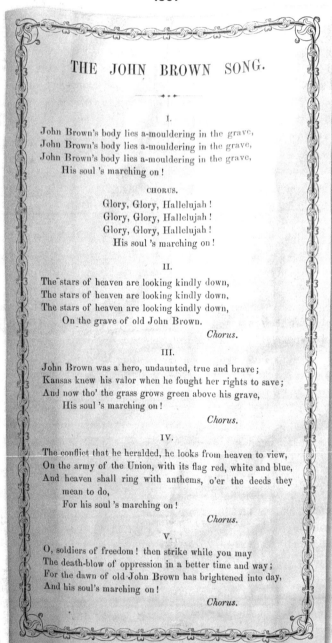

THE JOHN BROWN SONG.

I.

John Brown's body lies a-mouldering in the grave,
John Brown's body lies a-mouldering in the grave,
John Brown's body lies a-mouldering in the grave,
His soul 's marching on!

CHORUS.

Glory, Glory, Hallelujah!
Glory, Glory, Hallelujah!
Glory, Glory, Hallelujah!
His soul 's marching on!

II.

The stars of heaven are looking kindly down,
The stars of heaven are looking kindly down,
The stars of heaven are looking kindly down,
On the grave of old John Brown.

Chorus.

III.

John Brown was a hero, undaunted, true and brave;
Kansas knew his valor when he fought her rights to save;
And now tho' the grass grows green above his grave,
His soul 's marching on!

Chorus.

IV.

The conflict that he heralded, he looks from heaven to view,
On the army of the Union, with its flag red, white and blue,
And heaven shall ring with anthems, o'er the deeds they
mean to do,
For his soul 's marching on!

Chorus.

V.

O, soldiers of freedom! then strike while you may
The death-blow of oppression in a better time and way;
For the dawn of old John Brown has brightened into day,
And his soul's marching on!

Chorus.

Lyrics to "The John Brown Song," also called "John Brown's Song,"
that George Garrison clipped and added to his scrapbook.

CHAPTER 34

Charlotte Forten

SALEM
JANUARY 1860

"**C**an it be possible that so many months have elapsed since my pen last touch the pages," Charlotte had asked herself and her journal on January 1, 1860. She hadn't written anything since shortly after Daniel Webster had left her aunt and uncle's home in Byberry in late April 1859 once he'd been released from custody.

Time flies. She could say it so easily, but grasping what it meant was harder.

"How the months, days and hours *rush* along, bearing us on—on—upon their swift, unwearying wings?" she asked. "Too often past experiences, and high resolves for the future, are forgotten, swallowed up in the excitement of the present moment."

She had returned to Salem in September 1859 to work at the Higginson Grammar School, but that winter into spring, she wrote in her journal, "my eyesight failed." She could hardly read or study or teach. She became weak and frail again, like she had felt two years earlier. She had to stop teaching, and depression consumed her.

Excerpts from "The Two Voices" by Charlotte Forten

1859

In the dim December twilight,
    By the fire I mused alone;
    And a voice within me murmured
    In a deep, impassioned tone—

Murmured first, and then grew stronger,
    Wilder in its thrilling strain—
    "Break, sad heart, for, oh, no longer
    Canst thou bear this ceaseless pain.

"Canst thou bear the bitter anguish,
    All the wrong, and woe, and shame
    That the world hath heaped upon thee,
    Though it hath no cause for blame?

[. . .]

"Wouldst thou live, oh, foolish dreamer?
    What to thee are life and joy?
    Know'st thou not the cruel future
    All thy visions shall destroy?

[. . .]

To the earnest voice I hearkened,
    And within my troubled breast
    Deeper, stronger grew the longing
    For the blessed boon of rest.

"Grant," I prayed, "O gracious Father!
  Grant the simple boon I crave.
Let me leave this weary conflict,
  Let me rest within the grave!"

[. . .]

Then another voice spake to me,
  Spake in accents strong and clear;
Like the proud notes of a trumpet
  Fell its tones upon my ear.

"Shame," it cried, "oh, weak repiner!
  Hast thou yielded to despair?
Canst thou win the crown immortal
  If the cross thou wilt not bear?

"Hast thou nothing left to live for?
  Woulds't thou leave the glorious strife?
Know, the life that's passed in struggling
  Is the true, the only life.

[. . .]

"Live for others; work for others;
  Sharing, strive to sooth their woe,
Till thy heart, no longer waiting,
  With an ardent zeal will glow.

[. . .]

"Sweet the grave's unbroken quiet
  To thy aching heart would be;
But, believe, to live for others
  Is a higher destiny."

Ceased the voice; again in silence,
　　By the fire I mused alone;
　　Darkly closed the night around me;
　　But my soul had stronger grown.

And I said—"I thank Thee, Father,
　　For the answer thou hast given.
　　Bravely will I bear earth's burdens,
　　Ere I pray to rest in heaven."

CHAPTER 35

Lewis Douglass

**ROCHESTER
MARCH–APRIL 1860**

The sun shone brightly in a blue sky, green buds appeared on trees while purple crocuses and bluets dotted the ground, and robins chirped merrily. Friday, March 16, 1860, should have been as delightful a day as ever in Rochester. But no matter how pleasant the weather, Lewis could not be happy. He could only be devastated.

His little sister, Annie, the baby of the family, had died just days before her eleventh birthday. Today, friends came to the Douglass home for the funeral service.

Annie had been sick for months, and the last weeks had been the worst. She couldn't speak or hear, and at the very end, she couldn't even recognize her family that loved her so much. The doctors said Annie had "consumption of the brain." She'd been upset by their father's departure and John Brown's "murder," and maybe that had had something to do with her illness and death. The doctor couldn't explain the ailment or find a cure for it.

"Annie was a child of great promise—the darling of the mother, the pet of the father, and dearly loved by sister and brothers," Lewis's family wrote in Annie's obituary.

Lewis was the oldest son, and she was the youngest, and where he was responsible, she was excitable and happy. Where Lewis had to go to work, Annie went to school and was even studying German. "She was the light of the house," their father said. Everyone loved her—even John Brown, with his stern look and white beard, had let Annie sit on his lap as he entertained Lewis and his siblings.

Amidst the large numbers of friends gathered for the funeral, Lewis's mother moved weakly about the house, and his father wasn't there to provide any consolation. Frederick Douglass had gone to England after Brown's raid, and the family sent him a letter right after Annie's death, but he wouldn't get the news for weeks. Lewis's family would have to say goodbye to Annie without him.

They sang a hymn and said a prayer, and then they followed in a procession of thirty-five carriages and more people on foot to the cemetery.

———

Lewis's father came home in April. They didn't even know he was coming. When he had returned from his trip to Europe in 1847, Lewis and his brother Fred met their father at the train station, and their father scooped Fred into his arms and took Lewis's hand. They'd been so happy. Now, Douglass came back to a home of despair.

Lewis, Fred, and their sister, Rosetta, had been trying to keep the newspaper going in their father's absence, but it was difficult. They moved to only publishing *Douglass' Monthly*. Letters for publication or any business concerning the paper were now sent to Lewis. It felt like the paper could not survive much longer.

For Lewis, there did shine one ray of light: the formerly bloomer-wearing Amelia Loguen. In May, Lewis met her again, and they actually spoke to each other this time. Lewis wanted to exchange letters with Amelia, but she requested that they not do so yet. They were friends, maybe more like siblings than anything else, she said. Perhaps next May they could start a correspondence. Lewis could barely wait.

CHAPTER 36

Charlotte Forten

WORCESTER, MASSACHUSETTS
SPRING 1860

I n the spring of 1860, in hopes of improving her health, Charlotte traveled to Dr. Seth Rogers's water cure in Worcester, Massachusetts. The institute sat on the top of a hill overlooking the town, conveniently next to a stream. Hydropathic doctors believed the body needed water and that to get water into a body, a person needed cold compresses, showers, and baths. Charlotte liked this idea enough to try it: "I love the water, and sometimes think I could live 'on the ocean wave,'" she'd written once.

She could have gone to any number of water cure institutes or hospitals across the Northeast; there seemed to be more than ever. Dr. Rogers was a good man, though—this Charlotte knew. He advertised in *The Liberator* and was a close friend of women's rights advocate Susan B. Anthony and of Thomas Wentworth Higginson, who had financially supported John Brown.

At the water cure, Rogers intended to cure patients, often women, of the type of illness that Charlotte had: one that he couldn't trace to a particular disease or infection, one that just appeared as weakness, frailty, or tiredness.

Charlotte's treatment took all day.

Get undressed.

Get wrapped in a wet sheet, pinned or taped around her body.

Lie in bed for forty-five minutes.

Shower.

Sit in warm water with cool water poured over her shoulders.

Dry off.

Get dressed.

Exercise.

Wait a few hours and repeat.

Wait a few hours and repeat.

As grueling as it seemed, Charlotte thought it was making her better. Rogers promised to make her feel better, and she did feel better. He did "a world of good—spiritually as well as physically," Charlotte wrote. She'd enjoyed her time there, too, getting to know Rogers. She thought he was good and noble. She wanted to be well so she could make a difference, too.

The Liberator

MAY 1860

THE REPUBLICAN NATIONAL PLATFORM

☞ Such is the Platform adopted by the National Republican Convention at Chicago last week. It will be seen that it takes no issue with the Dred Scott Decision, or with the Fugitive Slave Law, or with slavery as it exists in the District of Columbia; and, by mission at least, surrenders its old non-extension of slavery policy, and this virtually endorses the 'popular sovereignty' doctrine of [likely Democratic presidential nominee] Stephen Arnold Douglas, so far as the admission of new States into the Union is concerned.

The Convention itself was unparalleled for the enthusiasm and numbers (estimated from thirty to fifty thousand) attending it. [. . .]

On the third ballot, the whole number of votes cast was 466; of which [Abraham] Lincoln obtained 354, and was duly declared nominated. Seward received 110 1/2. The result was received with the most tremendous demonstrations of applause, and the vote made unanimous by the convention. [. . .] So, the,

Hon. ABRAHAM LINCOLN, of Illinois—and

Hon. HANNIBAL HAMLIN, of Maine,

are to be the standard-bearers of the Republican Party in the pending Presidential campaign.

CHAPTER 37

Lucy McKim

**PHILADELPHIA
SUMMER 1860**

L ucy, like most abolitionists in the country, picked up the
newspaper on June 5, 1860, to read Senator Charles Sumner's speech. Lucy
was at home in Philadelphia for the summer and kept up with the national
news in the papers and with what her friends and acquaintances were doing
through letters.

Sumner spoke to the Senate "to insist upon the immediate admission of
[Kanas to] this Union, with a Constitution forbidding slavery."

Sumner was brave to get up and speak about Kansas again. Four years
earlier, when he had given a speech about a free Kansas, the pro-slavery South
Carolina representative Preston Brooks had beat Sumner unconscious on the
Senate floor. Now, Sumner wanted to speak about "The Barbarism of Slavery."

"Slavery must be resisted not only on political grounds, but on all other
grounds, whether social, economical, or moral," Senator Sumner said. He
mentioned the various excuses that Southern slave-owning politicians made
for slavery, and that both morally and politically, the practice was wrong and
should be illegal.

"It is only when Slavery is exhibited in its truly hateful character, that we can fully appreciate the absurdity of the assumption, which, in defiance of the express letter of the Constitution, and without a single sentence, phrase, or word, upholding human bondage, yet foists into this blameless text the barbarous idea that man can hold property in man," Sumner said. Lucy knew well "the barbarism of slavery" from the lessons her parents taught her—but then Sumner explained how "on the letter of the law alone Slavery must be condemned."

Lucy knew less about the law but trusted that Sumner knew of what he spoke. The free soilers had won out in Kansas, and the Kansas legislature had adopted a constitution explicitly outlawing slavery in 1859 and petitioned to become part of the United States. Now the Slave Power in the United States Congress was keeping Kansas from entering the Union.

Sumner's speech and the growing power of the Republicans made Lucy enthusiastic. She asked Ellen Wright if she was as excited about Sumner's speech: "Is't [sic] not splendid? Splendid is a big-hearted adjective, and includes eloquence, logical, bold, courageous, elegant, cause, etc. etc." Maybe there was yet hope to be had.

CHAPTER 38

George Garrison

MASSACHUSETTS
FALL 1860

George had been busy at *The Liberator* during the summer of 1860 as the political conventions had been taking place. Abraham Lincoln was the Republican candidate for president, while the Democratic Party had been unable to select a nominee during their first Democratic convention in the spring, and so in Baltimore in June, the party officially nominated Stephen A. Douglas, with a splinter group going in favor of John C. Breckenridge. The Democrats were even less in alignment that the Republicans, it seemed. This split might make it easier for Lincoln to win the election.

Reading the papers, George saw young men his age rallying around the Republicans. They called themselves the Wide-Awakes. In August, his brother Wendell had seen processions of the Wide-Awakes with their "black glazed caps and black oiled cloth capes" and torches, parading with anti-Democrat and anti-Douglas posters. They looked like a militia, and their military bearing scared Democrats and Southerners.

———

On October 16, the *Boston Evening Transcript* wrote that the Wide-Awakes were coming to Boston:

> To the Wide-Awakes and other Republican Organizations of
> New England. You are hereby invited to participate in a
> Grand Republican Demonstration and
> Torchlight Procession, at Boston,
> On TUESDAY EVENING, OCTOBER 16, 1860.

The parade would be on the one-year anniversary of John Brown's insurrection at Harpers Ferry. How could the grand procession to support the Republicans not remind every one of the martyr's work? That may have scared the Democrats even more.

On the evening of October 16, George and his family walked to a family friend's house to watch the parade. Outside the door hung an illuminated sign with the words *No compromise with slavery*.

Young men needed opportunity; George had felt that as he had traveled west. The young men who were part of the Wide-Awakes felt that, too, living as they did in times without reliable economic or political prospects. They wanted—no, they *needed*—to participate in elections.

The Wide-Awakes were even more impressive than the Frémont parade had been in 1856. Now, ten thousand men wore their black caps and capes, the oilcloth shining in the light of the torches they carried. They cried, "Wide Awake! Wide Awake!" only to be punctuated by fireworks going off in every direction. A band from Bangor, Maine, rode on a float drawn by four horses, proceeded by eight Penobscot Native Americans dressed in their regalia. Some banners George could quite appreciate.

The succinct: *No more Slave Territory.*

And the more nuanced: *The Election of Lincoln and Hamlin will check the spread of Slavery, Secure to Colored Citizens their full Constitutional Rights, Crush out Disunion and the Slave Trade, Insure a Ready Obedience to all Just Laws, and Restore to the Government a Respect for Liberty, Justice and Equality.*

A delegation of about two hundred Black Wide Awakes had a banner with the slogan: *God never made a tyrant or a slave.*

Even if the parade route had gone by Dix Place, George's house would only have been illuminated by their regular gas lamps. George's father still did not believe the Republicans would offer redemption or the end of slavery. George and everyone else along the route also saw the banners that declared, *We are Republicans but not Abolitionists.*

On November 6, George received news of Abraham Lincoln's victory.

"On Tuesday last, the Presidential struggle, which has been carried on with as much zeal and heat in all parts of the country, terminated in the triumph of the Republican Party by the election of ABRAHAM LINCOLN, of Illinois, to the Presidency," *The Liberator* reported.

Southern states warned that if Lincoln won, they would leave the United States. George knew many abolitionists thought as his father did: "No union with slaveholders." The United States would be better with disunion. George's friend in Minnesota, William Reed, wrote to George and said that any secession of the Southern states would be "like amputating a sick limb from a sick body." But amputation was messy and painful.

A certificate of membership to a Wide-Awake Club with the motto "Free Speech, Free Soil, Free Men." The young men who made up the Wide-Awakes gained prominence before the 1860 election and marched with the torches and oil-cloth capes in support of Republican candidate Abraham Lincoln.

Douglass' Monthly

DECEMBER 1860

THE LATE ELECTION

Our last monthly paper announced the probable election of ABRAHAM LINCOLN and HANNIBAL HAMLIN, the Republican candidates for President and Vice President of the U.S. What was then only speculation and probability, is now an accomplished fact. [. . .]

It was a contest between sections, North and South, as to what shall be the principles and policy of the national Government in respect to the slave system of the fifteen Southern States. [. . .] Mr. LINCOLN, the Northern Republican candidate, while admitting the right to hold men as slaves in the States already existing, regards such property as peculiar, exception, local, general an evil, and not to be extended beyond the limits of the States where it is established by what is called positive law. [. . .]

If Mr. LINCOLN were really an Abolitionist President, which he is not; if he were a friend to the Abolition movement, instead of being, as he is, its most powerful enemy, the dissolution of the Union might be the only effective mode of perpetuating slavery in the Southern States—since if it could succeed, it would place slavery beyond the power of the President and his Government. But the South has now no such cause for disunion. [. . .] There is no sufficient cause for the dissolution of the Union. Whoever lives through the next four years will see Mr. LINCOLN and his Administration attacked more bitterly for their pro-slavery truckling, than for doing any anti-slavery work. He and his party will become the best protectors of slavery where it now is, and just such protectors as slaveholders will most need.

DOCUMENT

The New York Herald

DECEMBER-JANUARY 1860

IMPORTANT FROM WASHINGTON
ANTICIPATED HOSTILITIES FROM SOUTH CAROLINA

WASHINGTON, DEC. 31, 1860

The Southern men openly declared to-day that all hope of adjustment or reconciliation is passed. The feeling and excitement is running very high, and it is predicted that an explosion will occur in either House of Congress in less than ten days. The general feeling in both houses to-day is indicative of trouble.

It is stated, on reliable authority, that several thousand men are already enrolled, and large accessions are daily made, both in Maryland and Virginia, to take possession of this capital. They declare that Mr. Lincoln never shall be inaugurated in this city. Many Republicans have been assured of this. If the present state of things go on, and there is no settlement, rely upon it the Capitol never will be permitted to pass into the hands of the Republicans.

THE SOUTHERN CONFEDERACY

(From the Charleston Mercury), Jan. 8.

We publish below the resolutions passed by the South Carolina Convention, recommending to her sister States of the South the assemblage of a Convention to form a constitution for a Southern Confederacy. [. . .] The probability is that the Northern people and statesmen will see the desperate folly of attempting the coercion of the Southern States; and that the Convention can proceed without haste, calmly and thoroughly, to lay the foundations of a Southern confederacy, which will last for ages to come.

is not Attic. Accept my friendly com-
miserations. May you accomplish the
Latin grammar, & obtain a goodly stock
of propriety. For me, I talk French;
I read Geo Sand; I play Beethoven with
notre cher M. Sezandie; I write rhymes,
and I watch the sunsets from the shore
alone. There, does not that sound idyllic?
But I confess, — & you may read the confession over
again for your comfort, if you should
long too much for these Academic shades,
— even at Eaglewood, where life is most
unlike the commonplace existence that
one passes anywhere else, one gets dissatisfied; & peevish, as a consequence —
One must choke down the cry of their
hearts, (or souls, whichever you please, —
I haven't yet learned the fine distinction)
with work, work. It wont do to stop
to think, or we shall grow wild, or melan-
choly, like poor Sode — Ah! now for
the drill; — that is real enough, at
any rate.
    I'm afraid you wont thank me for
this homily instead of a batch of news —
But there is nothing of any particular interest.
Dora sprained her foot on the ice some time ago,
& is quite lame. Got a delightful letter from
Annie yesterday, saying that she was having

Letter from Lucy McKim to Ellen Wright

FEBRUARY 1861

Eagleswood, Feb. 1st, 1861

Dear Elle,

[. . .] Your letter was as welcome as all your others have been. [. . .]

For me, I talk French; read [George] Sand; I play Beethoven with notre cher M. Fezandrié; I write rhymes; and I watch the sunsets from the shore alone. There, does not that sound idyllic? But I confess,—& you read the confession over again for your comfort, if you should long too much for these Academic shades,—even at Eagleswood, where life is most unlike the commonplace existence that one passes anywhere else, one gets dissatisfied; & peevish, as a consequence. One must choke down the cry of their hearts, (or souls, whichever you please, I haven't yet learned the fine distinction) with work, work. It won't do to stop to think, or we shall grow wild [. . .]

Lovingly,
Luce

CHAPTER 39

Lewis Douglass

ROCHESTER
FEBRUARY 1861

On February 18, 1861, it seemed as if nearly all of Rochester was gathered at the train station to watch President-Elect Abraham Lincoln's train pass through on his way to Washington, DC. Lewis and his family couldn't pass up the historic opportunity, as disappointed as they were in the president-elect. Lincoln had not said anything about the secession crisis because he felt it was not his place to do so yet. A mob in Rochester tried to stop Susan B. Anthony from speaking about disunion and abolition, and the specter of that mob seemed to be gagging Abraham Lincoln.

Two weeks later, Lincoln entered Washington "as the poor, hunted fugitive slave reaches the North, in disguise, seeking concealment, evading pursuers, by the Underground Railroad, between two days, not during the sunlight, but crawling and dodging under the sable wing of night," Lewis's father wrote in his newspaper. People made assassination threats, and the Southern-sympathizing city of Baltimore, Maryland, seemed especially treacherous for Lincoln. So the president-elect snuck into Washington under guard, at night, in a disguise.

In President Lincoln's inaugural address on March 4, 1861, he said what Lewis and his family feared: that, as president, he had "no purpose, directly or indirectly, to interfere with the institution of slavery in the States where it exists." Lincoln didn't have the "lawful right" to do so, he said. If one could never see an end to slavery in the United States, could one really stay here? Could this country really provide the best opportunity for a young Black man like Lewis?

After the inauguration, Lewis's father accepted an invitation from James Redpath to travel to Haiti. Redpath was the British man who had guided Francis Meriam to Haiti in 1859. He had long thought that Black Americans should move to the Caribbean Republic to leave the racism of the US behind. Lewis's father and sister Rosetta would take a steamer on April 25, 1861. Lewis would stay home and continue working on the newspaper during their travels. Maybe emigration *could* provide opportunity. What chance for work did Lewis have beyond his father's newspaper? His brother Charles had gone to work on a farm, something Lewis wasn't interested in. What if the newspaper failed? How could he make a living if he was treated as a member of a "servile and degraded caste," as his father said? What would happen if President Lincoln didn't see Black people in the United States as Black Americans? Would the war the Southern states seemed to be asking for change anything?

PART 4
1861–1862

The Rockets' Red Flare

"Ah, me—I'm afraid this war must break our hearts, before it liberates the slaves, whose hearts have for so long, been of no account."

—ELLEN WRIGHT TO LUCY MCKIM'S SISTER, ANNIE, AUGUST 21, 1862

CHAPTER 40

George Garrison

BOSTON
APRIL 1861

On Sunday, April 14, 1861, George's brother William was going to speak at an anti-slavery convention outside Salem, Massachusetts. There would be talk of the secession crisis and situation at Fort Sumter in Charleston Harbor. For the past few months, George had been printing news about the US Army at the fort, their dwindling supplies, and whether the troops would withdraw and surrender the fort to South Carolina troops or if the South Carolina troops would attack. The day before, Saturday, George would have read in the newspapers that the troops finally fired "cannonade all day" on the fort.

George and his younger brother Frank decided to stay home that Sunday. George might not have wanted to hear William speak, or perhaps he needed to be close to *The Liberator* office if news from South Carolina changed.

The early spring weather was fair, and George and Frank went for a walk on the Common. The trees had leaf buds, flowers sprouted from the ground, and the birds chirped.

Then they heard the news: the US flag flying above Fort Sumter was shot down. South Carolina troops had taken the fort.

George and Frank raced home. They needed to know if their father knew, and George would have to set to work on next week's edition of *The Liberator* immediately.

They would be nearly a week behind in the news of it, *The Liberator* only going to print once a week on Fridays. However, George and his father would put together some of the most interesting accounts from other papers to print on the front page. In an editorial, people across the country would be able to read what the great abolitionist William Lloyd Garrison thought about the impending conflict.

By Wednesday, George and the printer had set the largest type they had, rolled it over with black ink, and pressed the words into the paper:

CIVIL WAR BEGUN!

FORT SUMTER CAPTURED.

THE FEDERAL CAPITAL IN DANGER.

THOUSANDS OF TROOPS MUSTERING.

THE NORTH UNITED AT LAST.

CHAPTER 41

Lewis Douglass

ROCHESTER
APRIL 1861

Lewis's sister, Rosetta, and their father wouldn't be going to Haiti after all. Now that the war had started, Lewis's father publicly announced that his place was in the United States. He spoke almost every Sunday at the AME Zion Church or Rochester City Hall in favor of the war. "The cry now is for war, vigorous war, war to the bitter end," Lewis's father declared, "and war till the traitors are effectually and permanently put down."

Lewis could do little for the war. After the attack in South Carolina, President Lincoln called for seventy-five thousand men to enlist in the fight. With an enlistment term of only three months, one knew that the president hoped the rebellion of the Southern states could be quickly subdued. But Lincoln's call didn't matter to Lewis. Black men would not be accepted into the army.

CHAPTER 42

George Garrison

BOSTON
MAY 1861

Geroge and his brothers would not be in line to enlist in President Lincoln's army. Their family were nonresisters, abolitionists who did not believe in violence to end the war or slavery.

George's brother Wendell came home from studying at Harvard most weekends, and his classmates talked of joining the fight. No one could study or focus on classwork with a war happening. Wendell would echo his father's views when asked whether he would enlist. This was a war of keeping the union of the United States, not of abolishment of slavery; therefore, it was not their fight.

Abolitionist acquaintances of George and classmates of Wendell did not feel the same way. Their good friend Norwood Hallowell thought this proved to be a moral fight, where he could demonstrate his belief in abolition. Norwood left Harvard and enlisted.

By May, Harvard's campus was rather empty, although Wendell and Robert Todd Lincoln, the president's son, were both still there.

CHAPTER 43

Lucy McKim

PHILADELPHIA
MAY 1861

A midst the outbreak of war, Lucy kept writing letters to Ellen Wright, letting her know about what was happening at Eagleswood and with other friends. Ellen had told Lucy about brothers Dick and Beverly Chase. Ellen was smitten with them, their good looks, pleasant manners, Quaker upbringing, and strong abolitionist sentiments.

In mid-May, 1861, Lucy was invited over for dinner at a family friend's house, where she finally got to meet Dick and Beverly.

At the end of the evening, the boys walked Lucy and her sister, Annie, to the horse-drawn streetcars. "Beverly became insane at the mention of your name," Lucy wrote Ellen. Beverly told Lucy that he didn't make friends often, and then stumbled over his sentence talking about Ellen.

"Isn't she nice!" Lucy said, realizing how entranced Beverly was.

Beverly could hardly reply, and instead squeaked out: "I guess she is!"

When they got on the streetcars, Dick and Lucy talked. She knew that Dick liked her. Before they'd left the dinner, he'd cut off one of his curls and given it to her. Unlike Ellen, Lucy didn't believe in romantic gestures like that, so she left it on the table. She felt so wicked for leaving it there, but she wasn't ready to accept such an intimate gift from someone she'd just met.

Dick asked if he could write to her. Lucy knew that meant more than sending letters. Agreeing to a correspondence meant that she was interested in him as more than just a casual friend. Lucy was ready to tell him no. Then she looked into his big, black eyes and worried about upsetting him. She didn't want to make the commitment, but she did like him.

Lucy compromised: she told him he could write to her, but she wouldn't answer.

———————

From the spring into the summer of 1861, everything was both normal and not normal at all. Ellen told Lucy of her dreams about parties, of spending time together, and of going to Europe. Lucy wished Ellen could be at Eagleswood with her. They would learn, read, play music, and teach. They would spend time with Dick, Beverly, and their other remaining male friends. Some, like their friend Norwood Hallowell, had already enlisted.

The war was still not about emancipation. "We [are] considering how to spend our holiday, the 4th," Ellen wrote to Lucy in late June, 1861. "It seems to be less of a farce now to celebrate the freedom of this independent country. Won't it be glorious, if we can see the beginning of Emancipation?"

By July 4, 1861, there had only been one real battle since the fighting at Fort Sumter. A few months into the war, Lucy and Ellen knew that if emancipation ever became the goal, much more fighting lay ahead.

The Liberator

JULY 1861

THE FIRST GENERAL ENGAGEMENT!

The Conflict Desperately Contested— Great Losses on both sides—Defeat of the Federal Troops—Retreat towards Washington, panic stricken, with great loss of cannon, wagons, and other appurtenances— Reorganization and vast augmentation of the army—General McClelland [sic] called to its command—&c., &c.

WASHINGTON, July 21. A most severe battle was fought to-day at Bull's Run bridge [Virginia]. The conflict was desperate, lasting nine hours. The programme, as stated in our first dispatch, was carried out, until our troops met with a succession of masked batteries, which were attacked with vigor and success, after a severe loss of life. [. . .]

A large number of our troops on their retreat fell by the wayside from exhaustion, and were scattered along the entire route all the way from Fairfax Court House. The road from Bull's Run to Centreville was strewed with knapsacks, arms, &c. Some of our troops deliberately threw away their guns and appurtenances, the better to facilitate their travel. [. . .]

General McClellan has been summoned by the government [. . . to] take command of the army of the Potomac. [. . .]

The *corps d'armee* at Washington is to be instantly reorganized and increased. The orders have already been given. Offers of regiments already raised and being made, will be accepted with such rapidity as to insure that this will be accomplished.

NEW YORK, July 23rd.

Within the last 24 hours over 60,000 fresh men, with a number of batteries of artillery, have been accepted [into the army]. A number of regiments have arrived, and every day will bring immense reinforcements to the National Capitol. Ten new regiments will be in Baltimore by evening. The response from every quarter has been most gratifying, and truly patriotic.

CHAPTER 44

Lucy McKim

PHILADELPHIA
FALL 1861

After the enlistments and battles and questions about what the fighting really meant for emancipation in the summer of 1861, Lucy grew distant from the social activities that once occupied her days. She found the entertainment boring and people unsatisfying.

Lucy's brother and his friend played war, lining up bottles and spools of thread, announcing who was president of the Confederacy Jefferson Davis or Confederate generals Robert E. Lee or P. G. T. Beauregard. They made so much horrid noise when she was trying to read or write letters to her friends. They could play war because they were only fourteen.

Ellen Wright's brother was eighteen and, in mid-October 1861, enlisted in the New York 1st Independent Battery Light Artillery. He was proud of enlisting, and Lucy knew how important it was to his family, too. Ellen's mother told him that she'd rather him die fighting for the freedom of the enslaved than sit at home.

At the end of October 1861, Lucy's father took her to the Pennsylvania Anti-Slavery Convention in West Chester. When Lucy saw her father's friend William Lloyd Garrison at the meeting, she thought he really was "a perfect old darling," although she wasn't really impressed with William Jr. Lucy was much more drawn to Wendell, who was studying at Harvard.

Wendell drove Lucy and her sister, Annie, around in a carriage one afternoon, passing by the lovely scenery of the Wissahickon Creek. He was kind and smart, and her father would love if Lucy married a family friend.

The subject of the war couldn't be avoided, though. On the one hand, William Lloyd Garrison argued that if the war was bloody and deadly, but ended slavery, then it was justly done. If it ended in compromise, we were doomed. Lucy knew both William and Wendell were nonresisters. William had given speeches advocating for nonresistance, and Wendell wouldn't assault human life by going to war, he said.

Lucy's father could stay friends with William Lloyd Garrison even if they disagreed about the war, but Ellen wasn't so sure about staying friends with nonresisters.

After Lucy wrote to Ellen about meeting Wendell in West Chester, Ellen told her bluntly, "I wouldn't look at a nonresister." Ellen couldn't see herself being romantically interested in someone who didn't believe in fighting for abolition.

Ellen hoped "this dreadful war would bring people to their senses & make them see that slavery, as the cause of it, must be removed before anything like Peace can be accomplished."

"What do you think of my disguising myself & accepting an office [in Thomas Wentworth Higginson's unit]?" Ellen asked Lucy in a letter. After helping Anthony Burns and John Brown, Higginson was finally in a real army, fighting for abolition. "We might make excellent warriors," she told Lucy.

Enlisting was a fantasy, and instead, Ellen was sewing and mending clothing for fugitives whom her neighbor and family friend Harriet Tubman had helped escape. Lucy's mother wanted her to learn the ways of running a household, saying she'd have one for herself one day. "Likely prospect, when everyone is gone to the war!" Lucy told Ellen.

Ellen Wright and her brother William in his uniform after his enlistment in the New York 1st Independent Battery Light Artillery, December 1861.

CHAPTER 45

Charlotte Forten

PHILADELPHIA
FALL-WINTER 1861

In the fall of 1861, Charlotte took charge of her aunt's school in Philadelphia. It was "a small school—but the children were mostly bright and interesting," Charlotte thought. Mostly, she was "thankful to have anything to do."

Charlotte was glad to have the company of Henry Cassey that winter. Cassey was the stepson of Charlotte's family friend and fellow abolitionist Charles Lenox Remond, and Henry detested Philadelphia as much as Charlotte.

"He and I have many things in common," Charlotte confided in her journal, and so they saw each other often. People talked that they might be engaged, but "I should no more think of marrying him than of marrying my own brother," she wrote. Cassey read books to her, and they talked about French history and literature. The war didn't seem to preoccupy Charlotte's mind. And if it preoccupied Cassey, he couldn't do anything about it. Black men like him were still not welcome in the Union army.

CHAPTER 46

Lucy McKim

PHILADELPHIA
DECEMBER 1861

B y Christmas, Lucy got used to the back and forth of emotions that came with war. Sometimes, she was glad to have a good time with Dick and Beverly Chase and their friends or to go to an art reception with her father. Other times, she felt helpless. Christmas came and went, but Lucy didn't care much about the presents. Yes, she and her loved ones were alive, but they were also surrounded by death. Since July 4, 1861, more than eleven thousand young men had been killed in battles.

"What has the new year for us?" she wrote to Ellen. The war would go on and people would die and the people who were still alive would also have to go on.

"We shall dance at funerals next year & flirt across corpses," Lucy told Ellen.

The Liberator

NOVEMBER 1861

AID FOR THE CONTRABANDS

THE FOLLOWING APPEAL deserves the action of the charitably disposed. Contributions of old cast-off clothing which are not suitable for the soldiers, may be made available for the objects of this appeal:—[. . .]

There are about two thousand of these ex-slaves now at the Fortress [Monroe, VA], for whom a large amount of clothing is required, many of them being very destitute and dependent entirely upon charity, whole others will need more or less assistance beyond what they receive from Government, who furnish full rations for all, and some clothing for a portion. Clothing of every description of personal wear, and bedding, is needed *immediately*, and when received will be distributed [. . .]

DOINGS IN SOUTH CAROLINA

THE CORRESPONDENT at Port Royal of the *Times* thus reports on the contraband question:—

"The battle of Port Royal was terminated at about 3 o'clock on Thursday last; on Saturday, at the same hour, I saw eighty fugitive slaves, contraband of war, who had escaped from their masters, and hurried within the Union lines. This was on the southern headland of the bay, and on the northern side there are half as many more. They report that *the rest are coming.* They declare that, since last March, they have been waiting and watching for the Yankees. And this is in South Carolina— this is where the blacks are so contented, where they were so attached to their masters, where we were defied to seduce them away. No attempt has been made, or will be made, to entice them, much less to excite an insurrection, but those who come in will be welcomed, will be clad and fed, and set to work for the National cause. [. . .]"

DOCUMENT

Douglass' Monthly

JANUARY 1862

WHAT SHALL BE DONE WITH THE SLAVES IF EMANCIPATED?

[. . .] IT IS SAID, what will you do with them? they can't take care of themselves; they would all come to the North; they would not work; they would become a burden upon the State, and a blot upon society; they'd cut their masters' throats; they would cheapen labor, and crowd out the poor white laborer from employment; their former masters would not employ them, and they would necessarily become vagrants, paupers and criminals, over-running all our alms-houses, jails and prisons. The laboring classes among the whites would come in bitter conflict with them in all the avenues of labor, and regarding them as occupying places and filling positions which should be occupied and filled by white men; a fierce war of races would be the inevitable consequence, and the black race would, of course, (being the weaker,) be exterminated. In view of this frightful, though happily somewhat contradictory picture, the question is asked, and pressed with a great show of earnestness at this momentous crisis of our nation's history, What shall be done with the four million slaves if they are emancipated? [. . .]

Our answer is, do nothing with them; mind your own business, and let them mind theirs. Your doing with them is their greatest misfortune. They have been undone by your doings, and all they now ask, and really have need of at your hands, is just to let them alone. They suffer by every interference, and succeed best by being let alone. The negro should have been let alone in Africa—let alone when the pirates and robbers offered him for sale in our Christian slave markets—(more cruel and inhuman than the Mahommedan [Islamic] slave markets)—let alone by courts, judges, politicians, legislators and slave-drivers—let alone altogether, and assured that they were thus to be let alone forever, and that they must now make their own way in the world, just the same as any and every other variety of the human family.

DOCUMENT

The Liberator

MAY 1862

THE PORT ROYAL CONTRABANDS

LETTERS RECEIVED by the Educational Commission of Boston from teachers employed at Port Royal and its vicinity, speak very encouragingly of the present condition and the capabilities and disposition of the numerous negro population of the Port Royal Islands. The negroes are busily employed in planting cotton, corn, and potatoes [. . .] They all manifest an eager desire to learn to read, and make excellent progress. [. . .] The teachers speak of their pupils as apt and fast learners. One says that in three months his will be able to read the New Testament. Several plantations, comprising four to six hundred negroes are placed under the care of each teacher. The contrabands are still much in need of clothing [. . .] The teachers are favorably regarded by the army and military authorities, the climate of the island is excellent, and altogether the Port Royal mission seems to be a very pleasant and hopeful field for missionary labor. For the information of those who would like to aid in this noble effort to benefit the liberated slaves, we will state that [Massachusetts] Governor Andrew is President of the Education Commission, Wm. Endicott, jr., Treasurer, and Edward Atkinson, Secretary.—*Boston Journal*

CHAPTER 47

Lucy McKim

PORT ROYAL
JUNE 1862

L ucy could not sleep on June 1, 1862. She and her father were about to leave for Port Royal, South Carolina. She would board the *Arago*, and before long, she would be in Union-occupied territory in the South. Her father formed the Philadelphia Port Royal Relief Association in March 1862 to help the newly freed people—called "contrabands" or "refugees," depending on who you asked. The South Carolina Sea Islands were a small scale of what emancipation would bring, and Lucy's father and some abolitionists wanted to provide food, education, and religious instruction to the freed people.

Lucy would get to be her father's assistant and secretary as he toured the schools and services the association had set up. They would also meet with Laura Towne, a teacher and nurse who arrived in April and now ran a school.

———

Aboard the *Arago*, Lucy played cards and sang in a quartet with some of the soldiers. Lucy "was a little ill, but notwithstanding, she enjoyed the company," her father wrote back to Lucy's mother. Her father, on the other hand, was sick the whole week they were aboard the ship.

———————

On Saturday, June 7, 1862, the *Arago* arrived at Hilton Head Island as dark descended and storm clouds gathered overhead. Lucy and her father stayed aboard as thunder crashed and lightning flickered. Her father was glad that as the storm passed, it seemed to take away some of the hot and humid not-quite-summer air.

The next morning, Lucy stood on deck and looked toward land as they got ready to go ashore. A Hilton Head Sunday didn't look like a Philadelphia Sunday at all. White officers rode their horses up and down the dock as wagons transported the goods from the ships. Union troops had been here since November, and now protected the people—and the plantations. The North wanted to keep up the production of cotton with the labor of free people.

Newly freed men pushed barrels and carried boxes. Nearby, the 1st Regiment of South Carolina Volunteers looked dapper in their blue coats and red pants. They had formed in May 1862 and were the first Black regiment the country had ever seen. Although free Black men in the North were not allowed to join the Union Army, General David Hunter had basically commissioned the regiment without formal approval from the War Department and began enlisting newly freed men from the Union-occupied areas of South Carolina and Florida. Lucy's father's friend Thomas Wentworth Higginson had left his Massachusetts regiment to become their colonel.

A rowboat glided up next to the *Arago*, and Lucy climbed in. She was pleased to meet the Black men rowing: Joe, Jerry, Gabriel, Pompey, and John Cole. She was even more pleased that they sang the whole time they rowed to shore. In Philadelphia, Lucy saw copies of "O go down Moses." Her father's office sold music to the hymn abolitionists heard Black people singing to raise money for the efforts in Port Royal. But the song the rowers were singing was totally new to her, and Lucy realized there must be many songs she hadn't heard.

From Hilton Head, Lucy and her father were supposed to go to the Oaks, where they'd meet with Laura Towne and learn more about her work. Ten thousand people were now free on the Sea Islands. Lucy had met and helped the formerly enslaved people who arrived at their home in Philadelphia, but that wasn't *this*. *That* wasn't thousands of people, scared of her because she was a white woman. *That* wasn't visible malnourishment and maltreatment. *That* also wasn't religious practices, singing, and joy.

———————

The Oaks was like something Lucy might see printed on the cover of *Frank Leslie's Illustrated Weekly* as an image of a Southern plantation. There was the big house, where the white people lived. Spread around the grounds were the stables, a corn house, a cotton house, and a chicken house, and "the Quarters," the cabins where the enslaved—now free—people lived. There was something tidy about them: two rows of homes that faced each other, each with a garden patch and fig tree out back. But any neatness couldn't hide their horror. The houses were small and with only a dirt floor that people had to sleep on. Even Lucy could see how easy it was for the fleas, mosquitos, and vermin to get in.

"I couldn't make up my mind whether I wanted most to laugh or cry," Lucy wrote to her friend Ellen Wright after seeing the houses. On the one hand, people had been glad to see Lucy, her father, and Laura Towne and were thankful for freedom. She might laugh with joy because the Black people here were now free. On the other hand, how enslaved people were treated was worse than even Lucy—raised in the Northern abolitionist movement from birth—had imagined.

Lucy knew she needed to write to her mother. She grabbed her pen and wrote quickly, feeling like she didn't have enough time to write everything she wanted to say. But there was this, this most important thing she needed her mother to know. She was glad to be there, to see the aftermath of slavery for herself. She'd heard the pro-slavery people say, "Slavery isn't bad, we are kind slave owners, go see for yourself." She had known better than to believe them then, but now she had seen reality. Her views on slavery had been changed. They had never been radical enough. She had needed to come here, to see how bad it really was.

"How lukewarm we have been! How little we knew!" Lucy wrote to her mother.

———

After dinner at the Oaks, Lucy went back down to the cab-ins. She and her father were invited to "a praise" at the home of Aunt Phillis, a woman everyone respected who had the largest cabin in the area. By the time Lucy and her father arrived, the sun had descended into darkness and inside the cabin, the only light came from a tallow candle someone had stuck in a black bottle as a candle holder. Lucy realized they were late and that the service was already underway. The people inside crowded together to make room for Lucy and her father.

An older Black man started a prayer, and everyone knelt down. Lucy hadn't had a particularly religious upbringing, but she felt tears rolling down her cheeks during the prayer. It was "so simple, touching, & eloquent," she wrote Ellen later.

———

The next night, Lucy went to "a shout." It was completely
different from anything she'd seen before. Although the shout was a religious ceremony like a praise, Lucy's father couldn't find anything familiar about it and told Lucy and Laura Towne that he thought it must have been like "African worship." The dancers formed a circle and began to walk, hitching their legs forward. A leader sang out a line of a song, and everyone responded. There were no instruments, but people clapped their hands, patted their knees, or stomped their feet to add percussion to the melody.

The songs that Lucy heard the men singing on the boats and the people singing in the praise and shouts fascinated her. It was different from anything she'd heard, and she felt like she needed to preserve it. Lucy could read and write music, and when she heard the singing, she was able to write down the melodies and lyrics. "I have copied down a number of the wild sad songs" of the people she met, Lucy wrote her mother before she returned home later that summer.

A man named Uncle July and his family stand and sit outside their home on St. Helena Island in South Carolina. After seeing the conditions formerly enslaved people had to endure in South Carolina, Lucy McKim felt the abolitionists had been "lukewarm" and not nearly radical enough.

Charlotte Forten's Journal

JUNE 1862

Salem. June 22, 1862.

I went to Marblehead Beach. The tide was coming in, and never have I seen Old Ocean more gloriously beautiful. We had an afternoon of rare enjoyment; and it seemed to me as if I really could not tear myself away. I think I should have stayed all night if any one would have stayed with me. It was too much happiness to sit upon the rocks, and see those breaking waves, again. As they receded, my whole soul seemed drawn away with them, then when they rushed back again upon the steadfast rocks my being thrilled, glowed, with joyous, exultant life. Strange, strange, old sea, how something in the deepest depths of my nature responds to you, how the very fibers of my being seem to cling to you. But how can I describe the emotions which you awake in me? Words cannot do it. They fail, are worthless, absurd.

CHAPTER 48

Charlotte Forten

FRAMINGHAM, MASSACHUSETTS
JULY 1862

Charlotte boarded the train in Boston on the morning of July 4, 1862, and shortly after nine, it pulled away from the station. The train was full of abolitionists from the Boston area on their way to Framingham, Massachusetts, for the annual anti-slavery celebration. The weather lent itself to festivity, the summer sun shining as steam puffed from the train into the sky.

When they arrived, Charlotte and her friends walked down to the spot called Harmony Grove on the shores of the Farm Pond. For the last eight years, abolitionists had gathered here for speeches, but also games, boat rides, and picnics.

Amongst the thousands of people, Charlotte looked around and saw so many familiar faces. She saw William Lloyd Garrison with his wife, Helen, and their children, George, Wendell, Fanny, and Frank. They all looked so well and happy, Charlotte thought. Miller McKim had returned from South Carolina, and he would share how the relief efforts were going. Charlotte also spotted Dr. Seth Rogers and his wife. "How glad I was to see the Dr. again," Charlotte reflected later. She'd had bouts of bad health since being at his water cure, but this summer, she felt well.

After the opening of the meeting and a prayer, everyone joined together in singing a hymn:

For the sighing of the need, to deliver to oppressed,
Now the Lord our God arises, and proclaims his high behest;
Through the Red Sea of his justice lies the Canaan of rest:
Our cause is marching on!

The cause—and the soldiers of the Union—marched on as they gathered there in Framingham. Over the last week, newspapers reported almost continuous fighting around Richmond, Virginia, and that Confederate troops had retreated back into the city. Not quite a victory, but forward movement.

After the hymn, William Lloyd Garrison's voice boomed out, "Friends of Freedom!" as he began his speech. This wasn't a day for celebration, but reflection, Garrison declared: "The nation is reeling and staggering to-day like a drunken man; the nation is divided and torn asunder by civil war; the nation is bleeding at every pore; and the cries of enslaved millions are still fresh in the ear." But they should have hope, too. This war meant that things could not go back to how they had been two or ten years earlier.

Charlotte particularly liked Garrison's speech—how could she not when she thought so highly of him? She also thought Susan B. Anthony's speech one of the best of the day.

Anthony was a forceful, seasoned speaker, and stood before the audience. Unlike Garrison, Anthony thought that only abolitionists could celebrate the Fourth.

"Abolitionists, the sole representative of an oppressed class, the only true patriots of the country," sounded the alarm bells about the unjustness and lack of liberty in the United States, she told the crowd.

She reiterated the idea that had for so long been seen on *The Liberator*'s masthead: "No union with slaveholders." Anthony criticized President Lincoln for not emancipating the enslaved people as soon as fighting broke out at Fort Sumter. It was within his power, she told the audience, and it was only for fear of upsetting Southern slaveholders that he didn't do it. That was a disgrace.

"A privileged aristocracy of any kind, whether founded on blood, or wealth, or slavery, cannot exist in a democracy," she told the audience.

They had come to a turning point, though: "Generations will pass away sullenly protesting against wrongs they have not the courage openly to resist. But when the smoldering fires of discontent burst forth in revolution, the storm breaks upon the nation with a thundering power, just in proportion to the long moral torpor that has preceded it."

Anthony also told the audience that emancipation shouldn't be only about saving the nation. They needed to "demand emancipation simply as an act of justice to the black man," and it couldn't stop there—Black Americans needed "all the rights of citizenship." Charlotte should have been allowed to go to school or get an ice cream wherever she wanted.

At the end of what was an enjoyable and inspiring day, Charlotte took the train back to Boston, where she planned to stay a few days and enjoy the city.

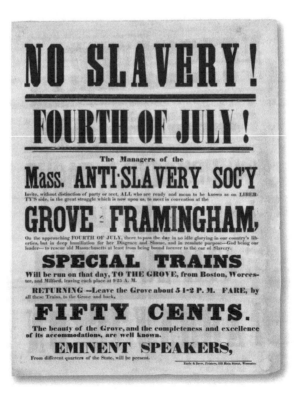

Charlotte Forten's Journal

JULY 1862

Sunday, July 6, [1862]

I was boarding [in Boston] with Mrs. R., a very good anti-slavery woman, and kind and pleasant as can be. Well, when I appeared at the dinner-table to-day, it seems that a gentleman took umbrage at sitting at the same table with one whose skin chanced to be 'not colored like his own,' and rose and left the table. Poor man! he feared contamination.

But the charming part of the affair is that I with eyes intent upon my dinner, and mind entirely engrossed by Mr. [Wendell] Phillips' glorious words, which were still sounding in my soul, did not notice this person's presence or disappearance. So his proceedings were quite lost upon me, and I sh'd have been in a state of blissful ignorance as to his very existence had not the hostess afterward spoken to me about it, expressing the wish, good woman—that my 'feelings were not hurt.' I told her the truth, and begged her to set her mind at ease, for even had I have noticed the simpleton's behavior it w'ld not have troubled me.

I felt too thorough a contempt for such people to allow myself to be wounded by them. This wise gentleman was an officer in the navy, I understand. An honor to his country's service isn't he? But his is not alone, I know full well.

CHAPTER 49

Lucy McKim

PHILADELPHIA
AUGUST 1862

After her visit to Port Royal and the Union victories outside Richmond over the summer of 1862, Lucy felt "a steady influx of patriotism." She was doing the little part that she could. Lucy scraped lint from old linen fabric so that doctors could use the material to pack wounds on the battlefield. She sewed shirts for the hospitals. She told people about the music that she'd heard at Port Royal, in hopes that they would support the schools there.

She still had a hard time being proud of this country when slavery was embedded at its core, and she told Ellen Wright that at this point, she was "not going to countenance young men who stay at home from purely selfish motivations."

"Seriously, the indifference of some people makes me indignant," Lucy went on. The North had to win. "Why are the men so sluggish?"

Lucy had let Dick and Beverly Chase know how she felt.

———

On August 11, 1862, Dick came over to Lucy's house tell her
that he and his brother were not sluggish. They had enlisted. Lucy was both

frightened for their well-being and incredibly proud of them. Lucy also envied Ellen for having a brother who was fighting.

"Noble boys!" Lucy wrote to Ellen. "God bless them for going, a thousand, thousand times! May His hand shelter them wherever they are!"

Now Lucy wanted to refuse any invitation to be social that didn't involve doing good for the war effort.

CHAPTER 50

George Garrison

BOSTON
AUGUST 1862

"**G**eorgie, I can't feel willing to have you go [to war] till the government declares emancipation," George's sister, Fanny, wrote to him in early August 1862. At seventeen years old, she could deliver their family's nonresistant line perfectly. Fanny was in Concord and must have heard what George told his parents.

All summer, George followed news of war and in his diary, noted how thousands of Union soldiers had died. There were rumors of a draft, and George told his father he was "inclined to think he shall go, if drafted, as he does not claim to be a non-resistant."

George's father still felt the war was about maintaining a country and a constitution that supported slavery, and that was not a war he wanted his sons to fight. His father's hope was "that George, though not a non-resistant, will take the penalties of disobedience as the friend and representative of the slave, until entire emancipation is the declared policy of the government."

When this was a war for freedom for the enslaved, George might have his father's reluctant blessing to enlist.

CHAPTER 51

Charlotte Forten

**AMESBURY, MASSACHUSETTS
AUGUST 1862**

C harlotte could not have asked for a better final Saturday in New England. The poet John Greenleaf Whittier invited her over to
his home on August 9, 1862. He was in "one of his most delightful genial
moods," Charlotte thought.

They talked about writing and art, a conversation that was "enjoyable
throughout."

Whittier also suggested that Charlotte apply to the Port Royal Commission
in Boston. Charlotte was substitute teaching classes in Salem over the summer, but soon she would return to Philadelphia and need a job. She always
struggled with how to help her "oppressed and suffering people."

It was an honor that Whittier—so smart, so talented, so forceful in his anti-
slavery beliefs—thought Charlotte should go teach the freed people in South
Carolina.

"I shall certainly take his advice," Charlotte wrote in her journal that night.

———

The rest of August 1862, Charlotte tried to see the commis-
sion in Boston to get a job in Port Royal, but "got little satisfaction" from them.

In the end, they claimed "they were not sending women at present," although white women like Laura Towne were already there and Lucy McKim had visited earlier that summer.

Charlotte was leaving for Philadelphia soon, and there, she could speak with Lucy's father about a job in Port Royal through his Philadelphia Port Royal Relief Association.

CHAPTER 52

Lewis Douglass

ROCHESTER
AUGUST 1862

The country had been at war for a year and four months, and in August 1862, Lewis was still at home in Rochester working at his father's newspaper. The fighting seemed as intense as ever, yet he could not be a part of it.

As soon as Union troops started freeing enslaved people in Confederate territory, President Lincoln said Congress should continue with plans of the voluntary migration of free and freed Black people. While Lewis's father had once written about Haitian emigration, by July 1862, he objected "to these schemes of emigration" because the plans suggested "the prejudice of the whites is invincible." And perhaps the president's perspective showed that Lewis would never be able to escape prejudice in the United States.

In late summer 1862, Lewis heard about a pamphlet Senator Charles Pomeroy of Kansas published: "Information for Persons Proposing to Join the Free Colored Colony of Central America." Pomeroy proposed a new emigration plan to Chiriquí, Panama, where one could receive passage to the colony, enjoy a wonderful climate, and receive a piece of land according to the size of his family or work in a coal mine.

Pomeroy asked Lewis's father for help promoting the plan, but Lewis's father would not do it. He hardly wanted to mention this plan in *Douglass' Monthly*.

"We are Americans by birth and education," Lewis's father said. That may have been true, but that didn't mean Lewis had opportunity by birth.

Lewis wanted his father to write a letter to Pomeroy to serve as an introduction so he could go to Panama.

Leaving wouldn't be an easy decision. Unlike his sister, Rosetta, or his brother Fred, Lewis had never left Rochester to live somewhere else. His mother often relied on her children at home, and his father relied on Lewis at the office. Lewis would be going to a place he'd never been, and he didn't really know what it would offer him other than what the senator promised. And he would be leaving dear Amelia behind. She had been his light. "Day after day freshens and brightens to respect the esteem and love I bear you," he told her. Would she forget about him in his absence? Lewis didn't even know how long he would be gone.

Lewis's father respected his son's choice and wrote the letter of introduction. Douglass was also sure to tell the senator that he did not approve of the colonization project.

Lewis decided he would leave in early October for Washington, DC, and from there travel on to Chiriquí.

George Garrison's Diary

1862 September 19.

A number of battles have been fought the past week in Maryland, and the rebels have been driven across the Potomac [River into Virginia] with great loss. Our loss is very heavy in killed and wounded. A great many of our Generals and officers have been killed and wounded. N.P. [Norwood] Hallowell has been wounded in the in the left arm.

1862 September 24.

Last Monday, Sept. 22nd, the President issued a proclamation of emancipation. It is to take effect January 1st, 1863.

CHAPTER 53

Lucy McKim

PHILADELPHIA
SEPTEMBER 1862

The Liberator **printed the full text of the proclamation:** "All persons held as slaves within any State, or any designated part of a State, the people whereof shall then be in rebellion against the United States, shall be then, thenceforward and forever, free."

"O! That proclamation! Is it not worth living for, selfish & imperfect as it may seem to abolitionists?" Lucy wrote to Ellen Wright.

Lucy knew it was both tremendous for the country and self-serving for the president. Ellen's mother thought it "not such a great thing after all" and William Lloyd Garrison was quick to point out the flaws, including the fact that it left slavery in place in Maryland, Delaware, Kentucky, and Missouri, and did nothing to combat "slave-hunting in the Free States, in accordance with the wicked Fugitive Slave Law."

Lucy thought that the most important thing was that the proclamation referred to *all slaves* in the rebel states, not just those in Union-occupied territory. If the proclamation meant a sooner end to the war, then it meant Dick Chase wouldn't be gone so long.

On Sunday, September 28, 1862—almost a week after Pres-ident Lincoln issued the preliminary proclamation—Dick Chase came to Lucy's house during a lint-picking circle. This still felt like one of the most practical things she could do for the war effort.

"Dick was quiet, and kept looking at his watch, I was on nettles," Lucy confided to Ellen. Lucy knew Dick wanted to talk with her and he would be leaving for the battlefield soon.

Before long, it was eight thirty, and Dick still hadn't said anything to Lucy. This might be the last hour that she saw him for three years, maybe forever. Her sister, Annie, kept chatting, and Dick was scribbling on cards. Finally, he passed her one.

"Do let me have half an hour," he wrote.

Lucy wasn't sure what to say. She didn't know where they could talk privately, so she said they could walk up and down the porch a bit. Her excuse was that she hadn't gotten any exercise that day, something she knew her sister would laugh at later.

Lucy and Dick really didn't have anything special to say to each other, but he noticed Lucy wasn't wearing the ring he'd given her. He said he was afraid she'd taken it off because he needed discouragement. They weren't officially engaged, but the ring told Lucy that he cared for her. She hadn't meant to discourage him, she said, and he understood. Dick was going away to war, and neither of them knew what would happen. He wanted to write her an occasional letter, and she let him.

A decorative version of the Emancipation Proclamation printed by F. W. Thomas in Philadelphia. Along with an image of President Abraham Lincoln at the top, the document has images of Lady Liberty freeing enslaved people.

CHAPTER 54

George Garrison

BOSTON
OCTOBER 1862

Massachusetts had not met the recruitment quota set by President Lincoln in August, and so the draft went into effect on October 15, 1862. George knew it would take several days before they finished the process. He suspected that if either of his brothers were called, they would not go. Draftees could hire a substitute or pay a fee of three hundred dollars to avoid service.

"Some 300 [white men] were drafted today," George wrote in his diary. "My name is not among the number," he added, disappointed. Now that emancipation was coming and a draft was in place, perhaps there might be a chance for him to join in the fight soon, after all.

CHAPTER 55

Lewis Douglass

SALEM, NEW JERSEY
OCTOBER 1862

L ewis thought he would be away for a long time when he
left Rochester on October 10, 1862. He said his goodbyes to his family and
Amelia. He had told her once that he hoped that "nothing [would] arise
that may in any way shake the firmness or overturn the foundations of our love
which we have each made known to one another"—not even Panama and the
opportunity that awaited him there.

———

When Lewis arrived in Philadelphia on his way to Washing-
ton, DC, he "saw by the papers that the day of departure from Washington to
Central America had been indefinitely postponed." He didn't know what was
happening.

William Lloyd Garrison's *Liberator* declared: *The Central American Colonization Scheme Abandoned*. Garrison had always been and still was against
colonization. Could Lewis trust him after the insults and falsehoods he'd spoken and printed about Lewis's father and Julia Griffiths?

The *New-York Daily Tribune* wrote on October 16 that "the colonization expedition going to Chiriquí had been approved and was happening."

Lewis didn't know what to do, and he "became fearful that the whole scheme had failed." Everything looked very gloomy, so he telegraphed Washington asking for details on the departure, but a week later the response was that it was "impossible to tell" when they could leave. Lewis felt so shocked, he could barely comprehend his own feelings. He felt "dejected and miserable." He "thought of home," but he did not feel homesick. For weeks, he had only thought about Panama, and the disappointment was great.

Lewis thought of Amelia, but in that moment, he "had not spirit enough to even pen a line" to her or his parents.

He wrote to Senator Pomeroy instead. He wanted to know when they would sail, and he wanted money Senator Pomery had promised him: twelve dollars for travel and twenty-four for four weeks of lost wages. When Pomeroy finally told Lewis they would not sail until the spring, Lewis went to Salem, New Jersey, where his sister, Rosetta, was teaching.

In Salem, Lewis wrote to Amelia.

"I merely write this to let you know that I am well, and to renew that correspondence which is the joy and pleasure of my life."

Lewis knew his father thought the whole expedition foolish. The fact that the Chiriquí scheme had failed was a "wise ending to a singularly foolish beginning," he said. Lewis would need to find a new opportunity.

CHAPTER 56

Charlotte Forten

PHILADELPHIA
OCTOBER–NOVEMBER 1862

C harlotte waited anxiously for news in her aunt's sitting room in Philadelphia. Miller McKim told her the Philadelphia Port Royal Relief Association was "perfectly willing" for Charlotte to teach in Port Royal, and she had been waiting almost a month to hear when she could depart.

On October 21, 1862, a note arrived from Miller McKim asking if she "could possibly be ready to sail for Port Royal, perhaps tomorrow."

Charlotte "was astonished, stupefied, and, at first thought it impossible." She left her aunt's house and went to McKim's office. He explained this "was an excellent opportunity to go."

"An old Quaker gentleman is going there to keep store, accompanied by his daughter, and he is willing to take charge of [you]," Miller McKim went on.

This would be the only opportunity Charlotte would have this winter.

"At any cost I will go," Charlotte wrote in her journal. "And so to the new work. In great haste."

Charlotte's boat pulled away from New York on the afternoon of Friday, October 24, 1862. She was finally on her way to South Carolina.

She was nervous that she might encounter trouble in being served meals on the boat, be harassed in some way, or have someone take umbrage with the fact that she received equal treatment on board. Although the other passengers had backgrounds similar to Charlotte's—well educated and well-read, and middle- or upper-class—they were also all white. To her surprise, the people aboard "were as kind and polite as possible," and she had interesting conversations with a few of them.

Being on the water calmed Charlotte. She "luxuriated in the glorious beauty of sea and sky" and thought it pleasant they "were far, far away from land." How fitting it was that her new adventure would begin on the water.

As the steamer neared South Carolina, Charlotte took pleasure in watching the ocean, the breaking waves, the foam and spray of the sea, and the silver moonlight glinting off the water.

Finally, they passed Charleston Harbor, then disembarked at Hilton Head before taking a smaller steamer to Beaufort.

———————

One more river to cross and Charlotte would be at her new home. She stepped into a boat rowed by now-free Black men "just at sunset—a grand Southern sunset; and the gorgeous clouds of crimson and gold were reflected in the waters below, which were as smooth and calm as a mirror."

Then the men began to sing "Roll, Jordan, Roll":

> *My brother, sittin' on the tree of life,*
> *An' he heard when Jordan roll;*
> *Roll, Jordan, roll*
> *Roll, Jordan, roll!*
> *O march the angel march,*
> *O march the angel march,*
> *O my soul arise in Heaven, Lord,*
> *For to hear when Jordan roll.*

The river Jordan: where Jewish people crossed to escape enslavement in Egypt, where John baptized Jesus, where people could be healed. A song of life, of rebirth, of freedom, of salvation. Charlotte could see those biblical ideas embodied by the newly freed people. People who had now been freed from enslavement could live their own lives, could be educated, and could fully embrace religion without the control of the enslaver.

Charlotte, the Quaker shopkeeper, and his daughter continued overland in a carriage, through the "pines and palmettos." Now, they jubilantly sang the John Brown song.

"Ah! It was good to be able to sing that *here*, in the very heart of Rebeldom!" Charlotte thought.

They couldn't make it all the way to the Oaks, the plantation where they would be living, so they stayed at the superintendent's house on St. Helena for the night.

The next morning, everything was almost as dreamlike as the night before had been. Live and white oaks lined the roads, and fuzzy, grayish-green moss tendrils draped from the tree limbs. It was as if someone had taken a gauzy, worn fabric and placed it over the branches. Charlotte thought it gave "a solemn almost funeral aspect to the trees."

The house at the Oaks, too, seemed as if it could have been in one of the Gothic novels that Charlotte loved to read. The house was dilapidated, Charlotte thought, and the area around it had "a very forlorn, desolate look." And yet, the place still had beauty. The roses, still blooming in late October, circled the garden, and the bright green ivy crept along the ground. In a way, the Oaks was the metaphor for slavery that some Northern artists and writers had tried to create: slavery caused moral decay, represented by the properties falling apart. The people held in bondage were like the roses and ivy, trying to create beauty and be free despite the oppression.

Laura Towne was still in charge at the Oaks, as she had been when the McKims visited during the summer. Towne took Charlotte down the road a mile to the Baptist Church she had converted into a school. It wasn't large or fancy, just a wooden building painted white with a few windows on the front and a little steeple that held a bell. Charlotte visited the class and was overcome with affection for the children. They were bright and eager to learn.

"Dear children! born in slavery, but free at last?" Charlotte wrote in her journal that night. The Emancipation Proclamation promised freedom, but it had not yet come to pass. "May God preserve to you all the blessings of freedom, and may you be in every possible way fitted to enjoy them," she prayed. Charlotte wanted to help them in every way she could, fulfilling a wish she had made so long ago to help "her people."

About two weeks after Charlotte arrived, when she'd set-tled into her house and teaching duties and met many of the people who lived around, she went with Laura Towne to the collection of houses known as the Corner to see Miss Susy.

Here in South Carolina, Charlotte saw the distance between her life and experience and that of the Black freed people she spoke with every day. Where once she had written "our oppressed people," she now felt they were different from her.

Towne introduced Charlotte to Miss Susy, who had been forced to work for others with no agency over her own life until Union soldiers had scared away her enslavers. Towne asked Miss Susy "if she wanted her old master to come back again."

"No indeed," Miss Susy said. She must have thought the question ridiculous. They'd taken every one of her children away from her. When she was sick and couldn't work, they'd taken her food from her. Anyone who wanted a master back "got no sense," Miss Susy declared with contempt.

Abolitionists had been asking people to imagine a life like Miss Susy's for decades. They'd written novels and painted works of art, delivered sermons and speeches, published photographs and memoirs. That would never be as real as sitting in front of a woman with a withered face, scowling at the idea that someone would want their children and grandchildren forcibly taken from them.

Charlotte longed for her own mother often, and that loss was simply a matter of misfortune. With President Lincoln's Emancipation Proclamation, slavery would never be the reason a parent lost a child or a child lost a parent ever again.

Charlotte awoke on Thanksgiving morning 1862 to cool fresh air, golden sunlight, and blue sky that danced with white clouds.

"Had we not other causes, the glory and beauty of the day alone would make it a day to give thanks for," Charlotte wrote. They did have other causes, though. General Rufus Saxton had declared it "a day of public Thanksgiving and praise" and now everyone was headed to the Baptist church.

So many people had gathered inside the church that people crowded outside at the doors and windows. They sang hymns, a reverend led a prayer and gave a sermon, and then Saxton used the opportunity to ask the Black men to join the regiment led by Thomas Wentworth Higginson. As soon as Charlotte heard Higginson's name, she was transported back to last summer and the streets of Worcester, where she'd seen Higginson lead the exercises of the 51st Massachusetts. Charlotte knew that he was one of the best people to lead a regiment of Black soldiers.

The day finished with more songs and a number of weddings, a commitment the freed people could officially make themselves. Charlotte reflected back on the many Thanksgivings she'd had and considered this to be "the happiest, the most jubilant Thanksgiving day of my life."

Charlotte received a package from home that included an old issue of *The Liberator*, a great treasure and reminder of why they were doing this work. She started a long letter to William Lloyd Garrison, telling him he could publish it if he thought it worth printing, which she didn't think it was.

A month later, Garrison wrote that Charlotte was "a highly accomplished" young woman from a prominent family and was delighted to print two of her letters in his newspaper for the whole country to read.

CHAPTER 57

Lucy McKim

PHILADELPHIA
NOVEMBER 1862

L ucy's father had been speaking on behalf of the Port Royal Commission, trying to get money to fund Laura Towne and her teachers. Part of one of his speeches appeared in *Dwight's Music Journal*, a weekly magazine Lucy enjoyed reading. Lucy and her father had both been struck by the music they'd heard in South Carolina. Miller McKim told audiences that he didn't dwell on the songs "as a matter of entertainment but of instruction." In the music—almost all in a somber, minor key—and the words— recounting their experiences and yearning toward freedom—he thought you could hear their mistreatment and sadness.

Since Lucy had returned from South Carolina, she had been thinking about this, too. Her father could share the words of the songs they'd heard, but he wasn't a musician. He couldn't bring those minor-key tunes into notation. Lucy could. As she picked lint, sewed, and taught piano lessons during the summer and fall of 1862, she kept coming back to what she'd heard in South Carolina. How boatmen and children working the cornmeal mill might sing the same song, but they'd change the tempo to the speed of their work. How one woman, who'd lost twenty-one of her twenty-two children, told her that you couldn't sing "Poor Rosy, Poor Gal" without "a full heart and a troubled spirit." How the songs all had a religious tone to them. How at the Baptist Church, they had heard the "grandest singing," with three hundred people joining in to "Roll, Jordan, Roll," their voices swelling up, a wave of a song that might have sounded sorrowful but was full of triumph, too. To Lucy, the songs showed the character and life of those who had been enslaved.

She had taken some of the songs she'd heard and set them to a piano accompaniment. Transcribing the music wasn't easy. These songs were so different from the hymns, European melodies, or popular songs she knew how to play. The notes almost didn't fit on the musical notation. Notes came from the throat, single voices coming in at different times. But the "striking originality" was what had caught her attention.

Since *Dwight's Music Journal* published her father's notes, Lucy thought that she should send them her transcription of "Poor Rosy," believing it would interest readers. People could learn of this music—and of the humanity of those not yet free.

"Mr. Dwight, SIR," Lucy began her letter. "My chief object in writing to you, is to say, that having accompanied my father on his tour to Port Royal, and being much struck with the songs of its people, I reduce a number of them to paper."

She continued that it was hard to "express the entire character" of the songs "by mere musical notes and signs," but she tried.

"The wild, sad strains tell, as the sufferers themselves never could, of crushed hopes, keen sorrow, and a dull daily mystery which covered them as hopelessly as the fog from the rice swamps," she wrote.

Lucy knew there were more songs, too, songs she hadn't even heard.

"I must remember that [the music] can speak for itself better than any one for it," Lucy concluded in her letter to Dwight. But people wouldn't hear the music if she didn't share it.

Lucy McKim published two songs she heard in South Carolina: "Poor Rosy, Poor Gal" and "Roll, Jordan, Roll." This sheet music cover suggests she planned to publish more individual pieces to support the Port Royal Relief Association, but she never did.

Charlotte Forten's Journal

DECEMBER 1861

December 3, 1861

*See that Lucy McKim has set music to some of the songs of
the 'contrabands' here. She has sent 'Poor Rosy, Poor Gal'
as the first of a series to 'Dwight's [Music] Journal.' It is
much liked.*

CHAPTER 58

Charlotte Forten

PORT ROYAL
DECEMBER 1862

"**M**erry Christmas! Merry Christmas!" Charlotte heard the chorus of voices around the Oaks ringing out as people knocked on her window. It would be a merry day. Soon, she'd be handing out red dresses to the babies, clothing and oranges to the children, apple pies to the workers on the plantation, and picture books and dresses and material for clothing to the boys and girls at the school.

When she was that age, her whole family would gather at her grandmother's house in Philadelphia. They'd wait eagerly for their Christmas presents and the big family dinner. Today, Charlotte could see the same joy on the faces of all her students, who she'd started calling her children. Since she was young, it had amazed Charlotte to think that across the country and world, people gathered together on the same day to celebrate Jesus's birth. One week from today, on New Year's Day, her new friends here in South Carolina, and her friends and family across the North would be gathering for something as momentous: freedom for millions of enslaved people. Seeing the happiness of this Christmas and feeling the anticipation of the coming week, Charlotte's heart swelled. She had dreamed of a new generation where slavery vanished into liberty. In less than a week, the Emancipation Proclamation would go into effect, and the people who had once been enslaved on these Sea Islands would be forever free.

Charlotte, Ellen Murray, and Laura Towne gathered with the children in the church. It was beautiful, so Christmas-like, Charlotte thought. They'd draped it with holly, pine, and mistletoe, just like the churches in Philadelphia might have been decorated. They'd also added the Spanish moss Charlotte adored and Southern holly, another plant she had never seen before coming to the Sea Islands.

The sun filtered through the moss on the oak trees and through the open windows of the church. It was as if God knew that this was a special Christmas and signaled the coming of a wonderful new year. The children beamed.

"It was very pleasant to see their happy, expectant little faces," Charlotte wrote. This "was a wonderful Christmas-day, such as they had never dreamed of before."

Charlotte's friend John Greenleaf Whittier sent her a Christmas Hymn he wrote for her children. They learned it easily and were ready to sing it for the whole crowd gathered.

> *O, none in all the world before were ever so glad as we!*
> *We're free on Carolina's shore, we're all at home and free!*

When the children sang the lyrics, Charlotte felt as though the message came from within them.

That night, music continued to fill the air. Charlotte was exhausted by all the joy, but too many people felt too joyful to stop. She could hear the singing, clapping, and stomping from the shouts around the plantation. Children came to the house to sing, and a six-year-old girl named Amaretta told Charlotte all she just wanted to do was sing and shout. Charlotte loved her voice and the dimples that appeared on her cheeks when she smiled. She thought that soon, Amaretta could shout and sing and do whatever else she wanted "to her heart's content." For Amaretta, slavery would be a childhood memory, not a current reality.

Sad Songs Made Happy

"There must come liberty and
there must come peace."

—LUCY STONE

CHAPTER 59

Charlotte Forten

PORT ROYAL
JANUARY 1, 1863

N ew Year's Day 1863 would be "the most glorious day this nation has yet seen, *I* think," Charlotte wrote in her journal. It was to be Emancipation Day.

Charlotte and Laura Towne were on their way to the camp of the 1st Regiment of the South Carolina Volunteers for the reading of the Emancipation Proclamation.

After what Charlotte thought an impossibly slow carriage ride, they boarded a steamboat to cross the Port Royal River. The flags snapped in the wind, and a plume rose from the smokestack as the boat started to move. Charlotte could feel the excitement on board. Everyone was dressed for the occasion. Charlotte loved the colorful head kerchiefs the women wore, a style that had stayed with the people of South Carolina since their ancestors had been taken from ports across Africa. Their aprons were also crisp and white, a symbol that now work would be on their own terms, not someone else's.

The steamboat's engine competed for sound with the band playing aboard, and people had to talk even louder to be heard over both. The sun shone in the blue sky and shimmered in reflections of the water. If this was not evidence that God smiled on this day, what was?

First, the ruins of the old British fort surrounded by large oaks came into view. Then Charlotte saw the soldiers. Their dark blue coats and red pants contrasted against the earthy tones of the sand, grass, oak trunks, leaves, and moss.

"Charlotte Forten," a familiar voice rang out as soon as she stepped onto the landing. She looked up and Dr. Seth Rogers grabbed her hand. Dr. Rogers was a close friend of Colonel Thomas Wentworth Higginson and had joined the 1st South Carolina Volunteers as a doctor.

"How delighted I was to see him; how *good* it was to see the face of a friend from the North, and *such* a friend," Charlotte thought.

Then, Charlotte was introduced to Colonel Higginson, a man she'd heard about for years but never met. She felt overwhelmed by his presence. No matter how well Charlotte could write when she had a pen and paper in front of her, words sometimes failed. She mumbled something and smiled in response to whatever Higginson said, immediately felt stupid that she didn't have something interesting to say, and went on with her tour of the camp with Dr. Rogers.

After they saw the makeshift hospital, the kitchens, and the rest of the camp, Charlotte took her seat on the platform the men had built under a large live oak tree. She looked out onto the crowd of Black soldiers, officers in "their handsome uniforms," and smiling Black men, women, and children. "I thought I had never seen a sight so beautiful," Charlotte reflected.

After everyone assembled, the chaplain of the regiment said a prayer. Then, Higginson introduced Dr. William Henry Brisbane—a South Carolina–born white abolitionist—who read the whole Emancipation Proclamation. At the end, the crowd erupted in cheers.

Other men gave other speeches, and at the end, some of the Black men spontaneously began singing, "My country 'tis of three, sweet land of liberty." Higginson received flags, and more men gave more speeches and the people cheered. They sang more hymns and the "John Brown Song."

After the speeches, Charlotte joined Dr. Rogers at the colonel's table for dinner. The meal would have been perfect if someone hadn't asked her to read John Greenleaf Whittier's "Hymn" for everyone. Charlotte wanted to pass the task on to Dr. Rogers, but she knew he would insist she do it. She was a poet and writer, but that didn't mean she enjoyed reading in front of people, even friends. "I believe the older I grow, the more averse I get to do anything in public," she thought. She read it anyway, and tried not to let it ruin her day.

A few hours later, the soft moonlight poured over the ruins of the old fort as Charlotte waited with Dr. Rogers for the next rowboat home, but she didn't want to go. She wanted to stay here with them, and she wanted to see the shout and "grand jubilee" the soldiers had planned.

As the boatmen rowed Charlotte from Beaufort to St. Helena Island, singing the hymns that had entranced Lucy McKim and other Northerners, Charlotte had another chorus singing in her soul: "Forever free! Forever free!"

For as long as she could remember, those words—the words in President Lincoln's Emancipation Proclamation—were what she had hoped for. Her heart again swelled with happiness. Victory had not yet come; the war was not over and not all enslaved people were free, but this day was a victory and had felt like one. Later, she'd think that the whole day "seemed, and seems still, like a brilliant dream." She knew that the government had much more to do, but, she thought, today, January 1, 1863, is the day freedom was born in our land.

CHAPTER 60

George Garrison

BOSTON
JANUARY 1, 1863

Despite the chill in Boston on January 1, 1863, George and his whole family made their way to the Music Hall in the afternoon. A fading light came in from the high windows, and a hundred gaslights began to illuminate the hall as people filled in the balcony seats.

As the Garrisons entered, people applauded George's father. Famous New England writers made up the audience, including Harriet Beecher Stowe and John Greenleaf Whittier.

How far the abolitionists had come. When his father founded *The Liberator*, the president of the United States had been Andrew Jackson, a proud slave owner. A pro-slavery mob almost killed George's father for his beliefs in 1835—a story George knew well, since his father retold it every October. This moral conflict became a political one, and the political conflict turned into a war, yet everyone in this room was jubilant.

The orchestra played Lobgesang—a most fitting piece for this elite abolitionist celebration. Felix Mendelssohn wrote the triumphant symphony in 1840 for the four hundredth anniversary of Johannes Gutenberg's invention of the printing press, and these abolitionists felt it was the printed word that allowed them to spread what they felt was God's moral opposition to slavery.

Right in the middle of the concert, they received notice of the official proclamation from Washington, DC, and people jumped up, waved their hats and handkerchiefs, and shouted with joy.

The proclamation was not perfect; George's father and their many abolitionist friends had made that clear. There would be no going back, however. Now that enslaved people in the rebelling states were forever free, it could not be long until the people in border states were also given their freedom.

"It has been a most magnificent day," George reflected.

BOSTON MUSIC HALL.

Grand Jubilee Concert,

THURSDAY AFTERNOON, JANUARY 1, 1863,

IN HONOR OF

THE DAY!

THE PROCLAMATION!

THE EMANCIPATION OF THE SLAVE!

THE SPIRIT OF THE FATHERS AND THE CONSTITUTION!

THE exigencies of the war have made necessary, in the judgment of the President, and as an exercise of the military power of the Government, the issue of a Proclamation, emancipating all persons held as slaves in such States as shall be in rebellion against the Federal Government on the first of January, 1863.

Confident in the belief that this first day of the new year will prove the complement of the 4th of July, 1776, and a new era in the history of the Republic, when the soil of America, hallowed anew by the sacrifice of so much heroic blood, shall no longer be trodden by the foot of a slave, we propose to celebrate the occasion by a MUSICAL FESTIVAL, at the BOSTON MUSIC HALL, on THURSDAY AFTERNOON, JANUARY 1, 1863, the proceeds of the sale of tickets to be appropriated to the benefit of the freed slaves, under the auspices of the Educational Commission.

H. W. LONGFELLOW,	R. W. EMERSON,	O. W. HOLMES,
JOSIAH QUINCY, JR.	WM. ENDICOTT, JR.	J. S. DWIGHT,
EDW. ATKINSON,	GEO. S. HALE,	JOHN G. WHITTIER,
MARTIN BRIMMER,	JAMES STURGIS,	JOHN P. PUTNAM,
R. W. HOOPER,	JAMES T. FISHER,	OTTO DRESEL,
JAMES M. BARNARD,	J. P. COUTHOUY, U. S. N.	E. P. WHIPPLE,
EDWARD E. HALE,	J. M. FORBES,	F. H. UNDERWOOD,
FRANCIS PARKMAN,	HENRY LEE, JR.	R. E. APTHORP,
JAMES T. FIELDS,	B. SCHLESINGER,	JOHN C. HAYNES.
S. G. WARD,	CHARLES E. NORTON,	

The Committee are happy to announce the cordial assistance of

THE GRAND PHILHARMONIC ORCHESTRA,

CONDUCTED BY

MR. CARL ZERRAHN.

A Full Chorus, under the Direction of Mr. B. J. Lang.

ALSO,

MR. OTTO DRESEL, and MR. AUGUST KREISSMANN.

☞ The Concert will commence at 3 P. M. punctually. Doors open at 2.

☞ Tickets, with numbered seats, for sale at Messrs. DITSON & Co.'s. Prices $1.00, or 50 cents, according to location.

S. Chism, — Franklin Printing House, 112 Congress Street.

A program for the Boston Music Hall's Grand Jubilee Concert, which George Garrison attended with his family on Emancipation Day.

CHAPTER 61

Lucy McKim

**PHILADELPHIA
JANUARY 1863**

L ucy could hardly believe what she was reading. Dick Chase was dead. His cavalry regiment had fought near Murfreesboro, Tennessee, on December 31, 1862, and he'd been hit. Another member of the cavalry wrote to Lucy:

> *Dick was struck in the left cheek. He just bent slowly forward to his horse's neck, & then rolled to the ground. He must have died very soon, for as our party fell back he was unconscious. I was not with him, having been sent back to bring up the reserves. The next day a party of five, of which I was one, started to recover the bodies. Bev had gone back to the wagon train. We found them & took them to Nashville, where in Nashville cemetery he is buried. 'Richard W. Chase, Co. E, 13th Penna. Cavalry.' He was the finest man I have met for many years, and he would have matured so well I think.*

Lucy wanted to cry. Dick had only been at war for a few months, and now he was dead. The newspapers said that 2,500 Union men died in those three days of fighting, but that didn't make Dick's death any easier.

Lucy wasn't allowed to cry over Dick, though. "Red eyes are not in the programme at Hilltop," according to her father. But what was more—Lucy and Dick were not officially engaged, so she could not mourn him as anything other than a friend. A dear friend, whom she would never see again.

Lucy thought that when her friends went off to war, she would be prepared to get a letter like this one. She would learn that her friend had died, and she would be sad, but she'd be "so well drilled" that she could be calm and philosophical about it. This was a bloody war. Everyone knew that. But it would be a bloody war for freedom for all of those people she'd met in South Carolina and so many more. The death of a soldier was for a greater joy.

She couldn't bring herself to that reasoning now. Since the moment when she read the words "Killed—R.W. Chase," Lucy realized she hadn't known what the death of a loved one would be like. She felt as though she'd been stabbed and had a gaping wound. "Death is the last Professor for us poor students," Lucy wrote to Ellen Wright.

Lucy also wanted to hug Dick's brother, Beverly, for herself and for Ellen.

"I wish you were here," she wrote to Ellen, "even though your presence would suggest the blank in our future more to me than anyone or anything else I know."

———————

A few weeks later, Beverly Chase came home. He, his sister Edith, and their mother came over to the McKim's house, and Beverly seemed the same as he'd always been. Only, he had a tendency to smile nervously and seemed distracted when Lucy talked to him. And if anyone mentioned Dick, he'd wince. Edith and Mrs. Chase seemed bizarrely cheerful—in black dresses and yet smiling and talking. Maybe they felt like Lucy, always thinking how real it was that Dick was gone and how unreal it was that they'd never see him again. So nobody was the same as before. They couldn't be.

Lucy kept thinking about the battles being fought, battles where she couldn't fire a shot, all the suffering happening that she couldn't ease. She knew that was selfish in a way, but it felt true to her. Ellen suggested that Lucy work in a hospital; Ellen had thought maybe she herself could be a doctor's assistant. Or, she said, Lucy could work in South Carolina at one of the schools for freedmen. Lucy didn't think she was really qualified to do either of those. Ellen's final suggestion was that Lucy pose as a man and enlist. They'd heard that their friend Norwood Hallowell was to be an officer in the Black regiment that was being drawn up in Massachusetts. Lucy wouldn't become a man to fight, though: "Womanhood is as good as manhood anyway," she told Ellen.

CHAPTER 62

Charlotte Forten

BEAUFORT, SOUTH CAROLINA
JANUARY 1863

Beaufort seemed to be an ancient town, made more desolate through the war, Charlotte thought. The large houses on the Main Street with their spacious piazzas had gone into disrepair. On the streets, Charlotte saw only freed people and soldiers—all of the white people who had once lived here had fled long ago. To her pleasure, the soldiers made the public library a shelter for freed people. She saw Black children "looking as merry and happy as children ought to look,—now that the evil shadow of Slavery no longer hangs over them."

When Charlotte went to Beaufort in late January 1863, she spent nearly all her time with Harriet Tubman, who many people called Moses. The biblical Moses led his people to freedom in ancient Egypt, while Harriet Tubman— after having escaped to freedom herself—had led enslaved people from her home state of Maryland to the North.

"She is a wonderful woman—a real heroine," Charlotte thought, and wanted to hear Tubman's stories of leading people to freedom. She told Charlotte the story of a man named Joe. Tubman hid Joe in the woods during the day, got him food to eat, and led him farther north at night. During the journey, Joe was very quiet, and even when they came to the bridge across Niagara Falls. While Harriet Tubman stood in awe of "the glory of the Falls," Joe wouldn't even look at them. Tubman told him they were in Canada, and then he shouted, clapped his hands, hurrahed, and even sang a hymn.

Tears began to form in Charlotte's eyes when she heard the story. How exciting to hear Moses tell this story and hear her sing Joe's hymn.

"I am glad I saw her—*very* glad," Charlotte thought.

CHAPTER 63

Lewis Douglass

ROCHESTER
FEBRUARY 1863

L ewis would be allowed to enlist. What a triumph. His father had been saying that the government should make use of Black soldiers since the beginning of the war, but President Lincoln had not officially allowed it, only turning a blind eye to rogue regiments like the 1st South Carolina Volunteers. On January 26, 1863, Secretary of War Edwin Stanton finally allowed Massachusetts governor John Andrew to form Black regiments. The first would be the 54th Massachusetts Colored Infantry, which now needed volunteers.

George Luther Stearns—a white abolitionist who had financially assisted John Brown and used his home in Massachusetts for the Underground Railroad—came to Rochester to speak to Lewis's father about helping recruit soldiers. Stearns assured Lewis's father that Black men would receive "the same wages, the same rations, the same equipment, the same protection, the same treatment and the same bounty secured by white soldiers." By enlisting, Black men could prove they deserved equal treatment from the United States government, that they were Americans.

Lewis's father began writing an essay for his newspaper encouraging men to enlist. He wrote to all young Black men, but the words were for Lewis and his brothers, too.

"The counsel I give comes of close observations of the great struggle now in process—and of the deep conviction that this is your hour, and mine," his father said. Fight for the enslaved, fight for peace, fight for "every aspiration which you cherish for the freedom and equality of yourselves and your children."

"Manhood requires you to take sides, and you are mean or noble according to how you choose between action and inaction," and Lewis needed to choose action.

"The Iron gate of our prison stands half open," his father said. "One gallant rush from the North will fling it wide open, while four million of our brothers and sisters, shall march out into Liberty!"

Lewis did not need much convincing. This was the chance to "wipe out the dark reproaches unsparingly hurled" at him because he was Black, to bring blessings to the family that he imagined for himself and his dear Amelia.

In the middle of March, Lewis boarded a train in Syracuse on his way to Camp Meigs outside of Boston. He had seventeen men with him, and by some accident they were able to ride in the first-class cars.

"The Syracuse men," Lewis told Amelia, "conducted themselves throughout the journey in a decorous and gentlemanly manner," even if they did start a chorus of, "John Brown's body lies a moldering in the grave, His soul's marching on! Glory, Glory Hallelujah!"

They were now the soldiers in the army of the Lord.

TO COLORED MEN.

54th REGIMENT!

MASSACHUSETTS VOLUNTEERS,

OF

AFRICAN DESCENT!

$100 BOUNTY!

At the expiration of the term of service.

PAY, $13 A MONTH!

AND

STATE AID TO FAMILIES.

RECRUITING OFFICE,

 ### Cor. Cambridge & North Russell Sts., Boston.

Lieut. J. W. M. APPLETON, Recruiting Officer.

J. E. FARWELL & Co., Steam Job Printers, No. 37 Congress Street, Boston.

A recruitment poster for the 54th Massachusetts Regiment, which Lewis Douglass and his brother would join. A number of different recruitment posters were printed across the North.

Recruiting poster, "Men of Color, To Arms!"

SPRING 1863

MEN OF COLOR
TO ARMS! TO ARMS!
NOW OR NEVER

This is our golden moment! The Government of the United States calls for every Able-bodied Colored Man to enter the Army for the

THREE YEARS' SERVICE!

And join in Fighting the Battles of Liberty and the Union. A new era is open to us. For generations we have suffered under the horrors of slavery, outrage and wrong; our manhood has been denied, our citizenship blotted out, our souls seared and burned, our spirits cowed and crushed, and the hopes of the future of our race involved in doubt and darkness. But now our relations to the white race are changed. Now, therefore, is our most precious moment. Let us rush to arms.

FAIL NOW, & OUR RACE IS DOOMED

On this the soil of our birth. We must new awake, arise, or be forever fallen. If we value liberty, if we wish to be free in this land, if we love our country, if we love our families, our children, our home, we must strike now while the country calls; we must rise up in the dignity of our manhood, and show by our own right arms that we are worthy to be freemen. Our enemies have made the country believe that we are craven cowards, without soul, without manhood, without the spirit of soldiers. Shall we die with this stigma resting upon our graves? Shall we leave this inheritance of Shame to our Children? No! a thousand times NO! We WILL Rise! The alternative is upon us. Let us rather die freemen than live to be slaves. What is life without liberty! We say that we have manhood; now is the time to prove it. A nation or a people that cannot fight may be pitied, but cannot be respected. If we would be regarded men, if we would forever silence the tongue of Calumny, of Prejudice and Hate, let us Rise Now and Fly to Arms! We have seen what Valor and Heroism our Brothers displayed at Port Hudson and Milliken's Bend, though they are just from the galling, poisoning grasp of Slavery, they have startled the World by the most exalted heroism. If they have proved themselves heroes, cannot WE PROVE OURSELVES MEN!

ARE FREEMEN LESS BRAVE THAN SLAVES

More than a Million White Men have left Comfortable Homes and joined the Armies of the Union to save their Country. Cannot we leave ours, and swell the Hosts of the Union, to save our liberties, vindicate our manhood, and deserve well of our Country. MEN OF COLOR! the Englishman, the Irishman, the Frenchman, the German, the American, have been called to assert their claim to freedom and a manly character, by an appeal to the sword. The day that has seen an enslaved race in arms has, in all history, seen their last trial. We now see that our last opportunity has come. If we are not lower in the scale of humanity than Englishmen, Irishmen, White Americans and other Races, we can show it now. Men of Color, Brothers and Fathers, we appeal to you, by all your concern for yourselves and your liberties, by all your regard for God and humanity, by all your desire for Citizenship and Equality before the law, by all your love for the Country, to stop at no subterfuge, listen to nothing that shall deter you from rallying for the Army. Come Forward, and at once Enroll your Names for the Three Years' Service. Strike now, and you are henceforth and forever Freemen!

CHAPTER 64

Lewis Douglass

READVILLE, MASSACHUSETTS
APRIL 1863

The bleak expanse of Camp Meigs stretched out before Lewis in early April 1863. The spring rain turned the military training camp into a pit of mud, the kind of mud that one gets sucked into. They were lucky to have wooden barracks, rather than the canvas tents that earlier regiments had used.

When Lewis arrived, he immediately went to be examined by one of the regiment's doctors to see if he was fit for duty. Then, an officer took down his description for official army records: "5 ft 9 inches Brown complexion brown eyes. Black hair. Printer." Finally, Lewis had to "promise to obey all orders from the President of the United States down."

Lewis Douglass was now officially in the 54th Massachusetts Colored Regiment, Company F, and promoted to sergeant major, the highest noncommissioned officer. After taking his oath, Lewis went to the quartermaster to get his uniform. His pants were a light blue, with one thick blue stripe down the side. He admired the dark blue coat with the three-striped golden triangle on the sleeves, which let everyone know his rank. As a sergeant major, Lewis would have respect, but mostly do paperwork rather than supervise the privates.

His rank also meant that he wasn't supposed to have to sleep with the privates in the barracks. "The rules are that I shall have a room of my own with writing materials &c," Lewis explained to Amelia. But his building was not yet ready, so he would have to bunk up with the other soldiers for the time being.

Since this was the only Black regiment in the North, men came from all over: western New York like Lewis, but also from as far west as Kentucky, as far north as Vermont, and as far south as North Carolina. Republican newspapers put out notices about the regiment, and Lewis's father and Amelia's father both made trips across the North to recruit soldiers.

Although Lewis found the men from Syracuse respectable, he was not particularly impressed with the overall conduct of men in camp. "The soldiers amuse themselves by fighting each other," he told Amelia. They also spoke up to the officers, for which they'd be "immediately punished, by chaining large balls of iron to them or making them hold heavy weights for long hours."

They all knew they could die fighting; that was part of war. They also understood that the Confederate army had no respect for them as people and definitely not as soldiers. If one was captured during battle, one could be killed or sold into slavery, even if one had been born free. They'd need get into good form quickly.

Lewis Douglass in his uniform after enlisting in the 54th Massachusetts.

CHAPTER 65

Lucy McKim

BOSTON
APRIL 1863

"**We shall dance at funerals next year & flirt across** corpses." Lucy wrote those words to Ellen Wright in 1862. Now it was true. Dick Chase died less than four months earlier, and here she and Ellen were in Boston, at a party. Their friend Norwood Hallowell's brother and sister-in-law had decided to host the Eagleswood alumni on an evening in April 1863.

They'd rented a hall in central Boston, hired musicians, and danced all night. They ate ice cream and cake and drank coffee. So many people were there, you might almost forget a war was happening. Norwood was there, even though he was now Lieutenant Colonel of the 54th Massachusetts and training at Camp Meigs outside Boston. Their old teacher Theodore Weld came, as did William Lloyd Garrison and his children George, William, Wendell, and Fanny.

George came to dance, although he seemed terribly shy. Ellen said she liked William better than anyone else. The last time Lucy had spent time with Wendell was in October 1861 at the Pennsylvania Anti-Slavery Convention in West Chester. Ellen thought she could tell that Wendell was still charmed by Lucy.

––––––––––––

Lucy and Ellen stayed with the Garrisons for a few days after the party. They visited friends around Boston, went to concerts and plays with Wendell and William, and had conversations about temperance and spiritualism. Lucy played and sang some of the songs she'd heard in Port Royal for the Garrisons, which fascinated them.

Wendell was smart and kind, and he enjoyed music and art like Lucy did. But even though they had fun together, Lucy couldn't bring herself to be smitten with Wendell. She wasn't over Dick, and she had so much life to live before she really gave her heart away.

CHAPTER 66

George Garrison

BOSTON
MAY 1863

Norwood Hallowell walked into the Garrison home at Dix Place on the evening of May 7, 1863. Norwood was slender, his full beard covering a face that still looked young at twenty-four years old. He had injured his arm at the Battle of Antietam, but he seemed better now.

George had immense respect for Norwood and saw him training with the 54th Massachusetts at Camp Meigs in April. George even donated two dollars in support of the regiment.

More Black men wanted to enlist than the 54th could accommodate, so now the 55th Massachusetts Regiment was forming at Camp Meigs. Norwood was going to be a colonel in the 55th, and told George and Wendell they needed officers. As young abolitionist men, George and his brother would make excellent candidates. Wendell immediately declined the offer of becoming quartermaster. He was a nonresistant and would not be in any part of the army, even if it was a more administrative position.

George declined to be a quartermaster, too. "I am unfortunately not qualified for it," he told Norwood. The quartermaster gave out supplies to the soldiers and kept logbooks and accounts, which George's father had told him he was not good at.

Norwood then said that George could "have a chance of being second Lieutenant."

"I shall try for it," George thought. He would never have a better opportunity than this to join the army.

———————

By May 11, George had made up his mind. He would enlist. George's brother William heard the news first from Norwood, but since their father was away in New York, no one had told him yet. George already knew what his father and mother were going to say. He would have to hold steady in his convictions.

When his father returned on May 16, George told his parents of his decision. First, his father was astonished, then took the news very hard.

"I could have wished that you had been able understandingly and truly to adopt those principles of peace which are so sacred and divine to my own soul," he told George.

But as much as his father hated the decision that George was making, he would not stand in George's way, if George was responding to his "own highest convictions of duty." If he was going because he was tired of printing in *The Liberator*'s office or because he wanted an adventure, however, he implored George not to think of going.

This was not about an adventure or a job; this was about George's moral duty. As a member of the 55th Massachusetts Regiment, George wanted to do his "full share towards suppressing the rebellion, and giving liberty to the enslaved," he said.

George's mother was more concerned with his safety. He could get sick, be injured, be taken prisoner, or die. As William Lloyd Garrison's son, he might "incur more risks," as his father put it, than other white officers in the Black regiments. But had not Frederick Douglass's own sons joined? Were all those

Black soldiers not under tremendous risk in fighting the rebels who wanted to make them slaves again?

George's conviction was not swayed by his parents, and on May 19, the *Boston Evening Transcript* announced his new position as second lieutenant.

———

On June 1, George spent one dollar on a ticket to Readville to start training at Camp Meigs. At least Fanny was proud of him. She wrote that she heard he was drilling soldiers and doing better than some officers who had been there much longer. Other family friends gave him presents, taking an interest in his involvement with the regiment.

George Garrison's portrait after enlisting in the 55th Massachusetts Regiment.

CHAPTER 67

Lewis Douglass

READVILLE, MASSACHUSETTS
MAY 1863

B y early May 1863, the sun had been shining for a few weeks and the mud had finally dried out at Camp Meigs. Lewis loved how the soldiers were "kicking up their heels," joking, and "making the camp ring with their hilarity."

On May 18, 1863, Lewis's father, mother, and sister all arrived at Camp Meigs. Lewis's father had been to visit in between his recruiting, and Lewis's mother and sister had been in Boston for a week and had been coming regularly to see him. This would be the final celebration before the 54th left for South Carolina.

In the barracks, Lewis and the other men put on their light blue pants and buttoned the golden buttons of their dark blue jackets. They fastened belts around their waists and placed blue caps on their heads. They looked as crisp and clean as—or maybe even neater than—any army regiment that had come out of Massachusetts.

Even though the proceedings wouldn't start until eleven o'clock, people had been arriving in carriages and on extra trains sent from Boston to Readville since early in the morning.

At eleven, Lewis marched in line with the hundreds of other men, and they formed a square around Massachusetts governor John Andrew, who was going to present flags to Colonel Robert Shaw, the leader of the 54th. After a prayer, Governor Andrew began to speak. For the abolitionist Andrew, this wasn't a political fight of a country trying to hold itself together. This was a moral fight, and having this Black regiment proved something. Now that they were in the army, Andrew declared, Lewis and his regiment could "help raise aloft their country's flag—*their* country's flag, now, as well as ours—by striking down the foes who opposed it, [striking] also the last shackle which binds the limbs of the bondmen in the Rebel States." Andrew didn't believe in what the Supreme Court had said almost ten years earlier in the Dred Scott decision. Lewis wasn't just a soldier, but a citizen of this country; this was his flag.

"We are fighting a battle, not merely for country, not merely for humanity, not only for civilization, but for the religion of our Lord itself," the Governor's voice boomed across the field. The last banner Andrew presented to Colonel Shaw was a blue flag with a white cross and the words in Latin *In Hoc Signo Vinces*, or "In this sign, thou shalt conquer." Their fight was a moral fight to abolish slavery in the United States, where God was on their side, the flag seemed to say.

"Remember that if I fall that it is in the cause of humanity," Lewis wrote Amelia a few days later, "that I am striking a blow for the welfare of the most abused and despised race on the face of the earth, that in the solution of this strife rests the question of our elevation, or our degradation, our happiness or our misery."

This was a war for freedom, and Lewis wanted to imagine that he would be "aiding in the glorious work of bursting loose those chains which [keep] the husbands, wives, children, lovers and friends" shackled, and overthrowing a system of tyranny "which degrades millions of human beings."

Lewis thought of the "inexpressible joy" freedom would bring and looked forward to being a part of "that joy, that happiness."

On May 28, Lewis and the 54th were ready to leave Camp Meigs for Boston. While at camp, the dress parades attracted "many visitors from the city of Boston every evening of both complexion, the paler brethren and sisters however predominating," Lewis told Amelia. When the governor spoke to the regiment on May 18, the crowd had been huge and supportive. Now the police feared that as the 54th paraded through Boston to the wharf, an unfriendly crowd might be waiting. There were people who didn't like the idea of a Black regiment or just didn't like Black people at all, and a hundred officers were ready to deal with any fighting that broke out.

In his neat uniform, Lewis marched in time with his company. They were all supposed to keep serious faces, but could they manage that when so many people had come out to cheer them on? The sidewalks were packed with well-wishers, and people stuck their heads out of windows and waited on balconies to see the men pass.

Red, white, and blue fabric seemed to flutter everywhere, and patriotic songs blared from the band at the front. As Lewis passed by the home of Wendell Phillips, William Lloyd Garrison and his daughter watched from the balcony. Garrison's hand rested on a statue of John Brown's head, and then the band began playing the "John Brown Song."

It took them almost four hours from getting off the train to arriving at the steamship *De Molay*, and it wasn't until four o'clock that they finally left the dock.

Sometimes, it could be nice to have such a prominent father. While everyone else waved from the wharf, Frederick Douglass was allowed to board the *De Molay* and ride out into the harbor with his son. When the sun began to set over Boston, Lewis said goodbye to his father, who got onto a tugboat back to shore. Lewis didn't know when, or if, they'd see each other again.

Letter from Lucy McKim to Wendell Garrison

JUNE 1863

Hilltop, June 6th, 1863

Dear Wendell-

[. . .] So, after all, Norwood Hallowell has accepted the colonelcy of the 55th. I am glad of it. And your brother George is advertised as one of the lieutenants. Will you give him my warm regards and—you see I am a resistant—congratulations? Is it not fortunate that some of us are resistants, since it is only by fighting, the black race can shake off the degradation of years? Certainly moral weapons are almost always better than carnal ones, but when a brawling nation thrusts our reason and gentleness back in our faces, it understates to say that one cannot hinder her from worse than murdering four millions of helpless beings, then—'better war, loud war!

'War with a thousand battles, & shaking a hundred thrones.' (I need not say 'vide Tennyson' by this time, I suppose.)

Above all is the instinct within us. Not the brute desire to kill, but the divine impulse which seizes us irresistibly as to become instruments of God's retributive justice. It is not necessary to take tigers for models; rather the beautiful archangel, whose picot we saw in the Athenaeum, with his foe beneath his foot, & his eyes kindled with celestial fury. [. . .]

With cordial remembrances to your parents & brothers. I remain very truly yours,

Lucy McKim.

Letter from Lewis Douglass to Amelia Loguen

JUNE 1863: ST. SIMONS ISLAND

Georgia, June 18, 63

My Own Dear Amelia:

I am now in the State of Georgia, "away down in Dixie." Our journey over the "briny deep" was fraught with no remarkable incidents, we were six sea-sick days coming from Boston to Port Royal or Hilton Head.

Our steamer the "De Molier" [sic] was tossed and pitched about by the waves like a play thing in the hand of a child, now away up up up, then down, down now on this side, now over that, frightening some while others had very serious expressions on their faces. To see the men huddled about on deck looking as though Death would be welcome visitor was sad enough, many wishing they never had gone for a soldier.

I stood it first rate, I was sick only a half hour. Arriving at Beaufort S.C. the first man to whom I was introduced was Robert Small. I there met Harriet Tubman, who is captain of a gang of men who pilot the Union forces into the enemy's country. We staid [sic] in Beaufort four days and then came to this place.

A week ago to day we went to Darien Georgia, expecting to have a fight. Darien lies on the Altamaha river, about 8 miles from its mouth, in going up the river our gunboats shelled the woods along the way, but could discover no enemy. We landed at Darien, took some $100,000 worth of different articles consisting of furniture which the Rebels had run away from a year ago and never came back after. We found two white women in the town and one white man [who] escaped, the women we left after burning every building or shelter in the place to the ground. I felt a little sympathy for [the] feminines. I hope to have more to write of soon. Oranges, lemons and peaches grow here.

Remember me to all at home, and to all enquirers if there are any.

Believe me ever

Your Own
Lewis

CHAPTER 68

George Garrison

READVILLE
JULY 1863

On Monday, July 13, 1863, George left Camp Meigs to visit home and friends. He thought this might be the last time he could do so before the 55th Regiment was sent south. At home, he heard that his brother Wendell had received a draft notice. In March 1863, President Lincoln signed a federal draft law to get more enlistments. Wendell told George what the whole family already knew: "my mind has long been made up" and he would pay three hundred dollars instead of going to war. Wendell believed hiring a substitute was morally the same as fighting himself. George and his fellow soldiers did not have much respect for men who stayed home, although George knew that his brothers had a moral reason for not wanting to fight and could afford the fee.

George also heard that the draft was causing a "tremendous riot in New York City." The news reports were sporadic, since the telegraph line had been cut. As always, he was anxiously waiting for news.

Finally, George heard that working-class Democrats and Irish immigrants—who had not voted for President Lincoln and did not support the war—attacked Republican Party buildings at first and then, believing that Black Americans had been the cause of the war, turned to destroying the Black community in Manhattan. The mob burned Dr. James McCune Smith's pharmacy, the Colored Orphan Asylum, and other buildings. The rioters murdered eleven Black New Yorkers.

In Boston, the mood was tense on July 14 as a group of Irish men gathered in the streets and violence broke out. The police and the military managed to subdue the riot, but not before five men died.

All this changed the plans for the 55th. They were supposed to take the train to New York City, parade through Manhattan, and board boats in that harbor. Deeming that far too inviting for another riot, the governor decided they would leave directly from Boston.

On July 21, George marched through the rainy streets of Boston with the 55th. The band still played the "John Brown Song," women still threw bouquets, and family, friends, and supporters still lined the streets.

George's family and friends, and the family and friends of many members of the 55th, had purchased tickets to see them parade on the Common. They were supposed say their grand goodbyes, with hugs, tears, and handshakes. This wouldn't happen, though. George heard the state authorities cancelled the parade because they felt it too risky in light of the riots.

"It was cruel and cowardly of the state authorities in not letting us go on to the Common after all the arrangements had been made for us," George told his mother later. "We feared no attack," he said, "and if there had been one [we] were abundantly able to take care of ourselves, as our muskets and revolvers were loaded and we did not lack in ammunition." As the 55th marched, George managed to see his siblings Fanny, Frank, and William for just a moment as he walked through the streets. The parade paused at the statehouse for a presentation of arms, and George managed to stop and shake William's hand in a final goodbye. Frank decided he'd walk alongside George to the docks.

George saw his mother and father but had no chance to say anything to them. They were one thousand men, marching in formation in the rain, and hardly anyone was able to say goodbye to their families. Even though George went to Dix Place just three nights before, he knew his father wanted to shake his hand once last time, to wish him well and offer a parting blessing.

As they approached the wharf, it seemed as if all of the Black residents of Boston had come to see them off. There must not have been a person who came out in that rain that did not feel a mixture of pride and fear. The rumors were already rampant: that captured Black soldiers would be sold into slavery and that the rebels would refuse to exchange any officers. No one could say whether this was true or not, not yet anyway, but the thought terrified many family members. They knew that joining this regiment was dangerous.

As fearful as the families of the 55th were for their future, they knew the fighting was now for a just cause. George's father told him he had "nothing but praise to give you that you have been faithful to your highest convictions, and taking your life in your hand, and willing to lay it down, even like the brave Col. Shaw and his associates, if need be, in the cause of freedom, and for the suppression of slavery and the rebellion."

By the time the troops reached the docks, the morning drizzle turned to a downpour. George climbed onto the steamer, rain soaked through his blue officer's coat and pants. The 55th Massachusetts Colored Regiment was on their way south.

CHAPTER 69

Lewis Douglass

SOUTH CAROLINA
JULY 18, 1863

The 54th Massachusetts had clear orders: take Fort Wagner. If Lewis and the other men could take this fort in South Carolina, they could take Charleston and extinguish the burning heart of the rebellion. Lewis slogged through sand, swamp, and sheets of rain, his boots sinking into silt and his uniform soaked, before taking a swaying steamer to the shore of Morris Island.

The evening air felt thin, and the storms and humidity had cleared from the sky on July 18, 1863. One might almost think that thunderheads still floated above the 54th Massachusetts Regiment. The bombs going off around the island sounded like thunder in the distance and created a thick smoke that hung over the water.

They kept moving forward, even though they hadn't received rations in two days, hadn't eaten since the morning, and had been marched for hours on hours.

In the light of dusk, they saw the slope of the fort. They formed columns, six hundred men strong, and Colonel Robert Shaw decided they would be the first to advance.

"Now I want you to prove yourselves as men," Colonel Shaw cried.

As they moved forward, the sky began to light up, a torrent of flames showering down on them. Lewis looked around and "not a man flinched." They would prove themselves as men.

It looked like a hailstorm, Lewis thought, but instead of balls of ice, they were balls of fire. Balls from cannons and shells from guns exploded up from the fort and rained down on them. And as the hail hit, men fell. And fell. And fell. They collapsed like stalks of grain under a scythe.

Men ran out of the way, the shell exploding and clearing a space, and then other men closed up into that space again. They lost formation but pressed on toward the fort.

Amidst the explosions and gunfire, Colonel Shaw called out, "Come on, men! Follow me!"

They climbed into a ditch outside the fort, then up the sloped walls to the parapet.

The energy in the air felt like a bolt of lightning touching down in the storm.

Lewis yelled for the men to press on.

The colonel stood atop the parapet, waving his sword. Men followed and drove the rebels from their guns. Then the colonel was tumbling backward. He'd been hit.

Something struck Lewis, and his sword sheath flew off. His leg was struck, too.

There was no way to move forward. For those who had not made it into the fort, the only way to go was back. Lewis didn't understand how he got out of there alive. One moment he was surround by those explosions, and the next he was away from the fort. They had to abandon their attempt to take it and formed a line instead. They didn't have any backup until the 10th Connecticut showed up hours later.

Around Lewis was a sea of bodies and body parts, and they hadn't taken the fort.

Two days later, Lewis wrote to Amelia. "I have been in two fights and am unhurt," he lied. Although they had not been able to take the fort, the newspapers reported that the 54th had fought valiantly and proved their worth as men and soldiers. Lewis didn't want Amelia to worry, but he also knew there was more fighting to come.

"Remember if I die I die in a good cause. I wish we had a hundred thousand colored troops we could put an end to this war," he told Amelia.

Charlotte Forten's Journal

Monday, July 20.

*For nearly two weeks we have waited, oh how anxiously
for news of our [regiment]. Which went, we know to Morris
[Island] to take part on the attack on Charleston. To-night
comes news oh, so sad, so heart sickening. It is too terrible,
too terrible to write. We can only hope it may not all be
true. That our noble, beautiful young Colonel [Shaw] is
killed, and the rest. Cut to pieces! I cannot, cannot believe
it. And yet I know it may be so. But oh, I am stunned,
sick at heart. I can scarcely write. There was an attack
on Fort Wagner. The 54th put in advance, fought bravely,
desperately, but was finally overpowered and driven back
after getting into the Fort. Thank Heaven! They fought
bravely! And oh, I still must hope that our colonel, ours
especially he seems to me, is not killed. But I can write no
more to-night.*

DOCUMENT
New York Herald
JULY 1863

WASHINGTON, JULY 25, 1863

Unofficial advices received from our forces operating in Charleston harbor to-day indicate that the second assault upon Fort Wagner, on Morris Island, was not a success. Our loss in this affair is not stated; but the dispatch from [P.G.T.] Beauregard, of the 22nd inst., putting it at two thousand in killed, wounded and missing, is of course a gross exaggeration, worth of his reputation acquired by previous similar official efforts. When the boat last arrived left the fight was still going on, with every prospect of final success. Further reliable advices from this quarter will be anxiously looked for.

CHAPTER 70

Charlotte Forten

**SOUTH CAROLINA
JULY 1863**

On July 21, 1863, Charlotte heard from Colonel Thomas Wentworth Higginson and Dr. Seth Rogers that the army desperately needed nurses in the hospital in Beaufort to take care of the wounded men of the 54th. Jean Lander, the supervisory nurse for the troops in Beaufort, was not sure that Charlotte could handle hospital life. Men would be bleeding and in pain. They would have open wounds or severed limbs. They would be dying.

Charlotte knew that she wasn't the strongest woman, but she could refill washbasins, keep the soldiers company, and help them write letters to their families at the very least. Colonel Higginson and Dr. Rogers both believed she could be of help, and Lander finally agreed.

———

Charlotte stepped into the large brick building—one of only a few in Beaufort. It had large windows and was rather airy, which made it suited to be a hospital. She started by sewing up uniforms. She had spent many nights mending clothes and sewing when she lived in Salem, but this job made her heart sink. Each hole was a where a bullet had struck a member of the 54th. Each rip a cut from a bayonet. One jacket was so torn up that Charlotte couldn't mend it. Could Dr. Rogers mend the man who had been beneath that jacket? Or was he gone forever, too?

She walked through the wards and was surprised by the cheerful faces of the men. Some had only flesh wounds, others were severely injured. They had just been through hell, and yet they were proud to fight, to have proven their mettle against the rebels.

"Brave fellows!" Charlotte thought. "I feel it a happiness, an honor, to do the slightest service for them."

Dr. Rogers was worried about Charlotte's health, though. That summer, she had felt her strength failing rapidly. Perhaps being in the hospital was not the best for her, and the unhealthy summer season, when people started to get fevers, was beginning. Charlotte found it hard to speak loud enough for her hundred students to hear her and to ride through the heat of the July days. Dr. Seth Rogers knew that if she exhausted herself now, she would only get worse.

"I take my good Dr.'s advice, therefore, and shall go North on a furlough—to stay until the unhealthiest season is over," Charlotte wrote in her journal on July 26, 1863.

Letter from George Garrison to his mother

AUGUST 1863

On board ship "Recruit" off the coast of North Carolina,
bound for Charleston, South Carolina.

August 3rd, 1863

Dear mother:

I very much regret that I did not have an opportunity to speak to you and Father, and to bid you both good-bye as we passed through Boston. [. . .]

We left Boston in the midst of a severe rain storm, but the next day and the rest of the voyage [. . . We] had clear and beautiful weather. [. . .]

At Hatteras Inlet we got New York papers giving us an account of the terrible fight at Fort Waggoner [sic] in which the 54th Massachusetts and other regiments got so terrible cut up. The 54th seems to have lost terrible in officers, almost every one being killed or wounded. I felt very sorry to hear of the death of Col. Shaw, and the wounding of Ned Hallowell and Capt. Appleton. If the fort is not taken before we get there, we shall have our turn at it, and I hope with little better success. The chances of our being badly cut up are, I suppose, as good as that of the 54th. All the officers and men of this regiment would prefer to die in an effort to take Charleston, than in a contest any where else. [. . .]

The men all have the utmost confidence in their officers in our regiment, which can be said of but few white regiments, I think. [. . .]

Give my love to Fanny, Franky, Wendell, William, + Father [. . .] Give my love to all friends who inquire after me. The papers will keep you posted in regards to our operations here.

Your loving son,
George T. Garrison

Letters from Lewis Douglass to Amelia Loguen

AUGUST 1863

Morris Island SC. Aug 15

My Own Dear Amelia: Your kind letters were duly received, finding my suffering slightly from a pain in the head caused by the climate. I have this far held out against the climate but I now fear that I am going to be sick [. . .]

You wish to know how to send a box to the sick and wounded of the 54th, you may direct to the Sick and wounded Hospital No 6, Beaufort S.C. send by Ailanis Express. The colored women of Beaufort have shown their appreciation of the cause by helping take care of our sick and wounded, under the irrepressible Harriet Tubman.

My head aches so bad that I scarcely [know] what I am writing, so you must excuse this disjointed scribble. [. . .]

I have got used to the music of shells the rebels are constantly throwing them from Sumter and Johnson. But we are all right we will have Charleston soon. Good bye

Ever Yours
Lewis

Morris Island, S.C. August 27, 1863

My Own Dear Amelia: Having some leisure moments, I know of no better, or pleasing way to use them than to write to you. I have got so much better as to be able to attend to my duties again, still I am in no wise enjoying perfect health. The weather here is chilly and the atmosphere damp. It is now fall in this portion of the earth, and like tropical countries the rainy season has set in, and night and day, we feel the chill damp of a southern fall shower [. . .]

We are still living in expectancy; Charleston is not yet ours, still we see no reason to be any thing but hopeful, all our movements tend to weaken the enemy and strengthen our own positions, and make the fall of Charleston a great deal more than a possibility, it is a certainty. What a day of rejoicing it will be the day that heralds the downfall of that city, from whose halls and streets rang first that treason and disloyalty which has overturned the nation, produced a great deal of evil, and yet been the source of much good unintended. [. . .]

This is fine to think of but before it can come to pass there must be work done, death must be dealt out, and must be received, some of us will live to see rebellion crushed and some of us will die crushing it. Either is glorious. [. . .]

Remember me to your mother and father, brother and sisters.

Ever Lovingly,
Lewis

CHAPTER 71

Lucy McKim

PHILADELPHIA
SEPTEMBER 1863

Wendell Garrison's letter lay on the table in front of Lucy. She'd received it the day before, on September 3, 1863, and she needed to figure out what to say in response. They had corresponded some after her trip to Boston in the spring, and that correspondence showed a certain level of intimacy. Wendell had come to the McKim's home in Philadelphia over the summer, and Lucy wished that he had told her how he felt in person rather than through this letter. There was so much she wanted to say, and she had to start somewhere.

Lucy picked up her pen, dipped it in ink, and began to write.

"Would that I could wholly and without reserve return at once the love you offer me." Lucy was honored that Wendell, who was smart and came from such a good family, loved her. But she had to tell him that she couldn't love him. She liked him very much; that she could tell him. She admired and respected him.

"But I love no one," she wrote. The first fact was that Lucy didn't want to be engaged to anyone at the moment. When she was alone, she felt strong and independent. Going to Port Royal with father had taught her that life was full of excitement and there was so much to do.

"The world seems wide before me," she went on. "I am so young: freedom is so sweet: I cannot part with it." Lucy had even spoken to Wendell's sister,

Fanny, about her desire to go back to Port Royal.

Then there was the matter of Dick Chase. In her and Wendell's conversations in March and over the summer, Lucy hadn't told Wendell about Dick and his death nine months ago, or what their relationship had been. Now that was part of why she couldn't return Wendell's feelings.

"For three years I had a dear and intimate friend" who died in battle, Lucy told Wendell. She explained that she and Dick were not engaged, and probably wouldn't have become engaged, but his death was a shock nonetheless. "Since then my susceptibilities seem to have been paralyzed," she told Wendell.

Wendell Garrison, posing for a portrait in 1861. He wanted to court Lucy McKim, but she was still unsure whether she could be with a nonresister.

As she wrote these words, Lucy wasn't even sure of them. She'd had dreams and omens that suggested she should change what she'd written, that she should have accepted Wendell's love. Lucy knew what she wrote would be devastating to receive.

"Forgive this hard, unsatisfactory letter. It contains the nearest approximation I can make of my sentiments," Lucy wrote, hoping he'd understand.

What she hadn't written was that Wendell was still a nonresister, someone who wasn't willing to go to war like his own brother George, who was now in South Carolina. Or Norwood Hallowell, who had been injured but wanted to keep fighting. Or like Ellen's brother, who had been injured at the battle at Gettysburg a month earlier. Or like Beverly Chase, who was now a prisoner of war. Or like Dick Chase, who was dead.

CHAPTER 72

George Garrison

SOUTH CAROLINA
SEPTEMBER 1863

The beach on Folly Island was the finest George had ever seen. The sand was smooth and extended for several miles in both directions from their camp. The waves were not rough, and George could wade out a long distance before the water came over his head. "The whole regiment goes bathing every morning," he told his father.

From when they'd arrived in August until now in early September, everything was rather grueling, though. George had been sick with diarrhea for his first three days in South Carolina. He did not find this unusual, since all he had consumed were stale, bland hardtack crackers and coffee. George liked drinking cold water, but the water here was not good, and bad water could make anyone sick easily.

"We are an entirely different look[ing] set of men from what we were when we left Boston," George wrote to his father in late August. In Boston, they had paraded around Camp Meigs in their uniforms. "The fuss and feathers are gone," George explained, and "many of the men go about for comfort in their shirts and drawers only—some only in their pants." No one wore their coat in the heat of a South Carolina summer with hardly any shade, and George would have to be careful not to get a sunburn with his fair skin.

Some have "not got a constitution strong enough to endure" being in the army, George thought. While his brother's Harvard classmate Lieutenant Leonard Alden could not deal with the heat and spare provisions, George had spent months eating potatoes when there was not much else to be found in Nininger, Minnesota, fought off rats during the Kansas winter, and dealt with the fever and ague that seemed to make everyone out west sick.

Right now, they also had the rightly named fatigue duty. The men would start work at five o'clock in the morning and work until eight or nine o'clock at night. They built fortifications and dug trenches, unloaded vessels of freight and ammunition, dragged cannons to the front and mounted them. They did this while the Confederate forces fired upon them, and George and his men had to dodge the bullets. Since they had not seen a battle, this shooting might do the men good, George thought. They would learn to keep cool under enemy fire.

This fatigue duty was only supposed to last three or four weeks, George had been told, but after a month in South Carolina, this seemed to be their only task.

"They enlisted with the understand[ing] that they were to be paid and treated the same as other Massachusetts regiments," George told his mother, and yet, the Black soldiers were not being paid the thirteen dollars a month they were promised, and they were being made to "do all the heavy work and drudgery but not [...] any of the fighting."

The work was hard, and seemingly endless, and many of the men seemed to be breaking down even though they had only been here a month.

CHAPTER 73

Lewis Douglass

NEW YORK CITY
SEPTEMBER 1863

L ewis arrived at the hospital in New York City on September 23, 1863. In his letters since the Battle of Fort Wagner, he promised his dear Amelia that he was okay, but in fact he was getting worse. The doctors deemed Lewis too ill to stay in South Carolina, so they'd placed him aboard a steamer and sent him north.

Lewis could scarcely admit how sick he was to anyone and was lucky to be under the care of Dr. James McCune Smith, an old friend of his father who was still recovering from the burning of his pharmacy over the summer by the white anti-draft mob. Although Harriet Tubman and the other women in Beaufort had done a splendid job taking care of wounded soldiers, their facilities were that of makeshift hospitals in a war zone. At Dr. Smith's hospital, Lewis had clean sheets, a dry bed, and a doctor who had been educated at a medical school in Europe.

Dr. Smith noted Lewis had diarrhea and cachexia—the loss of body mass, including fat and muscles. Those two symptoms were not that unusual for soldiers on the Sea Islands. Lewis also had what Dr. Smith called "spontaneous gangrene of the left half of the scrotum." Something had caused the tissue to die—either the injury Lewis sustained after he was shot during the Battle of Fort Wagner or an infection that developed afterward.

Lewis was too weak to leave the city, Dr. Smith thought, and it would be months before he could go back to military duty. Lewis's father rushed to New York and visited him every day, sitting by Lewis's bedside.

While Lewis was in South Carolina, his father met with President Lincoln to commend the president on the order that would make sure the fellow members of Lewis's regiment were not enslaved by the Confederacy if captured. Lewis's father also pressed the president on the equal pay that Lewis, his brother, and all the other Black soldiers were waiting for—the full thirteen dollars a month the white troops received.

Lewis wished he and Amelia were married now. He wished she were not far away teaching but could come be by his side as his wife. He would turn twenty-three years old in a hospital bed, not sure if he could return to the army and unsure of what came next. The only thing he knew for certain was his love for Amelia.

CHAPTER 74

George Garrison

SOUTH CAROLINA
NOVEMBER 1863

George would be able to enjoy a little bit of his family's Thanksgiving feast in South Carolina. The box his family sent him in September finally arrived, right in time for the holiday. George opened it with immense joy. To get a box from home was considered one of the best things that could happen to a soldier. Inside, he found cranberry jelly his mother made, sweet potatoes (his favorite food, and only one had rotted during the journey), soft crackers to provide variety against the hardtack, and some medicines to help combat sickness.

George learned that Wendell was now a traveling lecturer for the American Anti-Slavery Society, speaking in favor of a petition for the universal abolition of slavery. Their father printed parts of the letters George wrote to the family in *The Liberator*, with slight grammatical adjustments made by the fastidious editor.

George was not always honest with his family about his health or how he was doing in those letters, though. He would tell them he was fine, but he had many bouts of stomach illness and many days he could not be on duty. Thirty-two men had died since they arrived, including his brother's friend Leonard

Alden. George told his family he had tried to get Alden on a steamer for New York, but he didn't make it and died in a hospital in Beaufort from chronic diarrhea. Even without fighting, this was a treacherous war.

The Black soldiers still had not received their pay. At first, white officers of the Black regiments had said they, too, would refuse pay until the situation was settled. The troops felt this was about solidarity among themselves and requested that the white men accept what they were owed. George finally did receive pay for his first four months of service in November 1863.

George's brother Frank thought it a great victory that Massachusetts would make up the difference in pay between the thirteen dollars the men had been promised and the seven dollars they received from the federal government. Frank was eager and a bit naive and had not come to know the men of the 54th and 55th.

"There was hardly a bakers dozen of men in the regiment that would consent to take the seven dollars a month that was offered them by the government," George explained to his brother William.

The Black soldiers saw the flaw in what Massachusetts offered. If they accepted to be paid seven dollars by the federal government, the federal government would only ever pay them that for three years of service. Massachusetts might pay the difference this time, but they would have no recourse if the state did not pay it next time.

George and his fellow officers advised them to take the money. They refused. They would work three years without pay, they said, rather than take unequal pay. George thought they were mistaken, but he could not "but admire their unanimity in refusing" to be paid less than white men, George told William.

CHAPTER 75

Lewis Douglass

ROCHESTER
CHRISTMAS 1863

L ewis came back to Rochester in November to continue his recovery. He could sit in the quiet library of his family's home and read *David Copperfield*; he loved how beautifully family relations were described in Charles Dickens's novel. If his father was in the right mood, he might play some music on the violin. The family could sit around the tidy parlor and discuss the state of politics and the war.

This was the place where their family could return to and be together, and on Christmas Day 1863, it would be the place where Lewis's sister, Rosetta, married her sweetheart, Nathan Sprague, who worked as a gardener at the Douglass family home. Like their father, Nathan had been born enslaved in Maryland and now lived as a free man in Rochester. One could see Nathan as the self-made man of Lewis's father's speeches, or Nathan may not have been good enough for Frederick Douglass's oldest and now only daughter. In the end, neither mattered. Rosetta loved him and wanted to marry him, and their family would celebrate that love.

Rosetta had always thought their mother's plum-colored silk wedding gown was so fine, and she would want to look as elegant on her own wedding day. In the parlor, the reverend led the ceremony, and Lewis watched Rosetta and Nathan exchange their vows.

Although Lewis loved Amelia, on New Year's Eve, he took Jennie Morris to the ball in Rochester. Lewis didn't think much of it, but within a few days, folks around the city started whispering that he and Jennie had "been married slyly." Lewis did not understand. "There must be something extraordinary about us boys," Lewis wrote to Amelia, "for we cannot speak to a colored girl in this city but what she thinks we have fallen in love with her." Lewis didn't think Jennie had started the rumors this time, though. It was "others here" in Rochester, and Lewis found this amusing. He knew he only wanted Amelia.

"What will become of your promise to me?" Lewis wondered to Amelia. She told him that she thought of teaching for two or three more years, but if he was discharged from the army because of his injuries, would she change her plans? He would like if they promised to "love, obey, cherish and protect each other" as Rosetta and Nathan had done.

CHAPTER 76

Charlotte Forten

**SOUTH CAROLINA
WINTER-SPRING 1864**

Charlotte returned to South Carolina in October 1863, after the hottest weather abated. It was pleasant to see her friends Colonel Thomas Wentworth Higginson and Dr. Seth Rogers again, and to go to church and see all of the freed people she had come to know.

She slipped back into her Sea Islands life of teaching, but she couldn't bring herself to write very much during the winter months. Although the weather was better on the Sea Islands, it had never been her favorite time of year, and in the spring, her father had joined the army and died suddenly of illness. Depression and illness crept back into her own life.

She knew the plantation where she was living would not be good for her health during the summer, and so in late May 1864, Charlotte resigned her position and returned to Philadelphia.

CHAPTER 77

George Garrison

SOUTH CAROLINA
FEBRUARY 1864

Over the winter, George was acting quartermaster of the 55th Massachusetts, a job that he did well but grudgingly. They were still on fatigue duty, so they faced little danger, but also little excitement.

On February 6, 1864, George was pleased to learn that some abolitionist friends from Boston had come to South Carolina.

They told George that surely he must have known that Harriet Tubman was on Folly Island as well. George had not known that she was here but wished very much to see her. So after breakfast, George and the others went to the lookout and General Alfred Terry's quarters, where they found Tubman ironing some clothes.

"Here is George Garrison," someone said by way of introducing George, and Harriet Tubman "no sooner saw me than she recognized me at once," George explained to his brother William. She then gave George "quite an affectionate embrace, much to the amusement" of the others. Shy George was very surprised and slightly embarrassed.

Tubman had been on Folly Island three months, George learned, but previously was in Beaufort and other places around South Carolina. She took on this extra work of cooking and washing at the general's quarters to make a little money to send to her parents and pay some debts.

She wanted to return to the North, but General Quincy Gilmore thought "her services are too valuable to lose," George learned. People who had been freed by the Emancipation Proclamation arrived at camp from the interior of South Carolina to get the protection of the Union Army. Tubman "has made it a business to see all contrabands escaping from the rebels, and is able to get more intelligence from them than anybody else," George told his brother William. She learned where the Confederate troops were stationed and what places they had abandoned. She had even gone with some of the recently freed Black men into enemy territory to conduct more reconnaissance, returning with news of where they might find stores of cotton or ammunition.

Tubman even found people who were waiting to be liberated and led them to the safety of Union-occupied territory. In one particularly daring raid, she went with Colonel James Montgomery and eight hundred men from the 2nd South Carolina Volunteers up the Combahee River, and they managed to free nearly eight hundred more people and destroy Confederate property. Tubman was proud that some of the men they'd freed had joined the Union troops themselves.

It thrilled George to talk with Tubman, and he knew his family would surely like to hear of how she was doing.

CHAPTER 78

Lucy McKim

PHILADELPHIA
MAY-JUNE 1864

L ucy's visit to New York City was wonderful. During the
week of May 10, 1864, Lucy and her father traveled to the city for the meeting of the thirty-first anniversary of the American Anti-Slavery Society. The audience on the first morning seemed larger than in years previous, and attendees thought that there were more young people in attendance because of the war and the possibility of total emancipation.

As president of the society, William Lloyd Garrison presided over the meeting and told the people gathered, "We meet this morning under very cheering and hopeful circumstances, in view of what comes to us from the battle-field. The rebellion is reeling to its overthrow, and the cause which is dear to all our hearts is in full promise of triumphant success—the cause of impartial and glorious liberty."

A few months earlier, William Lloyd Garrison came out in favor of President Lincoln's reelection, and Lucy felt that "Mr. Garrison was right" in his perspective on what Lincoln could do with another term in office. Lucy knew of the "horrid... differences [that come] between the followers" of the abolition movement. Others who spoke at the meeting felt that there was no evidence full emancipation was near and did not support President Lincoln.

Even Wendell Garrison admitted that he "was not in favor of a second term for Mr. Lincoln," although he recognized that if the party was not unified for the election, that lack of unity would also "endanger the Union itself."

Lucy was glad to see Wendell in New York and hear his thoughts. Over the last half year, Lucy felt that "Wendell developed into a new creature." He was working at the *Independent* newspaper in Brooklyn, New York, and he had matured and grown since the fall. He had resolved to keeping aloof from Lucy until September, which would have been a year since he'd first confessed his feelings to her. Wendell knew Lucy liked him but wanted her to love him. Maybe she had changed, gotten over Dick Chase's death and realized she could be in love and have some independence.

"I fell in love with him desperately!" Lucy admitted to Ellen Wright when she returned home to Philadelphia.

It was not an engagement, Lucy told Ellen later that sum-
mer. "We have come to the decision to have nothing but an 'understanding,'" she wrote. This was what her Quaker mother would call it: nothing too official, but an agreement that they would become engaged. Lucy and Wendell would be officially engaged after Ellen and William Garrison were married in September.

Newspaper Letters

1864

CHRISTIAN RECORDER—APRIL 23, 1864

The question is this: What is the reason Congress will not pay the gallant and brave boys of the Fifty-fourth and Fifty-fifth Massachusetts Volunteers their thirteen dollars per month? They cannot say that they are not good fighting soldiers in the field. I rather think that it is the color and quality of citizenship of the United States that is the reason they want us to take ten dollars per month, three deducted for clothing. No, never will I take it. You may sever my head from my body first. Give us our rights, and we will die under the stars and stripes for the glorious old Union.

—Letter From a Soldier

WEEKLY ANGLO-AFRICAN—APRIL 30, 1864

It is also true we have been twice insulted by having the paltry sum of seven dollars per month offered us. But I thank God that we did not take it; for if we had our children would blush with shame to think their fathers would acknowledge their inferiority by taking inferior pay to that of the other soldiers, and the whole civilized world would look on us as being a parcel of fools, not fit to enjoy our freedom.

—De Waltigo

CHRISTIAN RECORDER—MAY 24, 1864

And I am not willing to fight for this Government for money alone. Give me my rights, the rights that this Government owes me, the same rights that the white man has. I would be willing to fight three years for this government without one cent of the mighty dollar. Then I would have something to fight for. Now I am fighting for the rights of white men. When men have never given me the rights that they are bound to respect. God has not made one man better than another; therefore, one man's rights are not better than another's.

—J.H.B.P.

CHAPTER 79

George Garrison

**SOUTH CAROLINA
JUNE 1864**

During the spring of 1864, George felt like his regiment "shifted about from one place to another continually" from South Carolina to Florida and back again. By June, George was glad to be back on Folly Island, sleeping near the ocean, hearing waves at night, and taking cool salty baths in the morning.

On June 1, 1864, George's commanding officer removed him from acting quartermaster without a reason as to why. George did the best he could but did not really enjoy the job. The responsibility was so large and he felt constant pressure to keep his accounts in order and make sure that the men had the supplies they needed.

In fact, it was a great relief to go back to his company, he thought. Although he was as quiet as ever, he enjoyed conversations with the men and the officers in the 55th. Commissary Sergeant Richard White was from Kansas, so they could talk about the West. White had "been in and through the troubles there," George wrote to his mother, and recounted White's amazing story.

White had been born in South Carolina to an enslaved woman and a white man who also owned him. Sergeant White was so light-skinned that he could have passed for a white man, George thought. George told his mother that when Sergeant White was just a baby, "his master and father" took him to what was now Wheeling, West Virginia, and while there, some Quakers managed to free him from his father. When Sergeant White last heard from his father, "he was alive and in the rebel army."

George asked Sergeant White what he would do if he met his father/master now, and he replied without hesitation, "Shoot him!"

In his conversations with the men, George could also tell that morale was low. The soldiers were "beginning to show signs of insubordination," George told his mother. They had still not been paid since first arriving in Readville a year ago.

"Please use your influence towards having these [regiments] paid," George pleaded with his father.

George's father said that he had private conversations with President Lincoln and Secretary of War Stanton, and that the problems were not "with them, in regard to the non-payment" of the 54th and 55th "but with Congress." George knew that the bill for equal pay had passed both Houses of Congress in May, so why was there still a problem? His father insisted that "full justice will be done them in the way of back payment."

George could update the men in his company with the information his father relayed. Everyone thought George kind, selfless, and earnest. If it was true and they would be getting paid soon, the soldiers would be jubilant. But another empty promise would be demoralizing.

Hopefully, the equal pay would be one step to fuller equality for his troops. George noticed that they had "done pretty much all the fatigue duty" in South Carolina, despite the fact that there were many white regiments that could have done that demanding work. George was beginning to feel the same as the men in his command: if they would not be paid equally, they should be mustered out of service and return to Boston.

George decided to copy some of his father's letter about his conversations with the president to circulate among the men.

"[I] hope it will do some good," he thought.

CHAPTER 80

Lewis Douglass

**SOUTH CAROLINA
LATE SUMMER 1864**

Lewis once again stepped onto the sandy soil of the South Carolina Sea Islands. He was no longer a soldier—he had been discharged because of his illness—but he was well enough to do something. He found work selling supplies to the troops and transporting shipments from the North to South Carolina.

Lewis and his employer worked on Hilton Head with the 144th New York and 32nd US Colored Troops from Pennsylvania, who were building a fort to protect the freedmen's town of Mitchelville. Lewis sold food and goods to soldiers, and then kept sales and inventory records. "I feel more self reliant, more independent, than I should had I forever hung around home," he wrote to Amelia.

In Mitchelville, the freed people built homes of wood-shake shingles with glass-paned windows, smartly raised a few feet off the ground to prevent flooding. Around the houses, they built wells, neat gardens, and fences.

Every night, Lewis could hear the people singing and praying, seeming so happy.

Lewis found he could share only a little bit of that happiness. He had enjoyed the bright and beautiful spring mornings at home, and now he missed his family and Amelia. Lewis wrote to her in one of his brief moments of leisure and told her he should have married her two years ago, before he started thinking of leaving the United States for Chiriquí, Panama.

"I was full of Africa, Central America, or any where to make a fortune and a name," he told her. Lewis admitted that he had felt unsettled since the trip to Chiriquí fell through. The army—the purpose of war—was supposed to fix that.

"I do not know where my home is, I have none," Lewis wrote. He also did not see how he would be able to earn a living, and he knew that without money, he was "like a ship without a helm, soon go to wreck on the rock of Poverty."

"If I did not love you above all else I would care for none," he confided. Maybe these feelings, that hope, could help him find a home and a purpose.

Republican Party Platform: June 1864

REPUBLICAN PARTY CONVENTION, BALTIMORE, MARYLAND
JUNE 7 AND 8, 1864.

RESOLUTIONS.

MR. HENRY J. RAYMOND, of New York.—I am instructed by the Committee and Platform to present for consideration and action of this Convention the following series of resolutions: [. . .]

That as Slavery was the cause, and now constitutes the strength, of this Rebellion, and it must be, always and everywhere, hostile to the principles of Republican Government, justice and the National safety demand its utter and complete extirpation from the soil of the Republic. [. . .] We are in favor, furthermore, of such an amendment to the Constitution, to be made by the people in conformity with its provisions, as shall terminate and forever prohibit the existence of Slavery within the limits or the jurisdiction of the United States. [. . .]

That we approve, especially, the Proclamation of Emancipation, and the employment as Union soldiers of men heretofore held in slavery; and that we have full confidence in [President Lincoln's] determination to carry these and all other Constitutional measures essential to the salvation of the country into full and complete effect.

George Garrison's Diary

June 21, 1864

Abraham Lincoln was renominated for the Presidency by the Baltimore Convention June 8th, and Andy Johnson, of Tenn., was nominated for Vice President. The Convention was very harmonious.

Letter to George Garrison
from Frank Garrison

SEPTEMBER 1864

Anti-Slavery Office

Boston, Sept. 3rd, 1864

Dear George:

Atlanta is ours! This is the glorious news that greets me as I come in from Roxbury this morning. [. . .]

The Emancipation plank is the strongest one in the Baltimore Platform, and is on this issue that we have got to fight & win. If Lincoln is elected, have not the slightest doubt that [James] Trotter & the rest will be commissioned [as officers]. Poor Trotter speaks of the disheartening coldness with which himself & the rest are treated by brother white officers. Men with such prejudices ought never to have been appointed in colored regiments. [. . .]

Good bye
Ever, Frank

CHAPTER 81

Lucy McKim

AUBURN
SEPTEMBER 1864

Lucy had agreed to the understanding that she and Wendell Garrison would become engaged, but she knew she was a "hard match," as Ellen Wright said. Both Ellen and Wendell accused Lucy of being too serious, but she just didn't gush with emotion like Ellen did.

"There are autumn strains in the air," Lucy wrote to Wendell in early September 1864 from Auburn, New York, where she was helping Ellen get ready for the wedding. Lucy admitted to Wendell that this weather "tantalize[s] me with half-caught remembrances, & suggestions of other places where I must have been, and another life I must have led; they recall strange solitariness." This must have been hard for Wendell to read, because Lucy admitted that he was "removed" from those thoughts and her desires were "quite incompatible with love-dreams" of their future.

Another place Lucy might have been was Port Royal. Lucy kept up a correspondence with Laura Towne, who she thought had "enough sense for a dozen uncommon women & enough independence for twenty." Towne could do what she did in Port Royal because she was unmarried and without children, and Lucy considered what "wifely obedience" might mean for her, what she might lose by marrying Wendell, and what she might gain.

On the evening of September 17, 1864, Ellen's family wasn't sure she would be well enough to get married. She'd been sick for weeks with headaches and fatigue, and William stayed by her side, hoping she would feel better. They'd reduced the invitations to the wedding, and Lucy and Fanny Garrison held Ellen up to get her into her wedding dress and veil.

They decorated the parlor with colorful autumn leaves and bright red mountain ash berries. Friends had sent bouquets of late-summer flowers that they placed throughout the room. Even without a reception, guests filled up the space and placed their presents by the piano. William and Ellen stood in front of Reverend Samuel May, the great anti-slavery lecturer, who kept the ceremony short and happy. Even though the reception was cancelled, Ellen's family was large, and so was the party. They ate a big supper and had an enormous cake.

After today, Lucy and Wendell's engagement would be more public, and they would have to set a date for their own wedding.

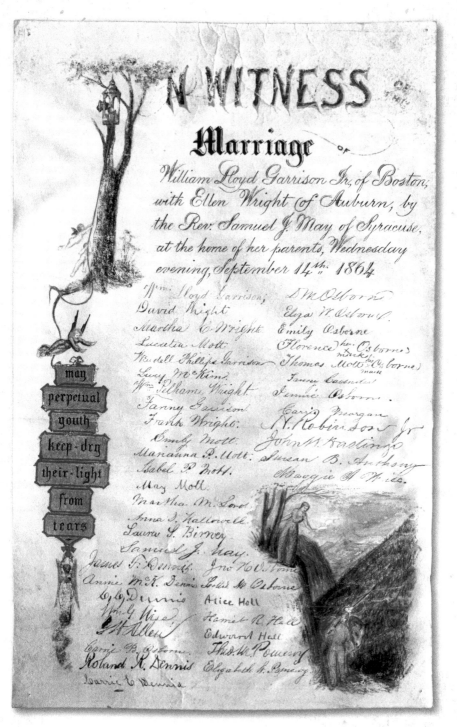

Ellen Wright and William Lloyd Garrison Jr.'s marriage certificate, signed by everyone in attendance, including Ellen's mentor and women's rights advocate Susan B. Anthony.

CHAPTER 82

George Garrison

SOUTH CAROLINA
OCTOBER 1864

A regimental doctor who just got back from a furlough in the North came into George's tent on October 4, 1864, with a letter from George's brother William and a piece of William and Ellen's wedding cake. William was such a good brother to him, and everyone said that Ellen seemed to make William so happy. George thought of them on the day they married, and now he read over William's letter and another from Wendell detailing the event.

George would have liked to have been there, but for the last months, the 54th and 55th had simply been holding their own outside of Charleston, and the Union Army seemed to be creeping toward victory. The newspapers and letters from his family brought the news that General William Tecumseh Sherman's troops had taken Atlanta, Georgia, and General Ulysses S. Grant's troops had gained ground from Confederate general Robert E. Lee in Virginia.

George's men had their own reason to celebrate. On October 5, 1864, George's company received the back pay for the full thirteen dollars a month they had been promised since they had mustered at Camp Meigs in the spring of 1863. George helped his men send back over nine thousand dollars to their families and friends.

Five days later, the men celebrated their achievement. Each company assembled, with the band playing popular songs between speeches. They adopted resolutions during the ceremony, including sincere thanks to "our friends at home who have stood by us throughout our trials and deprivations, and whose sympathy and practical kindness went far toward softening the rigor of our condition," and they gave special thanks to George's father.

George was always proud to be William Lloyd Garrison's son and felt that his father had done great things for the Black soldiers, enslaved people, and the country, and was good to him and his siblings. While outwardly, his father was still the great abolitionist orator, George thought his father was getting old and *The Liberator* seemed to be in a precarious situation. It was time for him and his siblings to take care of their parents, George thought.

George's brothers and sister wrote to him about the dire financial situation of the newspaper. Their father had lost subscribers and had not increased the price of subscription to properly cover his costs. His sister, Fanny, wrote that maybe it was time for *The Liberator* to cease, "now that its sentiments are echoed by every loyal paper in the land." She did see the need for their father's strong perspective and did hope it would last "till the Rebellion is crushed & freedom becomes not only a name but a fixed fact." George hoped that their father would at least try to keep the newspaper going until January 1, 1865, thirty-four years to the day after it began.

This was what tamped any celebration, though: the nation was still at war, and all the country had was the Emancipation Proclamation. George hoped that Abraham Lincoln's reelection would bring an amendment to the Constitution outlawing slavery.

DOCUMENT

Boston Evening Transcript

NOVEMBER 8, 1864

TO-DAY is to go into the history of the world as one of the great days that mark decided turning points in the world's destiny. Imagination cannot conceive of the influence on the future of the verdict to be rendered in this country as to men and measure before the sun sets. If free men, as no doubt they will, sustain free institutions by the irresistible force of an overwhelming vote, the great cause of humanity, will receive a new inspiration and be encouraged by a new hope. If the North solemnly, as no doubt it will, determines to save the nation, at all and every cost, from the assaults of armed rebellion, and the intrigues of those who, for a cowardly peace would sell their birthright, then it will be proved that the republic has the strength, in the intelligence of its people, in their willingness to be taxed, their readiness to shed their blood like water if need be, to maintain the integrity of its self and its democratic principles, against the treasonable policy that would sacrifice the political rights, the industrial interests, the supremacy of the many, to the usurping ambition of the few.

Shall fraud, perjury, cowardice, treason, rebellion, and civil war, inaugurated by traitors at the South, break up the Union and destroy its nationality? [. . .]

These are the questions that the ballot box is now meeting. We shall soon be able to record the answer. We shall know what it is in a few hours. We know now what it will be. [. . .]

The triumph in this contest is not to be that of a party, but of the people. There can be no failure in this triumph, if the people are true to themselves. And true we believe they will be till the victory is won.

CHAPTER 83

George Garrison

SOUTH CAROLINA AND GEORGIA
NOVEMBER–DECEMBER 1864

"There must be tremendous excitement tonight in the North," George wrote in his diary on November 7, 1864. "It is the most important President[ial] election since the formation of the [government]." He hoped that President Lincoln would be reelected by "an overwhelming majority," because the reelection almost guaranteed a "speedy ending of the war," as George's father put it, and the passage of the Thirteenth Amendment, abolishing slavery.

On November 16, George received news that "President Lincoln has been elected. He carried nearly every state." George thought the news "glorious" and that the rebellion could not hold out long after Lincoln's victory. He was expecting Confederate soldiers to desert and turn themselves over.

The men stationed on Folly Island also heard rumors that General Sherman and his army were advancing on Augusta, Georgia.

Soon, George could be back in Boston, going to Fanny's dancing parties, "for if there is anything I used to be fond of, it was dancing," George thought. He might see Annie Anthony in person, after having stared at the photograph she'd sent him for months and receiving cordial notes about her well-wishes for him through Wendell and Fanny. He could listen to his father and Fanny sing hymns in the new house in Roxbury and finally see for himself how his mother was doing after her stroke last year.

On November 27, 1864, George and the 55th Massachusetts were ordered to leave Folly Island and travel inland to destroy the Savannah and Charleston Railroad, which would hopefully trap Confederate troops in Charleston, South Carolina, as General Sherman and his army advanced on Savannah, Georgia, burning and destroying everything behind them.

The 55th marched at daylight. George knew his men were well trained and well drilled, yet they had not seen much real fighting.

At first, it was calm. Then, about three miles into the dense woods around the railroad, rebel forces began to attack. The 55th stopped and prepared to fight, though the trees made it hard to see what was happening—and to hear orders.

They were ordered to advance, but George's company and two others did not hear the command. Those who moved forward began falling down. The rebels had four or five battery guns firing, which mowed the men down like blades of grass. They could hardly see the enemy, or the other companies to their sides.

George's company was ordered to stay where they were, and then to retreat behind a ditch. In it, they were somewhat protected from enemy fire.

They remained there until dark, holding the Confederates at bay.

Then they had no choice but to retreat. George and his company came to where the wounded had been taken. He saw so many bodies. Without ambulances or wagons, they had to carry the men through the woods to where the boats had landed. It was awful and harrowing to carry the men back. Some of the wounded died before they could reach the boats that would take them to the hospital.

"It was a perfect massacre of our men," George noted in his diary after the fighting. He knew his family would read about the battle in the newspapers. "If I am killed or wounded at any time you will hear of it by the newspapers," George wrote his mother and father after what had become known as the Battle of Honey Hill.

In the following days, the men of the 55th fortified the line, holding strong against the enemy. From the south, George could hear heavy firing, and hoped that it was General Sherman approaching. But for days, then weeks, the 55th just held the line.

"Everything here is dull and tedious, and we are anxious for orders to leave," George thought as they went on picket duty after picket duty.

On December 23, George received the news that Sherman had finally taken Savannah, Georgia, and with eight hundred rebel prisoners was making his way to Charleston, South Carolina. A Christmas present for the troops.

CHAPTER 84

Lucy McKim

WASHINGTON, DC
DECEMBER 1864

A rainy day wouldn't dampen Lucy's mood. She felt so lucky that she, her father, and Wendell were in Washington, DC, together. Lucy's father had been traveling to and from Washington during the fall. He was trying to get Congress to create a federal agency that would do similar work to what his association had done in Port Royal. When the Freedmen's Association realized that forty thousand Black people around the nation's capital had no formal education, they set up schools just as they had in Port Royal. Just as he had in South Carolina, Lucy's father asked Lucy to come see the schools, and he thought that Wendell should come along, too.

It was strange to think that Lucy was more well traveled than Wendell, but it was true. Wendell had traveled around New England giving lectures and traipsed through Pennsylvania and New Hampshire, but he had never been to the South like Lucy had.

Lucy walked with them around the city, her father on one arm and Wendell on the other, and they came to one of the schools the association ran. The Association modeled the schools on the ones they had been running for almost three and a half years on the Sea Islands, and it looked like a regular school with books, maps, blackboards, and a small keyboard instrument called a me-lodeon. They also gave out blankets, shoes, clothing, and basic medical sup-plies. Lucy, Wendell, and Lucy's father could see how excited the children were to learn, too, when they sang, "One, two, three! Don't you see where we love to be!"

They visited five of the Freedmen's Association schools, which probably had a thousand students in all. As in South Carolina, Lucy was eager to speak with the newly freed people she met. To imagine that slavery had been legal in the nation's capital until April 1862—a full year into the war. Now, they hoped that freed people would receive the "advantages of education" and "possess those rights which are now cruelly withheld from them," as Wendell wrote in *The Liberator*.

Lucy's father had also come up with a plan for Wendell's future. While William Lloyd Garrison worried about the future of *The Liberator*, Wendell thought that when slavery was abolished, they would need a newspaper to "contend against prejudice and wrong" and support freed people and rights for Black Americans. Wendell told Lucy he didn't think he could work for *The Liberator* because it was so wrapped up in the persona of his father. "It is better for young blood to begin altogether anew," he told her.

Lucy's father thought there might be an opportunity to start a newspaper in Baltimore, Maryland, that would advocate for the rights of Black Ameri-cans. "The moment is critical, and the opportunity for starting a liberal news-paper is eagerly sought," Wendell wrote to his brother George after their trip.

At one point in Washington, Wendell gave an impromptu speech, which Lucy thought "was not only worthy of his father, but exactly like him." She had made the right decision to marry Wendell.

Just like Lucy's father, Wendell could speak about these important issues and truly understood what was at stake for the country. When the December 15 issue of the *Independent* arrived at Lucy's home in Philadelphia, there was Wendell's report on their trip to Washington visiting "The Freedmen and Their Friends," showing how dedicated he would be to these issues.

"The debt which the people of the North owe to the disenthralled is one which centuries could never repay," he wrote in the newspaper. "All the amends of this generation for its own and its fathers' crime of human enslavement, and all the recompense of our children's children, will fail to equal the suffering" of Black Americans.

DOCUMENT

The Liberator

FEBRUARY 10, 1865

FREEDOM TRIUMPHANT!

—

GRAND JUBILEE MEETING IN THE MUSIC HALL,

To Rejoice over the Amendment prohibiting Human Slavery in the United States forever.

A large and brilliant audience were assembled in the Music Hall on Saturday evening last, to rejoice over the passage by Congress, and the ratification by the Legislatures of many of the States, of the Constitutional Amendment prohibiting Human Slavery in the United States hereafter and forever. The meeting was one of the most enthusiastic gatherings of the friends of freedom ever held in this city, and was in every respect eminently worthy of the great event in national history which had called it forth.

George Garrison's Diary

FEBRUARY 1865

Feb. 11th

The [regiment] was carried over to Folly Island this afternoon [. . .] and upon landing marched up and encamped upon an old camp ground again. [. . .]

The amendment to the Constitution abolishing slavery has passed Congress—a great event.

Feb. 18th

Tonight we have received word that Charleston was evacuated by the Rebels last night together with James and Sullivan Island. Glory, glory hallelujah.

Feb. 19th

Broke camp at daylight this morning and commenced to march at once.

CHAPTER 85

George Garrison

SOUTH CAROLINA
FEBRUARY–APRIL 1865

George and the 55th Massachusetts marched toward Charleston on February 21, 1865. As they walked along roads where Union troops had not been, Black people—mostly older men, women, and children who had not been able to escape to Union-held territory earlier—came out to greet them. If they had heard about the abolishment of slavery or not was of no importance. They were being freed and told of their freedom now.

One woman ran up to the troops and praised them, letting out a gasp of "Great God!"

Another woman cried, "Joy, Joy, Joy!" as they passed.

One sergeant found thirty people locked in a house near their camp. The overseer tried to prevent the people from escaping to safety at the Union camp and tried to keep them enslaved. George did not curse on principle but could not help thinking that the overseer was "an old scamp," and was happy that the sergeant had made him a prisoner.

On the evening of February 21, they marched into one of the principal streets in Charleston. The last city the 55th had been in was Boston, when they walked to the steamer that carried them south. Much of Charleston had been destroyed by fire two years earlier and suffered damage from Union gunfire, and it did not quite feel like a city, George thought.

The men of the 55th were overjoyed, though, and sang the "John Brown Song." George had never heard such shouting and never seen the soldiers so full of excitement. And the Black residents of Charleston were as excited as the soldiers, cheering and yelling words of support.

As they paused on one street, George was surprised to see Francis Meriam's friend James Redpath. Redpath told George he had been in Charleston for two days already, walking around and taking in the scenes. He had not returned to Haiti and was now a correspondent for the *Boston Journal*. Meriam had never been arrested after Harpers Ferry and, after returning to the United States from Canada, became an officer in the 3rd South Carolina Colored Infantry. It was almost surprising George had not seen him down here somewhere.

What an eventful day, George thought as they made camp that night.

For the next two months, George's company marched through South Carolina, letting people know about their freedom. They were just as joyous as other freedmen had been, jumping and cheering or staring in wonder and astonishment.

The men of the 55th responded by telling the freedmen to "Come along with us!" and "Get your bundle!" And some did.

On one plantation, some of the women wanted to have a dance. A colonel found a fiddler, and the Black soldiers and now-free women danced. On another, an officer told the sad man who owned the plantation to blow a horn and summon all the people he claimed to own. He complied. The officer told the people they were free and asked them to assist him in carrying off food and supplies for the soldiers and freed people that had joined their march.

"That there was joy on that plantation, I need not tell you!" George told his sister, Fanny.

Rebel soldiers and overseers still roamed the woods and plantations, trying to recapture people and enslave them or brutalize them in some way. So many

of the freed people joined the procession of the 55th, following along and hoping to get to safety and opportunity in Charleston.

"The end of this most accursed rebellion now seems near,"
George thought when he heard news of General Robert E. Lee's surrender to
General Grant at Appomattox, Virginia, on April 9, 1865. From *The Liberator*,
he also learned his father was probably in Charleston now. His father had been
invited by the secretary of war to be present at the celebration for the recapture
of Fort Sumter, four years after South Carolina troops fired on it, starting the
Civil War.

George wished he could be there now, but they were still miles outside of
the city.

As they marched toward Charleston the next day with nearly two thousand
people they had liberated from plantations across South Carolina, George
heard cannons booming from all of the forts in the Charleston harbor and
from the navy's ships. He paused to listen. He could not see it, but he could
imagine it. The tattered United States flag hoisted above Fort Sumter.

"It sounded good to my ears and as we rested I listened long and attentive
to it," George wrote in his diary. Cannons to signal the end of the fighting, not
the beginning or continuation of it.

George also received a furlough to take leave from the 55th for thirty days.
He could see his father in Charleston and travel home to Boston to see the rest
of his family.

George's father was, of course, very glad to see his son.
But William Lloyd Garrison was also in South Carolina as the editor of *The
Liberator* and one of the most prominent voices in the abolition movement. So
when his father arrived at George's camp, they had no chance to talk because
his father wanted to meet and talk to the formerly enslaved people at the camp.
Then, when George went to the Charleston Hotel that night, his father had gone

out. Finally, the following day, George found his father in the ladies' parlor of the hotel, occupied with guests. George waited nearly an hour and, in the end, only spoke to his father for a few minutes before he had to return to camp.

Before returning to Boston for the rest of George's fur-lough, his father wanted them to visit Beaufort, Port Royal, Savannah, and St. Augustine, Florida.

George and his father began the day on April 18, 1865, by taking a carriage ride on Lady's and St. Helena Islands to see the freed people working on the farms there. George was slightly surprised that most of the workers were women, but they seemed to work just as well as men, he thought.

They returned to Beaufort and got back on board the *Delaware* steamer to continue their tour of the South. At about two o'clock, they sat down to have dinner.

Then, Senator Henry Wilson, who was traveling with them, received a telegraph: President Lincoln and Secretary of State William Seward had been attacked on the night of the fourteenth, the same day that they had raised the flag over Fort Sumter. The details in the telegraph were not clear, and it seemed they had little hope of the president recovering. Everyone felt they needed to get back north immediately.

As the steamer came back to Hilton Head, George saw the flag at half-mast, and he knew President Lincoln was dead.

"President Lincoln had been shot in the head at Ford's Theater at Washington on the night of the 14th and died the morning of the 15th," General Quincy Gilmore explained. Secretary Seward and his two sons had been stabbed in bed the same night.

"The news deeply affected all of us, as we felt that there was no one who had such a strong hold upon the confidence of the people as the president had, or who could fill his place so well," George reflected in his diary that night.

George and his father boarded the boat bound for New York, anxious to be home.

George stood outside of the new Garrison home in Rox-
bury. He was home, but not at the home he had known. They'd sold 14 Dix
Place long ago, it seemed.

George stepped inside, and his family was overjoyed to see him. They had
no idea he would be coming home with his father. Nearly six years ago, he had
returned home from the West, a journey that had not been nearly as dangerous
as the last almost three years at war. The world had changed.

Now that full emancipation was almost ratified, his father said he would
shut down *The Liberator*. This would be a United States without slavery, where
all men, women, and children would be free.

PART 6

After

"Are we who are alive
spared for some purpose?"

—ELLEN WRIGHT GARRISON

CHAPTER 86

Lewis Douglass

TALBOT COUNTY, MARYLAND
SUMMER-FALL 1865

Even if the war was over, this was really just the beginning. Lewis wrote to his sweetheart, Amelia Loguen, that "there will be a great deal to do for some time to come, in the way of entirely crushing the mob spirit which will prevail at the south." He didn't admit that there was a great deal to be done in Rochester, too. He had tried finding work as a printer for months, but was turned away, and he came home "sad and dejected." Lewis had plenty of experience as a printer, and surely there was work to be found, so his father couldn't help but feel that this was because of "his color and race."

Lewis yearned for more. He confessed to Amelia that he sometimes felt lost, without a home. And yet was this not the time of opportunity? The end of the war should have brought joy, but Lewis saw the next great battle—equal rights for all Americans, regardless of race or gender—ready to be fought. Those schools and opportunities for education that the abolitionists had set up in South Carolina and Washington, DC, needed to be replicated across the South.

Maryland beckoned to Lewis. It had once been his father and mother's home, and for the family Lewis's father left behind, it was still home. And perhaps he could find something there that he couldn't in Rochester.

On Monday, June 5, 1865, Lewis set out from Ferry Neck,
Maryland, along a road used for walking, rolling barrels of tobacco, and the
occasional carriage ride toward the town of St. Michaels. The little peninsula
where Lewis planned to start a school was bordered by rivers that flowed into
the brackish water of the Chesapeake Bay, and he walked by flat fields of tobacco, swamp grasses, and stands of shallow-rooted pine trees.

He thought it might be four miles from Ferry Neck to his aunt Eliza's house
in St. Michaels. As he walked, he saw two people on the road. When he asked
how far it was to town and got to talking with the strangers, he realized they
were his aunt Katy and his cousin, Eliza's son. Eliza's husband had been born
free and bought Eliza and their children's freedom more than twenty years
earlier, although they continued to live and work in this little part of Maryland.

Lewis continued on to St. Michaels, where he found the street full of the
town's Black residents. It was the Pentecost holiday, and everyone seemed out
to celebrate. Aunt Eliza found him and immediately introduced him to the
crowd, and "I soon became a lion," Lewis wrote to his father. They knew of his
father, maybe remembered him from childhood, and so they revered Lewis,
too. As they walked to Eliza's house, they stopped at others so that Eliza could
"show the people, she said, that her brother's family were not too proud to
come and see her."

For the next few days, there was a flurry of visitors: his father's cousin,
some of his cousins, and people who had known his father as a child. Even a
white relative of his father's former owner, Thomas Auld, came by. His father
once wrote a public letter to Auld, proud that Lewis and his siblings were free
and belonged only to their parents, who could "train them up in the paths of
wisdom and virtue, and, as far as we can, to make them useful to the world and
to themselves."

That was what his father had done, but how different was Lewis's life from
that of his family in Maryland? Lewis and his siblings had gone to school,
while there was no school for Black Marylanders here in Talbot County—yet.
Lewis had learned a trade, but had no job from it, while here were oystermen

and farmers among his family and their friends who earned good money. Yet they couldn't buy anything with it.

"The white people will do any thing they can to keep the blacks from advancing," Lewis wrote to his father. They refused to sell their land, even though many Black men seemed to have enough money to purchase farmland. When one Black man suggested Black folks in the area should start businesses and Black residents should only buy from those business, a white mob attacked him. Lewis told his father he felt St. Michaels was "one of the worst places in the South."

That same June, Lewis's father would speak about "Reconstruction" in Baltimore. Lewis was proving to his father that the South needed to be rebuilt in a new way, one that would "protect loyal men, black and white, in their persons and property [. . .] and make a man from New England as much at home in Carolina as elsewhere in the Republic," as his father said. His father thought this must come from the government. Lewis knew it couldn't come without education and agitation from the Black community.

On June 12, 1865, Lewis would open his school and see if some part of Reconstruction could be achieved from the people.

———

Lewis worked the rest of the summer and fall at his school, and the week after Christmas, he went to Baltimore for the State Colored Convention. With pride, Lewis told Amelia he had been "made chairman of the business committee" and prepared to "address to the Legislature of the State which was received very flatteringly by the Convention."

The convention's goal was to organize for Black civil rights, through both individual and government action. They passed a resolution to fund rebuilding Black churches "burned in this State by the rebels and malicious persons" and adopted an address that encouraged Black Marylanders, among other things, to "educate your children . . . for if ever we are raised to that elevated summit in life for which we are striving, it must be done by our individual exertion: no one can do it for us," a statement Lewis's father would have been fully behind.

They also planned to bring a lawsuit against the State of Maryland to allow Black citizens the right to testify in court.

Lewis was also elected to represent Maryland at the national convention in Washington, DC, that January and returned to Ferry Neck elated.

"This I conceive to be the highest eminence that I have ever yet attained," Lewis wrote Amelia, "and places me still nearer that high mark to which I am aiming." That mark to make a difference, to make something of himself, to serve a purpose. He imagined himself climbing higher, "and when I get up I can look back and say that I have come up not without trials and tribulations, but come up I will."

CHAPTER 87

Charlotte Forten

BOSTON
SUMMER-FALL 1865

harlotte had not been well since she returned from South Carolina in May 1864. Her health problems had returned, and in the summer of 1865, she thought that Dr. Dio Lewis might be able to help her. He had once run a gymnasium in Boston, and many young people, including William Lloyd Garrison's children, had found benefits in his calisthenic exercises. Dr. Lewis had advertised for his new school in *The Liberator*, and Charlotte had written to her friend John Greenleaf Whittier about the possibility of trying Dr. Lewis's training.

Young women were weak and fragile because they had spent too much time on intellectual training and not enough on "physical culture," Dr. Lewis believed. Gymnastics, a proper diet, warm and cold baths, walks, and dresses that did not hinder the body would give women "strength, endurance, and grace." Dr. Rogers's water cure had once worked for Charlotte, and she knew that when she felt strong, she felt physically better, and perhaps Dr. Lewis could now help her.

Charlotte was too advanced for the school, really. Most of the girls were around seventeen years old, and almost all between twelve and twenty-three. She would turn twenty-eight in August. She could have been a teacher and not a pupil, but Whittier thought that if she tried to fund her time at the school by "literary efforts," she could not focus on the exercise. Whittier asked Theodore

Dwight Weld, who was now teaching there, if Charlotte could go "at [a] reduced price."

Charlotte yet again faced the limitations of people who were supposed to be progressive. Even if she could have paid for her stay, the parents of other students did not want a young Black woman at the school. Dr. Lewis couldn't accept her. "To take her at all would I fear be hazardous to his enterprise," Whittier wrote to another friend, "and I am sure Charlotte would not wish to run the risk of that." Slavery might have been over, but Charlotte's ancestry could still be a reason she wasn't allowed into a school, job, or business.

New England was still better than Philadelphia, though, and Charlotte had friends like Whittier with whom she could engage with intellectually and who could help her find a job. In October 1865, Charlotte began working for the Teacher's Committee of the New England Branch of the Freedmen's Union Commission in Boston. Like the school Charlotte had worked for in South Carolina, the privately funded Freedmen's Union Commission's goal was to improve the condition of people in the South, "upon the basis of industry, education, freedom, and Christian morality." What they included now that the war was over was that this wouldn't just be for people who were formerly enslaved. They would not deny this education to anyone on the basis of color, meaning that white Southerners could go to these schools, too.

Charlotte's job was to communicate with the close to two hundred teachers that the New England Branch employed across the South, and to make sure that donated clothing and supplies made their way to the over twelve thousand students in those schools. Charlotte believed in the cause, but it wasn't easy work. She, too, saw how white people fought back against the education of Black Americans. In Maryland, it was hard for white teachers to go to rural counties because "no white families will take them to board," which meant they really needed to hire Black teachers. The government in Charleston, South Carolina, had made no effort to establish schools for Black children or allow Black children into white schools, and "there [doesn't] appear any immediate disposition to do so." In North Carolina and Virginia, white mobs attacked Black schools. The mobs prevailed.

NATIONAL PROTECTION FOR WHITES AND BLACKS.

[. . .] The Thirty-eighth Congress made itself immortal by the passage of the Constitutional Amendment abolishing and forever prohibiting slavery. The Thirty-ninth has the no less glorious, but much more arduous, task of organizing the victory of the nation over its rebels into institutions assuring for ever the safety and happiness of all the inhabitants of that chastised region, and the prosperity, honor, and glory of the whole Union.

[. . .] Slavery was the occasion of the war. Slavery had practically abolished the clauses of the Constitution securing freedom of speech and of the press, and the right of the citizens of one State to claim the privileges of citizenship in every other State. And slavery had defied the general Government to enforce the Constitution in these particulars within its sacred domain.

There can be no question as to the duty of Congress to provide for the protection of all the good people of the United States in travelling whithersoever they will in the Southern country, and of saying and printing whatever they choose there, subject to the laws of the land constitutionally expounded, without danger from lynch law, whether administered with or without the walls of a court-house. This it was always the duty of Congress to do, and it is not to be supposed that it will permit the old reign of misrule to be established anew, now that the opportunity of reformation is forced upon it.

[. . .] The nation has given them [the enslaved] their freedom; it is to see to it that they are secured in the perfect enjoyment of that freedom by all guarantee, which wisdom and experience can devise.

CHAPTER 88

George Garrison

BOSTON
JANUARY 1866

Even though he was no longer in danger of being killed in battle, George's family had likely worried about him every day since he left the army. First, there had been the matter of Annie Anthony. She had happily sent him a photograph and well-wishes when he was in South Carolina, and upon his return to Boston in September 1865, agreed to marry him. Then she said she did not love him. She claimed that Wendell had said she was too good for George, although their sister, Fanny, believed Wendell would never have said such a thing. Fanny was grateful he would not marry such a selfish person, but George had always had a hard time talking to women, and he didn't seem to have anyone else he was interested in.

George also returned to help his father print the last issues of *The Liberator*. As when he returned from the West, the family business—and his father's shadow—was waiting, but George could not work there forever. They printed the final issue the last week of December 1865, almost exactly thirty-four years since the first. George needed a new place to work, a new vocation.

George's mother worried about how little he socialized. He had always been shy, but before the war, he went ice-skating with friends, went to dances and parties, and spent time with the family. Now he would not go anywhere and would not spend time with guests who came to the Garrison house. He had seen the world transformed, and yet nothing seemed to have changed for him. His friends and fellow soldiers had died, and what would become of him?

George Garrison (on the left) with his father and brothers Frank (standing), William Jr., and Wendell.

CHAPTER 89

Lucy McKim Garrison

NEW YORK
JANUARY 1866

❝ I think I should start to hear you called Mrs. Garrison," Ellen wrote Lucy. How much had changed in such a few short years. They were now both Mrs. Garrison, and their mother-in-law they called Mother G. In December 1865, Lucy and Wendell had finally married in front of many friends and family in Philadelphia. The day had been sunny and warm for the end of fall, and Lucy thought she was "just foolish enough to regard the fact with the popular superstition that as your wedding-day, so will your life be." That meant a wonderful prophecy for her and Wendell, she thought.

In their first months of marriage, they lived in Manhattan, where Wendell had begun working as the literary editor for *The Nation*. In a way, the new weekly magazine was envisioned as taking over where *The Liberator* would leave off. *The Nation* would diffuse "true democratic principles in society and government [...] to promote a more equal distribution of the fruits of progress and civilization," and work toward providing "education and justice" for African Americans in the South.

Lucy helped Wendell with his work and even wrote book reviews although she didn't sign her name. But she still couldn't get the remarkable music she'd heard in South Carolina out of her head.

By the fall of 1866, Lucy was pregnant. Soon, more of her time would be taken up by the wifely and motherly duties that her mother had worked to prepare her for. But the songs still beckoned to Lucy. After she had returned from South Carolina, she had written to Laura Towne about collecting more of the songs, but Towne didn't have Lucy's musical skill to write down the songs. Lucy also read Charlotte Forten's articles in *The Atlantic* about her time teaching in the Sea Islands, and Forten had included words to seven songs she'd heard. General Thomas Wentworth Higginson had been paying attention to the music he heard at Camp Saxton, too. And in the summer of 1865, an educator named William Frances Allen began writing for *The Nation*. He'd spent nine months in South Carolina teaching, and, like Lucy, had written down some of the songs he heard.

Lucy knew she had to make the collection of music of the enslaved a reality soon, since Reconstruction would bring the promise of a changed South. Although Lucy was well-read and very musically literate, at only twenty-four years old, she didn't feel like she could do it all on her own. She told Wendell what she wanted to do, and while she wrote letters to people she knew personally, Wendell thought men who might help would respond better to him—an editor and William Lloyd Garrison's son.

Wendell met with Allen, who agreed to provide his songs, and Allen contacted his cousin Charles Ware, who had collected about fifty songs from St. Helena Island, where he still lived and worked with Laura Towne. Ware was eager to share the music. They also received songs from General Higginson and others, including Charlotte Forten. For each song that would go into the book, they recorded where it was heard and who had transcribed it, creating a written record of Black music that had never before existed. They wrote about the music in general, although sometimes it was clear they didn't fully understand the culture they were trying to preserve. As Lucy got closer and closer to her due date, Allen took over editing.

On May 4, 1867, Lucy gave birth to a son that they named
Lloyd. Wendell wrote to his mother that, "Lloyd certainly resembles his name-
sake more than any known person," which was almost hard to believe since
George had always looked so much like their father. "Lucy mischievously says
that she sometimes feels very much embarrassed in handling" the baby because he looked so much like Grandpa G, Wendell admitted.

On November 21, 1867, *Slave Songs of the United States* was published.
Lucy wrote an unsigned review for the *Independent* (it wasn't unusual at the
time for authors to anonymously review their own books). "We welcome the
volume before us," she wrote, "the first collection of songs, words and music,
that has ever been attempted [of Black music]," saving music that was "now
rapidly passing away under the influence of the new civilization."

A portrait of Lucy McKim Garrison, from after the war.

CHAPTER 90

Charlotte Forten

BOSTON
1867–1872

I n the fall of 1867, Charlotte got a copy of *Slave Songs of the United States*. She knew that Lucy McKim Garrison had been working on the book and was pleased to see the work Lucy, Frances Allen, and Charles Ware had done.

"We are very glad that these songs, which are too rapidly losing favor among the freedmen—are thus collected and preserved, for they make a most striking, curious, and valuable addition to the history of slavery in the country," Charlotte wrote in her review for the *Freedmen's Record*.

The first time she'd heard that singing five years earlier, Charlotte wrote to her friend John Greenleaf Whittier's sister Elizabeth that the songs had a "peculiar wilderness and solemnity about them, which cannot be described." Now, from a chilly Boston, the songs reminded Forten of the sunsets and golden glows of the Sea Islands, the moss-draped oak she stood before on Emancipation Day, and the shouts and praises she attended.

Even without Dio Lewis's school, something in these postwar years had given Charlotte energy. She visited Whittier and went to plays with him; she translated a novel from French into English; she wrote articles for the *National Anti-Slavery Standard*; she attended meetings related to women's suffrage; and she worked at the Freedmen's Union Commission.

In 1870, Charlotte tried to get a job at the Boston Library, with the support of Whittier, her friend Thomas Wentworth Higginson, and the writer Ralph Waldo Emerson. No matter the success Charlotte experienced, though, there would always be the question of whether she wasn't allowed to do something because of her ancestry. She did not get the job.

Charlotte worked for the Commission in Boston until 1871—the longest she'd worked anywhere. Then she returned to South Carolina to teach at the Robert G. Shaw Memorial School, which was run by the Commission. Teaching would always be something that Charlotte could do and something that would help her people, as she had once written.

Her people were now free in Charleston, and Black Union soldiers marched on Emancipation Day and the Fourth of July, but the city was not Reconstructed. Charlotte found that "old reign of misrule," as *The Nation* described it, in full force. Here, Charlotte noted that the white elite were still celebrating the Confederate generals and began telling a myth of "The Lost Cause," the myth that the South could never have won the Civil War and that the war was never about slavery, but about "self-governance" and "states' rights."

After a year, Charlotte began teaching at a Black high school in Washington, DC. This was still the South, but in the years after the war, the city was also becoming a place for Black Americans to find education, opportunity, and prosperity. Charlotte only taught at the school for a year before getting a job as a clerk in the Treasury Department, and in Washington, DC, Charlotte would find the closest thing to contentment she had ever found.

A portrait of Charlotte Forten. After moving to Washington, DC, Charlotte married Reverend Francis James Grimké, the Black, formerly enslaved nephew of Angelina Grimké Weld and Sarah Grimké.

Brooklyn Daily Eagle

JULY 21, 1868

SECRETARY SEWARD has issued a proclamation declaring that the Fourteenth Amendment to the Constitution of the United States has been ratified [. . .]. For the information of those who may have forgotten what the Fourteenth Amendment is it may be stated briefly that it provides, first, that all persons born or naturalized in the United States shall be citizens thereof and of the State wherein they reside; secondly, that when the right to vote shall be denied any class of adult male citizens of any State, the basis of representation of such State shall be proportionally reduced; third, that no person who, having taken an official oath to support the Constitution of the United States, afterward engaged in the rebellion, shall hold State or national office [. . .].

An undated portrait of Lewis Douglass after his marriage to Helen Amelia Loguen, his "dear Amelia."

CHAPTER 91

Lewis Douglass

1866–1869

In January 1866, Lewis attended the National Convention of Colored Men in Washington, DC. Still in search of making something of himself and without a wedding date offered by Amelia, Lewis and his brother Fred traveled to Colorado, where they continued working for Black civil rights. Lewis started teaching at a night school for Black adults, with "general instruction in the common branches of an English education, and also by inducing a thorough reading of the Constitution of the United States, and investigating the general principles of the government; and by reading the newspapers of the day and explaining their political significance." He wanted informed Black voters.

By 1867, he was working for an African American mining company and campaigning to integrate Denver's public schools. When he wanted to get work as a printer again, however, he was denied membership to the local union because he was Black, and therefore he could not find work in that trade.

In the following years, he returned east and lived in Rochester, New York City, and Washington, DC, where he finally got a job as a printer at the Government Printing Office in 1869 and married Amelia Loguen. This was what he had wanted for so long: good employment, opportunity, and his own dear Amelia by his side.

Letter to Lewis Douglass

JULY 21, 1869

My dear Lewis:

I have just read with satisfaction in the Tribune, your brief but comprehensive and pertinent note acknowledging your election to honorary membership in the Soldiers and Sailors Union of Philadelphia.

I watch with intense interest all that concerns you and emanates from you in this struggle and am deeply gratified by every well aimed blow you deal the selfishness and meanness which seeks to humble, degrade, and starve you.

In the effort now making to chase you down, and through you to chase down and destroy your race, shall serve to place you before the country as one of the leaders of your people, and a representative of their cause, your experience will only conform to that of many other men who have risen to distinction in the world of persecution.

I send you this only to let you know that I am vigilant and observe all that is passion. We are all well here—Miss Assing read your letter aloud at the table to day.

Make my love to Charles and Frederick and to "Libby."

Your affectionate Father,
Frederick Douglass
Write "early and write often"

CHAPTER 92

George Garrison

1868–1872

I n August 1868, George accepted his brother Wendell's offer to work for *The Nation* and moved to Brooklyn, New York. The change of job and scenery did him well. He went to Women's Rights Society meetings and on a trip with his aunt and Wendell. Mostly, he replaced time alone in his room with time at the magazine, working more than he needed to.

But nothing ever seemed to stick for George. He did not enjoy his work, and before long, he had dreams of returning to Minnesota, where he still owned land. He moved back to Boston instead, and his brother William helped him open a paper box factory, which did not flourish before a fire destroyed the factory and many other businesses on November 9, 1872.

The fire could not have come at a worse time. George had restarted his courtship with Annie Anthony, and she had agreed to marry him, but without a job, they couldn't set a date to be married.

The fire and once-again-broken-off engagement depressed George. At thirty-six years old, he had yet to make something of himself.

George had planned on being at a dinner of the Association of the Officers of the 55th Massachusetts Infantry four days after the fire. In his postservice years, these reunions were one thing that George looked forward to, a time that he did want to socialize. So he went, regardless of the fire and what had happened.

George knew that his regiment and the 54th were both special, part of the Black regiments that had shown the nation that Black men were worthy of full citizenship. He also knew that the men he had served with were discriminated against, no matter where they lived now. The Fifteenth Amendment extended voting rights to African American men, yet just as the soldiers of the 55th had struggled to get paid their full salary in a timely manner, the injured veterans of the 55th had trouble securing their pensions. Men would write to George, asking him to vouch for their service and injuries they sustained while on duty so that they could receive their pensions. Up until his death, George would help his fellow veterans in any way that he was able.

CHAPTER 93

Lewis, George, Lucy, Charlotte, and Me

Throughout his life, Lewis Douglass continued working with his father for Black civil rights and with his brother Charles for the benefit of Civil War veterans. He and Amelia never had any children, which some scholars believe was because of the injury he suffered during the war. Lewis Henry Douglass died on September 19, 1908, in Washington, DC.

In the years that followed the publication of *Slave Songs of* *the United States,* Lucy lost pregnancies to miscarriage, which left her both physically disabled and isolated at home in New Jersey, where she cared for her sons, Lloyd and Philip, who was born in 1869. She wanted to become more involved in the women's rights movement, but she simply couldn't.

By the time her daughter, Katherine, was born in 1873, Lucy's health had only gotten worse. It was tough to take care of the children without help, Lucy confessed to Wendell once, relating that Lloyd and Philip had both held on to her skirts so tightly that she couldn't answer the door when friends came by the house. She had no time to play music or teach students, as she once had.

Lucy's health continued to get worse, and she suffered a stroke in December 1875, which was followed by fainting, headaches, and weakened eyesight. Everyone kept hoping for a recovery, but Lucy died on May 11, 1877, essentially paralyzed after suffering more strokes. She was only thirty-four years old.

———

In 1878, Charlotte began a courtship with Francis James Grimké, another member of the Black elite in Washington, DC. He had been born enslaved in South Carolina, the nephew of Sarah Grimké and Angelina Grimké Weld, the abolitionist sisters who ran the Eagleswood School. He had a contentious relationship with his white aunts but found support among them and other former abolitionists for his education. Francis had arrived in Boston after the Civil War, finally free of enslavement, taught at freedmen's schools, and graduated from Princeton University's seminary in the spring of 1878. Charlotte and Francis married in December 1878 and were a well-respected couple in the city. Charlotte was present in 1884 when Francis performed the wedding ceremony for Frederick Douglass and his second wife, Helen Pitts, although Lewis and his siblings were not.

Charlotte had one daughter, Theodora, in 1880, who died as an infant. Charlotte helped Francis with his work. Francis didn't believe that married women should have work of their own. Charlotte continued to write poems and essays, and she helped found the National Association of Colored Women. She died in Washington, DC, on July 23, 1914.

———

George had also been keeping newspaper clippings re-lated to the 55th, including achievements of the Black officers, which he pasted into his copy of *Record of the Service of the Fifty-Fifth Regiment of the Massachusetts Volunteer Infantry*. In 1895, George loaned his diaries to Captain Charles Soule, who was working on a history of the regiment. "In reading it over, for the first time in thirty years, I am surprised how much matter of interest I have left out that impressed itself upon my mind at the time, and which I still retain," the ever-humble George admitted. He never revised those diaries to include more detail or write memoirs of his time in the army, but did become part of the executive committee of his veterans' association.

George and Annie Anthony finally did marry in 1873 and had three children. George's businesses never did well, although for a time he made money in the stock market, and his family always worried about him. George died in 1904.

Lewis, Lucy, Charlotte, and George had been educated the way their parents wanted them to be: to not just believe in abolition and equal rights, but to make achieving those goals their life's work. They may not have been able to imagine that more than a hundred years later, *abolition* has taken on a new meaning: a movement to undo the injustices that Reconstruction never did.

It was a warm August night in 2023 as my partner, Pete, and I walked to the worker-owned bookstore and cafe in our neighborhood. Our mutual love of history and books is one thing that sustains our relationship, and when we move through Baltimore, we often consider what has happened in these spaces. We walk by the old Victorian houses, the vestiges of our neighborhood of Waverly being a summer retreat from the city. Just a block from the bookstore is a sign and a statue that point out where a schoolhouse for Black students once stood. We live on one side of Greenmount Avenue, a thoroughfare that is redlined, where homes are valued at one hundred thousand dollars less than on the other side of the avenue simply because banks once said these would be Black neighborhoods and they would not back loans to white homebuyers. We're still sandwiched between majority-white neighborhoods, and all the amenities of the Johns Hopkins University undergraduate campus are just a few blocks away.

Our past echoes through the present. In the summer of 2020, when so many other cities experienced protests after the murder of George Floyd in Minneapolis, our streets were quiet. Our uprising had happened in 2015, with the murder of Freddie Gray after he was arrested by Baltimore Police officers and put in a police van.

We were walking to the collective-owned Red Emma's bookstore to hear Justine Barron speak about her book *They Killed Freddie Gray: The Anatomy of a Police Brutality Cover-Up*. Rather than just talk about what she found, Barron chose to be in conversation with community activists. Barron uncovered evidence that the Baltimore Police Department and Baltimore city officials knew that they had caused Gray's death and then covered up the murder. Sierria Warren was there to recount seeing the police van stop and to attest to policing in their West Baltimore neighborhood in general. Tawanda Jones's brother Tyrone West was also killed in police custody in 2013, and she spoke about her protests, which demand police accountability, held every Wednesday. Ray Kelly, executive director of the Citizens Policing Project, and Eze Jackson, a community activist, discussed what the role of police really should be.

Many members of the audience were white. Some seemed to regularly attend Jones's West Wednesday protests; others I'd seen in front of the Quaker meetinghouse holding signs that said things like *Honk If You Want Peace* and *Black Lives Matter*.

Somehow, this space and these people felt familiar to me. I had just started doing research for this book and was reading about the abolitionist movement as it had started in the 1830s. In small spaces across the North, William Lloyd Garrison, Frederick Douglass, Miller McKim, Charles Lenox Remond, and other relatives and friends of George, Lewis, Lucy, and Charlotte advocated for abolition. Like Barron, Garrison published the truth for all to read. Like Jones, Douglass told a personal story of abuse and escape. Like Warren, Kelly, and Jackson, McKim and Remond spoke to the changes being made and what still needed to be done.

These are the abolitionists, I thought.

When we talk about abolition today, we often talk about abolishing the police and getting rid of a taxpayer-funded force that can stand on a street and murder Jones's brother and cover up their murder of Freddie Gray. Abolishing the police was part of the discussion at the bookstore that night. Journalist Ruairí Arrieta-Kenna writes that there are three different levels of "abolish the police." The first, he writes, "is a cry of frustration, a more civil version of 'f*** the police.'" In Baltimore, our police are under a federal consent decree after the US Department of Justice found that they were violating the civil liberties of Baltimore residents. Here, we know that the police are a problem and something has to be done. Saying "abolish the police" simply starts the conversation about change in a very loud way.

Some people, including many of the activists who visited Red Emma's for the book talk, don't think words are enough. According to Arrieta-Kenna, some activists believe that "scrapping our current police forces [would] allow a new and better version to emerge" or that less money for current police departments "would create a new and better balance of police and the other services that keep communities safe and peaceful." Ray Kelly and his colleagues at the Citizens Policing Project interviewed Baltimore residents and found that only thirty percent of city residents they spoke to were in favor of defunding the police. To compare, in the late 1830s, less than one percent of the free population in the United States was actively involved in the movement to abolish slavery. This percentage increased in years leading to the Civil War, but it was never as high as thirty percent, and Lincoln—who was not an abolitionist—won the 1860 election with a little less than forty percent of the vote.

Today, Kelly writes, reimagining the police force "isn't about less or abolishing police, but more about investing in community-based solutions and programs that reduce or prevent crime, reduce recidivism, and address the root causes of these issues."

Finally, there are those who believe we should not have police. Full stop. They literally mean get rid of police. Arrieta-Kenna writes that "[the] new movement to abolish the police is a direct outgrowth of the prison abolition movement." In *Slavery By Another Name*, Douglas A. Blackmon explores how the prison system in the United States was used after the Civil War to essentially re-create the forced labor—slavery—that the Thirteenth Amendment rendered unconstitutional. Only there was a catch: Slavery and involuntary servitude were acceptable as "punishment for crime." You just had to find—or create—a crime that required incarceration, and you got cheap and free labor. Black men were arrested and sentenced to hard labor for simple misdemeanors like vagrancy, owing someone money, or "speaking loudly in the presence of white women."

Blackmon's book ends with World War II, but the problem persists today. Prison labor produces less expensive American-made goods, while the people making them don't have a choice if they want to do these jobs, and they may face dangerous and unsafe working conditions. Americans are being forced to work for nearly nothing so that we can have cheap goods and food. In the 1850s, the McKims refused to wear cotton and the Douglasses refused to eat sugar because of the forced labor involved. We could refuse forced-labor goods today, too. Some folks already do.

Abolition is larger than dismantling a prison system that is the legacy of slavery, because our police are part of the legacy of slavery, too. While police forces existed throughout the world before the founding of the United States, modern policing as it now exists in the US would not exist without slavery. In 1854, the same year that Anthony Burns was arrested under the Fugitive Slave Act in Boston, that city created a police force. And while slave patrollers once arrested fugitives like Burns or enforced the laws that governed the behavior of enslaved people, after the Civil War they did not protect Black Americans but rather enforced segregation laws. Today, Black Americans are arrested, incarcerated, and shot by police at higher rates than any other group of Americans. Men like Tyrone West, Freddie Gray, and George Floyd—a few names that barely scratch the surface of Black Americans killed by police in the last twelve years—die at the hands of police before any evidence can even be presented against them.

After the Civil War, the children of abolitionists realized that while emancipation had come, what many had truly sought—equality among the races—was still far off. They may not have anticipated that many Black Americans would be effectively re-enslaved by other means or that the police would become a source and enforcer of oppression. Today, we are closer to equality than we were in 1865 or 1965, but there is still work to do.

We can meet in bookstores and discuss abolition in its full historical context. We can boycott prison-made goods, mindful of the country's legacy of forced labor. We can protest and be vocal with our opposition to the police and the way prisons are run in the United States because we know how they came to be run the way they are. But what ultimately ended slavery in 1865 was the ratification of the Thirteenth Amendment by three-quarters of the thirty-six state legislatures, after passing Congress with two-thirds majorities in the House and Senate. Without the tireless and often deeply unpopular pressure of abolitionists, the nation may have never cleared this high constitutional hurdle, or it may have taken another generation, as it did in Brazil, which didn't outlaw slavery until 1888.

As I looked around the bookstore and listened to the audience questions, I was awed by the abolitionists' dedication to changing a system that feels impossible to change. We need the new William Lloyd Garrisons and Frederick Douglasses, and we need the next generation after that to look at abolition not as an insurmountable challenge, but as something that can, and will, happen in their lifetime. In 1855, Samuel Tappan told George their generation couldn't just ignore slavery. Today, the generations that came before us left the "accursed system" of prison labor and policing, and we suffer because of it. If we speak loudly enough, gather support, and bring that change to the government, then we won't "leave it for those who come after us."

The 1846 book *The Anti-Slavery Alphabet* ends with:

Z is a Zealous man, sincere,
Faithful, and just, and true;
An earnest pleader for the slave—
Will not you be so too?

ACKNOWLEDGMENTS

Pete: thank you for your love and unrelenting belief in me. None of my writing would be without you keeping me sane.

This book wouldn't be possible without support from arts organizations. The Maryland State Arts Council gave me a project grant to develop the book proposal in the fall of 2022; I had an incredible residency at The Mastheads, where this book started taking shape in the summer of 2023; and I (mostly) finished the book at a residency at Hedgebrook in February 2024. We need the arts, we need arts organizations, and we need funding for the arts both through the government on the state and local level and funding for amazing private arts organizations.

I am always thankful to my writing friends for providing humor, insight, and grounding. Danny Lavery, Elisa Gonzalez, Auyon Mukharji, and Julia Mounsey—I'm so glad we got to be in community together at Ms. Hall's and in Melville's field. I'm grateful to my Goucher writers—Rachel Dickinson, Ginny McReynolds, Memsy Price, Neda Semnani, and Parisa Saranj. Special thanks to Stephanie Gorton for letting me stay with her while on a whirlwind research trip. And to Elizabeth Evitts Dickinson for conversations, thoughts on writing, and writing support.

Becky Hill—I somehow forgot to thank you last time, so that's not happening this time. Thank you for dance parties and friendship that make writing easier. I'm so lucky to have friends (you know who you are!) who show up and are excited about my work.

Thank you to the librarians and staff at the Massachusetts Historical Society, Harvard College libraries, National Archives, and Smith College—especially to Nanci Young, who saw me getting interested in Smith College's banjo club and bluntly asked if that was the research I was supposed to be doing. I had boxes of Garrison family papers on my table; it was not was I was supposed to be doing.

Thank you, Andrew Karre, for seeing the vision of the book and making it better, and for being as in love with Lucy McKim as I am. Thank you to the team at Dutton/Penguin Young Readers, including Anna Booth, Rob Farren, Ilana Jacobs, Madison Penico, Julie Strauss-Gabel, Rye White, Vanessa Robles, and Natalie Vielkind.

Thank you to Diego Mallo for bringing the Dadaesque cover of my dreams to life.

Thank you to my agent, Jenna Land Free, for just being wonderful.

Thank you to everyone in my family; I felt our closeness in some of the stories of the families I write about. Mom, thank you for your continued support and love. Dad, I can never ask for a better first reader. Thomas and Linn, tack för allt. Benjamin and Matney, I do hope Sidney, Ellis, and Bo may be trained up in the way they should go, but maybe be more understanding than William Lloyd Garrison.

BIBLIOGRAPHY

LETTERS, DIARIES, JOURNALS, AND SELECT NEWSPAPERS

FOR THE DOUGLASS FAMILY PAPERS:

Bernier, Celeste-Marie, and Andrew Taylor, eds. *If I Survive: Frederick Douglass and Family in the Walter O. Evans Collection.* Edinburgh University Press, 2018.

"Letters of Negroes, Largely Personal and Private." *The Journal of Negro History* 11, no. 1 (1926).

The archives of the various version of the newspapers published by Frederick Douglass are hosted by the Library of Congress at https://www.loc.gov/collections/frederick-douglass-newspapers/

FOR THE GARRISON, MCKIM, AND WRIGHT FAMILY PAPERS:

Merrill, Walter, ed. *Letters of William Lloyd Garrison, Volume II.* Harvard University Press, 1979.

Garrison Family Papers (including Ellen Wright's diary), Sophia Smith Collection of Women's History, Smith College.

Garrison Family Papers, Massachusetts Historical Society.

Garrison Family Papers, Houghton Library, Harvard University.

The archives of *The Liberator* are hosted by the Library of Congress at https://www.loc.gov/item/sn84031524/

FOR CHARLOTTE FORTEN'S PAPERS:

Stevenson, Brenda, ed. *The Journals of Charlotte Forten Grimké.* Oxford University Press, 1988.

ARTICLES AND BOOKS

Abzug, Robert H. *Passionate Liberator: Theodore Dwight Weld & the Dilemma of Reform.* Oxford University Press, 1980.

Allen, William Francis, Charles P. Ware, and Lucy McKim Garrison. *Slave Songs of the United States.* New York, 1867.

Alonso, Harriet Hyman. *Growing Up Abolitionist: The Story of the Garrison Children*. University of Massachusetts Press, 2002.

Armstrong, Erica. "Voices from the Margins: The Philadelphia Female Anti-Slavery Society 1833–1840." In *A Fragile Freedom: African American Women and Emancipation in the Antebellum*. Yale University Press, 2008.

Arrieta-Kenna, Ruairí. "The Deep Roots—and New Offshoots—of 'Abolish the Police.'" *Politico*, June 12, 2020.

Barker, Gordon S. *Fugitive Slaves and the Unfinished American Revolution*. McFarland, 2013.

Bernier, Celeste-Marie, and Andrew Taylor, eds. *If I Survive: Frederick Douglass and Family in the Walter O. Evans Collection*. Edinburgh University Press, 2018.

Blight, David W. *Frederick Douglass: Prophet of Freedom*. Simon & Schuster, 2018.

Brown, Clair H. "How Corporations Buy—and Sell—Food Made with Prison Labor." *The Counter*, May 18, 2021.

Brown, Francis. *Harvard University in the War of 1861–1865: A Record of Services Rendered in the Army and Navy of the United States by the Graduates and Students of Harvard College and the Professional Schools*. Boston, 1886.

Brown, Henry. *Narrative of the Life of Henry Box Brown, Written by Himself*. Manchester, 1851.

Brown, Ira V. "Miller McKim and Pennsylvania Abolitionism." *Pennsylvania History: A Journal of Mid-Atlantic Studies* 30, no. 1 (1963): 55–72.

Browne, Joseph. "'To Bring out the Intellect of the Race': An African American Freedmen's Bureau Agent in Maryland," *Maryland Historical Magazine* 104, no. 4 (2009): 374–401.

Byrd, Dana E. "Northern Vision, Southern Land: Designs for Freedom on Hilton Head Island, 1862–1880." *Studies in the History of Art* 81 (January 2016): 15–30.

Carton, Evan. *Patriotic Treason: John Brown and the Soul of America*. Free Press, 2006.

Charters, Samuel. *Songs of Sorrow: Lucy McKim Garrison and "Slave Songs of the United States."* University Press of Mississippi, 2015.

Cohen, William. "James Miller McKim: Pennsylvania Abolitionist." PhD dissertation, New York University, 1968.

Cox, Clinton. *Undying Glory: The Story of the Massachusetts 54th Regiment*. Scholastic, 1991.

Douglass, Frederick. "The Dred Scott Decision." In *Two Speeches, by Frederick Douglass; One on West India Emancipation, Delivered at Canandaigua, Aug. 4th, and the Other on the Dred Scott Decision, Delivered in New York, on the Occasion of the Anniversary of the American Abolition Society, May 1857.* Rochester, 1857.

Douglass, Frederick. *Life and Times of Frederick Douglass.* Boston, 1892.

Douglas Jr., Joseph L. *Frederick Douglass: A Family Biography: 1733–1936.* Winterlucht Books, 2011.

Doy, John. *The Narrative of John Doy, of Lawrence, Kansas: "A Plain, Unvarnished Tale."* New York, 1860.

Drew, Thomas Boston, ed. *The John Brown Invasion.* Boston, 1860.

Egerton, Douglas R. *Thunder at the Gates: The Black Civil War Regiments That Redeemed America.* Basic Books, 2016.

Fought, Leigh. *Women in the World of Frederick Douglass.* Oxford University Press, 2017.

Goodrich, Thomas. *War to the Knife: Bleeding Kansas, 1854–1861.* Stackpole Books, 1998.

Greene, Bryan. "America's First Black Physician Sought to Heal a Nation's Persistent Illness." *Smithsonian Magazine*, February 26, 2021.

Greenidge, Kerri K. *The Grimkes: The Legacy of Slavery in an American Family.* Liveright, 2022.

Grimké, Francis J. "The Second Marriage of Frederick Douglass." *The Journal of Negro History* 19, no. 3 (1934).

Grinspan, Jon. " 'Young Men for War': The Wide Awakes and Lincoln's 1860 Presidential Campaign." *Journal of American History* 96, no. 2 (2009).

Hallowell, Anna Davis, ed. *James and Lucretia Mott: Life and Letters.* New York, 1890.

Hinton, Richard J. *John Brown and His Men.* Arno Press, 1968.

Jabir, Johari. *Conjuring Freedom: Music and Masculinity in the Civil War's "Gospel Army."* Ohio State University Press, 2017.

Jones, Jane Elizabeth. *The Young Abolitionists, Or Conversations on Slavery.* Boston, 1848.

Kashatus, William C. *William Still: The Underground Railroad and the Angel at Philadelphia.* University of Notre Dame Press, 2021.

Kelly, Ray. *The Long Game: Defund, Divest, Reform and Abolish: The Resident*

Perspective of the Current Debate on Where We Should Invest Our Public Safety Dollars. The Citizens Policing Project, March 2022.

Lapsansky, Emma Jones. "Feminism, Freedom, and Community: Charlotte Forten and Women Activists in Nineteenth-Century Philadelphia." *The Pennsylvania Magazine of History and Biography* 113, no. 1 (1989): 3–19.

Legan, Marshall Scott. "Hydropathy in America: A Nineteenth Century Panacea." *Bulletin of the History of Medicine* 45, no. 3 –(1971): 267–80.

Lepore, Jill. "The Invention of Police." *The New Yorker*, July 13, 2020.

"Letters of Negroes, Largely Personal and Private [Part 2]…" *The Journal of Negro History* 11, no. 1 (1926): 87–112.

Levy, Leonard W. "Sims' Case: The Fugitive Slave Law in Boston in 1851." *The Journal of Negro History* 35, no. 1 (1950): 39–74.

Ling Lee, Christina Choon. "Therapoetics in Late Nineteenth-Century American Literature." PhD dissertation, UNC–Chapel Hill, 2021.

Logue, Larry M. and Peter Blanck. "'Benefit of the Doubt': African-American Civil War Veterans and Pensions." *The Journal of Interdisciplinary History* 38, no. 3 (2008): 377–399.

Long, Lisa. "Charlotte Forten's Civil War Journals and the Quest for 'Genius, Beauty, and Deathless Fame.'" *Legacy* 16, no. 1, Discourses of Women and Class (1999): 37–48.

Mayer, Henry. *All on Fire: William Lloyd Garrison and the Abolition of Slavery*. St. Martin's Press, 1998.

McGlone, Robert E. *John Brown's War Against Slavery*. Cambridge University Press, 2009.

McPherson, James M. "Abolitionist and Negro Opposition to Colonization during the Civil War." *Phylon* 26, no. 4 (1965): 391–99.

Reynolds, David S. *John Brown, Abolitionist: The Man Who Killed Slavery, Sparked the Civil War, and Seeded Civil Rights*. Knopf, 2005.

Richards, Leonard L. *"Gentleman of Property and Standing": Anti-Abolition Mobs in Jacksonian America*. Oxford University Press, 1970.

Robbins, Gerald. "The Recruiting and Arming of Negroes in the South Carolina Sea Islands—1862-1865." *Negro History Bulletin* 28, no. 7 (1965): 150–51, 163–67.

Rucker, Walter C. "Unpopular Sovereignty: African-American Resistance and the Kansas-Nebraska Act." In *The Nebraska-Kansas Act of 1854*, ed. John R. Wunder and Joann M. Ross. University of Nebraska Press, 2008.

Scheips, Paul J. "Lincoln and the Chiriqui Colonization Project." *The Journal of Negro History* 37, no. 4 (1952): 418–453.

Smith, John David, ed. *Black Soldiers in Blue:* African American Troops in the Civil War Era. The University of North Carolina Press, 2002.

Sprague, Rosetta Douglass. "Anna Murray-Douglass: My Mother as I Recall Her." *The Journal of Negro History* 8, no. 1 (1923): 93–101

Sterling, Dorothy, ed. *We Are Your Sisters: Black Women in the Nineteenth Century.* W. W. Norton & Company, 1984.

Stevens, Charles Emery. *Anthony Burns: A History.* Boston, 1856.

Still, William. *The Underground Rail Road.* Philadelphia, 1872.

Sturdevant, Katherine Scott, and Stephen Collins. "Frederick Douglass and Abraham Lincoln on Black Equity in the Civil War: A Historical Rhetorical Perspective." *Black History Bulletin* 73, no. 2 (2010): 8–15.

Sumner, Charles. *The Barbarism of Slavery: Speech of Hon. Charles Sumner on the Bill for the Admission of Kansas as a Free State.* New York, 1863.

Theiss, Nancy Stearns. *A Tour on the Underground Railroad along the Ohio River.* The History Press, 2020.

Townsend, Hannah and Mary Townsend. The Anti-Slavery Alphabet. Philadelphia, 1846, printed for the Anti-Slavery Fair.

Trudeau, Noah Andre. *Like Men of War: Black Troops in the Civil War 1862-1865.* Little, Brown and Company, 1998.

Trudeau, Noah Andre, ed. *Voices of the 55th: Letters from the 55th Massachusetts Volunteers, 1861-1865.* Morningside House, 1996.

von Frank, Albert J. *The Trials of Anthony Burns: Freedom and Slavery in Emerson's Boston.* Harvard University Press, 1998.

White-Perry, Giselle. "In Freedom's Shadow: The Reconstruction Legacy of Renty Franklin Greaves of Beaufort County, South Carolina." *Prologue* 42, no. 3 (2010): 18–26.

Winch, Julie. "'You Know I Am a Man of Business': James Forten and the Factor of Race in Philadelphia's Antebellum Business Community." *Business and Economic History* 26, no. 1 (1997): 213–228–.

Winston, Celeste. *How to Lose the Hounds: Maroon Geographies and a World Beyond Policing.* Duke University Press, 2023.

NOTES

ABBREVIATIONS IN CITATIONS

Garrison Family

   FG: Fanny Garrison

   GG: George Garrison

   HG: Helen Garrison

   WeG: Wendell Garrison

   WGjr: William Garrison, Jr.

   WLG: William Lloyd Garrison

McKim Family

   LM: Lucy McKim

   EW: Ellen Wright

INTRODUCTION

2 "We shall dance at funerals next year & flirt across corpses": Lucy McKim to Ellen Wright, Dec. 29, 1861, SC.

PROLOGUE

5 His name was Henry Brown...: Cohen, 264.

5 Her father was Miller McKim...: Ira Brown, 62–63.

6 He had "escaped the lash almost entirely"...: Henry Brown, 18.

6 The main reason Brown wanted to escape...: Ibid., 50.

6 With nothing to lose, Brown...: Hallowell, 89.

6 "A is for abolitionist...": Hannah Townsend, 1.

7 "Yes, my daughter, the slaveholders...": Jones.

PART 1

9 "May he be trained up in the way he should go—for he has been brought into a most perilous world": WLG to HG, Boston, April 18, 1836.

CHAPTER 1

11 Out the window of their home...: Blight, 291, 241–245.

12 A woman from Kentucky...: Theiss, 113. A father from farther south...: Bernier, 44. A man might tell...: Barker, 6. These people had traveled...: Winston. Behind their visitors was slavery...: quoted in Blight, 71.

13 His father hid...: Blight, 71–72. When the people were safely...: Bernier, 14. For every person...: Mayer 407.

CHAPTER 2

14 his family's home on Dix Place...: The Garrisons lived at 14 Dix Place; G.P. Reed's store was at 13 Tremont. Mayer, 460. "Another Triumph of the Slave Power": *The Liberator*, May 26, 1854. At the store, George was...: GG diary, September 7; 11; 13, 1854 (George didn't start keeping a diary until September 1854, so it is hard to know his exact movements during the week of May 1854, but he was working at Reed's). To pass the bill: Rucker, 130.

15 Since the bill had already passed...: Barker, 9. For him and those with similar...: WLG to Miller McKim, Oct. 14, 1856. Abolitionists like George's father...: Mayer, 222. George felt stubborn and independent....: Ibid., 250. George was supposed to be....: Alonso, 110.

16 A police officer named Asa Butman...: Barker, 138–139 (The 1854 Boston Directory has Butman's profession as constable, but he's often referred to as a "slave catcher."). The news of a man...: Barker 9 and von Frank 8. Three years earlier, Butman...: Levy 39–74. Unlike George's father...: Barker 11.

CHAPTER 3

17 Slavery had effectively ended in Massachusetts in the 1780s...: Elizabeth Freeman ("Mumbet") and Quock Walker argued in court in the 1780s that their enslavement went against the new Massachusetts constitution, which the court agreed with, effectively ending slavery in the state. https://www.masshist.org/features/endofslavery/end_MA.

18 "Men had taken Charlotte's...": Julie Winch, 213, 278–80 (Winch says that the background of Charlotte's mother, Mary Virginia Wood, was not really known, other than that she was well educated, Black, and from North Carolina). Charlotte's father did not think...: Lapsansky, 11 and Grimké, 17. He "was arrested like a criminal".... and "I can only hope and pray...": Grimké, 61.

19 "Remember the poor slave...": Stevenson, 81.

CHAPTER 4

21 "to the burning and eloquent words...": Charlotte Forten, "Glimpses of New England,"

National Anti-Slavery Standard, June 19, 1858. She thought today would be different: Stevenson, 62.

21 But as Charlotte walked...: Charlotte is with a friend from Salem in Boston. Von Frank thinks it is Sarah Remond, but in the journal transcription, Brenda Stevenson adds that it is Sarah Cassey Smith. Charlotte only writes "Sarah," so to avoid confusion, I've omitted the presence of the friend.

22 Charlotte continued around the corner to a concert hall...: Stevenson, 63–64. People said the Committee had been meeting...: von Frank, 56. "I do think reading one's composition...": Stevenson, 92.

23 The law said Burns could not present a defense...: Barker, 15.

23 Stone asserted that before long...: *The Liberator*, June 16, 1854.

24 "I do not know what bloody tragedies...": Ibid. "minions of the South...": Stevenson, 64. But here, he would get down on the floor...: Alonso, 96. Helen Garrison was lovely...: Mayer, 463. Helen didn't want to speak in public...: Ibid., 252.

25 The soldiers made Charlotte's heart sick...: Stevenson, 64. "I cannot hope to reach [that highest Christian spirit...] for I believe...": Ibid.

CHAPTER 5

26 Many of the shops in the center of Boston...: Barker, 19.

27 Along the route, people leaned out of windows...: von Frank, 206–8. Along the route, the bells mixed with horse hooves...: Barker, 20. Someone else threw a bottle of sulfuric acid...: von Frank, 215.

28 George's father thought that the judge's decision...: Mayer, 441. George's father wasn't as radical as Higginson...: Barker, 50.

CHAPTER 6

29 "a government which proudly": Stevenson, 66.

CHAPTER 7

30 A party from the New England Emigrant Aid Company...: GG diary, September 21, 1854.

31 "They are very much opposed to my going there...": GG diary, September 24, 1854. His father did not believe that these emigrants would do anything...: Murphy, 25.

31 "and as a matter of course we their children must suffer...": Samuel Tappan Jr. to GG, December 17, 1855.

CHAPTER 8

33 When they'd fixed any mistakes, the press started humming...: Sprague, 98. This was the first week in years that Julia Griffiths...: Fought, 142, 128; Blight, 253, 195, 219, 225, 225; Leigh, 133.

34 There were too many people who wanted to discredit his father...: In *Frederick Douglass: Prophet of Freedom*, David Blight explores the relationship between Julia Griffiths and Frederick Douglass, which is hard to sort out since Douglass was so private about his inner life. There was also an amazing coincidence...: *Frederick Douglass' Paper*, June 22, 1855 (Rosetta was in the preparatory department, like a high school). After Burns had been returned to Virginia...: Stevens, 213, 216. Lewis knew he'd never go to college...: "Letters of Negroes, Largely Personal and Private [Part 2]...", 206. Come up, friends, body to the work...: *Frederick Douglass' Paper*, June 22, 1855.

35 "The object of this Convention is...": Quoted in *New-York Daily Tribune*, June 28, 1855. "human Slavery unconstitutional, illegal and wicked...": *New-York Daily Tribune*, June 28, 1855. "well known as an active and self-sacrificing abolitionist...": *Frederick Douglass' Paper*, July 6. For years, Brown had been thinking of ways to liberate enslaved people...: Reynolds, 105. Brown thought the Allegheny Mountains in Virginia...: McGlone, 226. "well armed and thoroughly organized...": 15. *New-York Daily Tribune*, July 2, 1855.

CHAPTER 9

40 There were also reports that men simply crossed into Kansas...: Goodrich, 12, 28.

40 Free soilers burned the cabins...: Ibid., 89, 105, 106.

42 VALEDICTORY POEM: "Charlotte Forten Valedictory Poem, Salem 1856," Using Essex History, https://usingessexhistory.org/documents/charlotte-forten-valedictory-poem-salem-1856/.

CHAPTER 10

43 Sometimes, Lewis or his brother Fred joined their father...: Blight, 253. "deadliest blow upon slavery...": quoted in Blight, 275.

CHAPTER 11

45 "a close and desperate struggle…": GG diary, November 3, 1856.

46 "all beholders must have been convinced of the prevalence of free sentiments in our community…": *Boston Evening Transcript*, October 30, 1856. His supporters were Frémonters…: Mayer, 450, 4525. George's father did not approve of the Frémonters…: *The Liberator*, October 31, 1856.

CHAPTER 12

49 The setting autumn light cast a glow…: Henry David Thoreau's journal, October 26, 1856. Here, she could spend almost as much time as she wanted…: Letter to Ellen Wright from Mary Wright, May 20, 1857. Lucy's attendance at the school…: Abzug, 265.

50 The sisters had been Quakers…: Lapsansky, 11. Lucy's mother had not been allowed to sing…: "In Memoriam Sarah A. McKim, 1813–1891," MHS. "I wish to speak a word for Nature, for absolute freedom…": Quotes from Thoreau's lecture are from the published version of "Walking" in *The Art of the Personal Essay*, which was likely revised from the lecture that he gave at Eagleswood in 1856. He first delivered a lecture with this title in 1851, and continued to revise it until the essay's publication after his death. For more discussion of this, see the Walden Woods Project: https://www.walden.org/what-we-do/library/lectures/thoreaus-lectures-after-walden-lecture-52/ He had already given one lecture the previous Sunday…: Bronson Alcott to Abigail Alcott, November 3, 1856.

51 She and Ellen loved to sit on the steps of the bathhouse…: EW diary, January 1860. "perfectly lovely and fresh…": LM to Mary Byrne, August 30, 1857.

CHAPTER 13

54 Charlotte loved Christmas…: *Boston Evening Transcript*, December 26, 1856, 2; December 24, 1856. Set upon the tables in front of Charlotte…: *The Liberator*, December 19, 1856. At the fair and in free labor stores…: Armstrong, 88.

55 "the noblest and best women…": Stevenson, 174–175. Charlotte only wished that she could accept…: Ibid. The day after Christmas, *The Liberator*…: *The Liberator*, December 26, 1856.

PART 2

57 "How strange it is that in a world so beautiful, there can be so much wickedness…": Stevenson, 66.

CHAPTER 14

59 The defense argued that Scott could not sue at all because he wasn't a United States citizen…: *New-York Tribune*, March 9, 1857. "The question was simply this…": "The Dred Scott Case," *New-York Tribune*, March 9, 1857.

60 "colored men of African descent are not and cannot be citizens of the United States…": Douglass, *The Dred Scott Decision*. In Rochester, Lewis was now the foreman…: Douglas, J., 47. In his speeches that spring and summer, Lewis's father said…: Blight, 278. "the white flag of freedom…": Douglass, *The Dred Scott Decision*.

CHAPTER 15

64 "Hip! Hip! Hurrah!" George wrote in his diary…: GG diary, February 6, 1857. But George's friend had written to him…: Alonso, 121. "seemed to be the best opening for the young, the enterprising…": GG to Miss [Maria Weston] Chapman, April 26, 1857. His father and mother gave him their blessing in the end…: WLG to George Thompson Garrison, April 28, 1857. But George wanted to labor as a pioneer…: GG to Miss [Maria Weston] Chapman, April 26, 1857.

65 Truth traveled and spoke about abolition…: Sterling, 250–53. "gave me a great deal of pleasure at seeing her…": GG to Richard B. Merritt, July 15, 1857. From there, he got on the steamboat City Belle…: GG to HG, May 10, 1857. All in all, it had been a very pleasant journey…: GG to George [Benson?], May 27, 1857.

CHAPTER 16

66 The boat pulled out of the docks in Philadelphia…: Stevenson, 229. She was on her way to visit her aunt Harriet and uncle Robert…: Kashatus, 57; Stevenson, 11.

67 As fortune would have it, Griffith…: Stevenson, 113. She had not grown up with or even heard abolitionist teachings as Charlotte had…: *The Liberator*, August 14, 1857. "plain and unpretending…": Stevenson, 190.

68 "I cannot help feeling it very often, it intrudes upon my happiest moments, and spreads a dark, deep gloom over everything…": Ibid., 111.

CHAPTER 17

69 "a great deal of drinking during the day, and several [people] got dead drunk...": GG to WLG, July 8, 1857. George noticed men did not really shave here...: GG to HG, December 6, 1857. "make worldly success, or the accumulation of property...": WLG to George Thompson Garrison, April 28, 1857. In the summer of 1857, George got a job...: GG to WeG, August 16, 1857.

70 "that you were getting what you needed more than money, just now, and that was experience and self reliance...": WLG Jr. to GG, September 16, 1857. "not the slightest idea of returning home...": GG to George [Benson?], May 27, 1857; GG to HG, September 20, 1857

71 New lyrics to "The Star-Spangled Banner": Alonso, 122–23

CHAPTER 18

73 The three and a half story brick house...: Insurance maps of the city of Philadelphia, 1857, via Library of Congress. As a child, Charlotte had spent Christmases and Easters...: Greenridge, 58. William Still was there, too...: Kashatus, 57.

74 "No, sir, I never wrote any...": Steveson, 236. Even when Garrison published her recent poem...: Ibid.

CHAPTER 19

76 "able to dance...": GG to WGjr, December 13, 1857. "bashful when with women...": GG to HG, July 20, 1857. We danced the cotillons...: GG to HG, January 10, 1858. "Your 'great West' will be soon reeling...": WLG to GG, October 15, 1857.

77 "I shall never be able to [be successful] anywhere...": GG diary, January 1, 1858. "His friend Francis Meriam returned from France...": WeG to GG, November 4, 1857. "but his mother and grandfather forbid such a step...": WLG to GG, January 1, 1857. Back in Boston, Massachusetts senator Charles Sumner...: Mayer, 453; WGjr to GG, December 27, 1857. At Tremont Temple, the great orators spoke...: Charlie Cram to GG, March 15, 1858. "some very handsome young ladies...": WGjr to GG, December 14, 1857. "animal appetites and passions...": WLG to GG, January 1, 1858. "it seemed like old times to hear him...": GG to HG, December 6, 1857.

78 "My country 'tis of thee, Stronghold of Slavery...": Mayer, 348. The men concluded

that citizens deciding...: GG to WLG, January 17, 1858. "You are in an excellent position to let your light shine...": WLG to GG, January 1, 1858. He saw the necessity of it...: GG to WGjr, January 10, 1857.

CHAPTER 20

79 "I cannot bear to think how I have misspent...": Stevenson, 275. Her stepmother was a free Black woman from South Carolina...: Winch, 341. "rather die ten thousand times...": Stevenson, 289–90.

80 "I must need some great emotion to arouse...": Ibid., 276.

CHAPTER 21

81 That month, his father's friend John Brown...: Blight, 296. He'd grown a large white beard...: McGlone 183. One couldn't help but feel his religious presence...: Blight, 284. At the Douglass house, he would stand up...: Ibid.

82 "God has given the strength of the hills to freedom...": Quoted in McGlone, 226. "Thou shalt not deliver unto his master...": Quoted in Blight, 283. Take the people from the plantations...,: Blight, 298, Douglass, *Life and Times*, 385. That was the essence of the plan...: McGlone 226. Lewis and his brothers sat enraptured...: Blight, 298, Douglass, *Life and Times*, 385–386. Even Lewis's little sister, Annie...: Fought, 170. Lewis's father, on the other hand, saw flaws...: Blight, 282. Brown might counter with moral arguments...: Ibid., 298; Reynolds, 105, 107. Brown wrote letters to his sons in Kansas...: Blight, 296.

83 He talked of his constitution all day...: Douglass, *Life and Times*, 385–86. And yet, his father still helped John Brown...: Blight, 298–99. "If there is no struggle, there is no progress...": quoted in Blight, 285–86.

CHAPTER 22

84 She had time to write...: Forten, "Glimpses." "a mingling feeling of sorrow, shame...": Stevenson, 315.

CHAPTER 23

86 In June 1858, his father had been invited...: *Frederick Douglass' Paper*, July 23, 1858; McGrawville is now McGraw, New York.

86 It took hard work, too...: The Frederick Douglass Papers project notes that, "The first versions of the [Self-made Men] speech date from a tour of Illinois and Wisconsin in February 1859." However, in *Frederick Douglass' Paper* (which Douglass himself edited), it says this was the title of the speech he gave that day at McGrawville. He would continue giving versions of his speech into [the 1890s]. "The Trials and Triumphs of Self-made Men: An Address Delivered in Halifax, England, on January 4, 1860," *Halifax Courier*, January 7, 1860.

86 Two years ago, the Loguens came to Rochester...: Lewis Douglass to Amelia Loguen, June 1, 1861, reprinted in Bernier and Taylor. The younger brother is likely Fred, since he would have been working at the newspaper office then. "that near-masculine approach to men's unmentionables...": Ibid. She also sang...: Ibid.

CHAPTER 24

90 A year and a half into...: GG to WGjr, September 30, 1858. If only his father would have let him...: GG to WGjr., October 16, 1859. "to go back and work in...": GG to HG, March 14, 1858. "Everything is dead, dead, dead...": GG to WGjr, September 30. On October 18, fifty dollars arrived...: GG diary, October 18, 1858.

CHAPTER 25

94 George also quickly learned to avoid...: GG to HG, September 17, 1859. His father said he appreciated George's...: WLG to GG, February 11, 1859. George had suffered...: GG to WGjr, December 26, 1858.

95 "I am sure if I had it could have done...": GG to WLG, November 28, 1858. In December 1858, John Brown returned...: McGlone, 211. George understood the man to be a fugitive...: *Western Home Journal* (Lawrence, Kansas), February 3, 1859. The man was supposed to travel...: Doy, 23.

96 George was anxious to hear news of Brown's party...: GG diary, January 30, 1859. On his birthday—February 13...: GG diary, February 13, 1859.

CHAPTER 26

97 They had followed the harrowing...: Blight, 300. Brown was a hero...: Ibid., 301. But when Brown asked...: Ibid.

CHAPTER 27

98 "Heard to-day that there has been another fugitive...": Stevenson, 356. The marshal brought Webster...: Quoted in *The Liberator*,

April 8, 1859; *The Daily Evening Express* (Lancaster, PA), April 5, 1859.

99 "The Commissioner said that he released him...": *The Liberator*, April 15, 1859. "Others are inclined to believe...": Stevenson, 357. Sansom Street Hall...: Charlotte writes in her journal "Samson Hall" even though there's no venue in Philadelphia named that. I'm assuming she's making a play on words between Samson and Sanson. "A crowd of Southerners was present...": Stevenson, 357. Her uncle and Miller McKim had been...: Richards, 38. Charlotte knew she would remember that night...: Stevenson, 357–58.

PART 3

101 "He who looks upon a conflict...": Frederick Douglass, Why Should a Colored Man Enlist? *Douglass' Monthly*, April, 1863

CHAPTER 28

103 "attempted to seize the Arsenal...": *Frederick Douglass' Paper* October 21, 1859.

CHAPTER 29

106 "Tell Lewis (my oldest son) to secure...": Douglass, *Life and Times*, 378. So Lewis grabbed a chisel...: Ibid. Lewis destroyed the papers...: Fought, 171.

107 He'd almost been arrested...: Blight, 305. Six hours later, the federal marshals knocked...: Ibid., 3.

CHAPTER 30

109 "the death of Francis J. Meriam...": GG diary, November 1, 1859.

110 Meriam was not getting along with his family...: WGjr to GG, January 30, 1859. "I hoped to get George for my executor...": Ibid. William was worried Meriam meant...: Goodrich, 105 (William also let George know about the publication of Redpath's memoir). Meriam, newly back from Haiti...: WGjr to GG, October 28, 1859. Redpath had been interested in the possibility...: Reynolds, 107. Meriam heard about Brown's plans...: WGjr diary, October 19, 1859. George looked at the notice...: GG diary, November 1, 1859. The news of the insurrection and Meriam's death...: GG diary notes, September–November 1859. Now, no one could talk of anything else...: Mayer, 496.

111 Was Brown trying to take a group...: McGlone, 239. George could not simply look

out...: WGjr diary, November 23, 1859.
The troops arrived too quickly...: McGlone,
258. People sounded alarms...: *New York
Herald*, October 25, 1859. Rumors circled that
Northern friends...: McGlone, 317.

CHAPTER 31

112   "A good head...": Annie McKim to EW,
November 16, 1859.

113   Rebecca Spring was one of the Quaker...:
Carton, 328. "I charge you all never...": Drew,
48. "May we not feel that such worth...": Annie
McKim to EW, November 16, 1859. Like WLG,
Lucy's father...: *The John Brown Invasion*,
75, Cohen, 286. Garrison called the attack...:
The Liberator, October 21, 1859, *The Liberator*,
October 28, 1859. Brown was a hero...:
Quoted in Cohen, 286. He thought it would
all be too upsetting for her...: Mary Anne
Day Brown to Thomas Wentworth Higginson,
Eagleswood, Perth Amboy [N.J.], November
15, 1859.

CHAPTER 32

114   George had his beard...: WGjr diary,
November 23, 1859. William thought
Brown a martyr...: WGjr diary, December
1, 1859; WLG to GG, February 11, 1859.
During Brown's trial...: *The Liberator*,
October 28, 1859. "BUT LET NO ONE WHO
GLORIES...": Ibid. This was why many
questioned Meriam's sanity...: *The Liberator*,
November 11, 1859. Meriam confided that he
was... WGjr diary, December 2, 1859.

116   In the fall, Meriam heard...: Hinton, 569;
McGlone, 255–56. Less than a week before
the insurrection...: McGlone, 267, 274, 569.
When Meriam arrived...: Ibid, 256. Then
friends helped him...: Ibid., 257. Meriam's
friends had contacted...: WGjr diary,
December 2, 1859. That friend would take
Meriam...: Mayer, 500–502.

CHAPTER 33

117   It would have been improper...: Charters,
57

CHAPTER 34

121   "Can it be possible that...": Stevenson, 361.

122   Excerpts from "The Two Voices": C.L.F.,
National Anti-Slavery Standard, 1959.

CHAPTER 35

125   He could only be devastated...: *Douglass'*

Monthly, April 1860. His little sister, Annie...:
Fought, 172; Bernier and Taylor, 8. She'd been
upset by their father's...: *Douglass' Monthly*,
April 1860. Where Lewis had to go to work...:
Blight, 319. They sang a hymn and said a
prayer...: *Douglass' Monthly*, April 1860.
They'd been so happy...: Blight, 179–80.
Lewis, Fred, and their sister, Rosetta...:
Fought, 171. They moved to only publishing
Douglass' Monthly...: Frederick Douglass'
Paper, April 6, 1860. They were friends, maybe
more...: Lewis Douglass to Amelia Loguen,
December 8, 1861. Perhaps next May...: Lewis
Douglass to Amelia Loguen, December 22,
1860.

CHAPTER 36

127   Dr. Seth Rogers's water cure in Worcester,
Massachusetts...: Sometimes called Worcester
Hydropathic Institution, sometimes called
Worcester Water-Cure Institute. Hydropathic
doctors...: Legan, 267–80. "I love the
water...": Steveson, 74. He advertised in
The Liberator...: Smith, 317; Ling Lee.
Charlotte's treatment took all day...: Based
on Susan B. Anthony's account of her time at
Rogers's water cure, quoted in Sande Bishop,
"Historical Perspective: 19th Century Water
Cures," Worcester Medicine, Summer 2003.

128   "a world of good—spiritually as well as
physically...": Stevenson, 361.

CHAPTER 37

130   Senator Charles Sumner's speech...:
Sumner.

131   "Is't [sic] not splendid?...": LM to EW,
June 1860.

CHAPTER 38

132   In August, his brother Wendell...: WeG
diary, August 14, 1860; August 16, 1860. They
looked like a militia...: Grinspan, 357–78.

133   Outside the door hung an illuminated
sign...: *Boston Evening Transcript*, October
16, 1860. A band from Bangor, Maine...:
Boston Evening Transcript, October 17, 1860.
A delegation of about two hundred Black Wide
Awakes...: *The Liberator*, October 19, 1860.

134   Even if the parade route had gone by
Dix Place...: WeG diary, August 16, 1860.
George and everyone else along the route...:
Mayer, 513. "On Tuesday last, the Presidential
struggle...": *The Liberator*, November 9, 1860.
George's friend in Minnesota...: William B.
Reed to GG, December 6, 1860.

CHAPTER 39

140 On February 18, 1861...: Blight, 337. Two weeks later, Lincoln entered...: *Douglass' Monthly*, April 1861.

141 In President Lincoln's inaugural address...: Sturdevant, 8. How could he make a living...: Ibid., 8.

CHAPTER 40

145 The day before, Saturday...: *The Liberator*, April 19,1861.

CHAPTER 41

147 He spoke almost every Sunday: Blight, 342. "The cry now is for war...": Quoted in Blight, 346.

CHAPTER 42

148 Their good friend Norwood Hallowell...: Ireland. Norwood left Harvard and enlisted...: Brown. By May, Harvard's campus...: Egerton, 34.

CHAPTER 43

149 Ellen was smitten...: EW to LM, March 16, 1861. In mid-May, 1861, Lucy...: LM to EW, May 16, 1861.

150 "It seems to be less of a farce now to celebrate...": EW to LM, June 29, 1861.

CHAPTER 44

153 At the end of October 1861...: LM to EW, November 11,[?]1861, Smith College; *The Liberator*, November 8, 1861. Wendell drove Lucy and her sister...: WeG to family, October 31, 1861. If it ended in compromise...: Mayer, 520. William had given speeches...: Alonso, 156, 159. Ellen hoped "this dreadful war...": EW to [William] Beverly Chase, November 13, 1861. "What do you think of my disguising myself...": EW to LM, November 16, 1861.

154 Enlisting was a fantasy, and instead...: EW to LM, November 16, 1861.

CHAPTER 45

155 The war didn't seem to...: Stevenson, 363–64

CHAPTER 46

156 "What has the new year for us?...": 156: LM to EW, December 29, 1861.

CHAPTER 47

160 The South Carolina Sea Islands were a small scale...: Cohen, 304. Her father, on the other hand, was sick...: Charters, 98–100.

161 Her father was glad...: Ibid., 102. Although free Black men in the North...: Robbins, (General Hunter also enlisted men against their will).

CHAPTER 48

166 She saw William Lloyd Garrison...: GG diary, July 4. "How glad I was to see the Dr. again...": Stevenson, 367.

167 "The nation is reeling and staggering...": "Anti-Slavery Celebration at Framingham, July 4, 1862," *The Liberator*, July 18, 1862.

168 Black Americans needed "all the rights...": Susan B. Anthony Papers, 1815–1961, manuscript speeches, Fourth of July address, Framingham, Massachusetts, 1862, A-143, folder 29, Schlesinger Library, Radcliffe Institute, Harvard University, Cambridge, Massachusetts.

CHAPTER 49

170 Lucy felt "a steady influx...": LM to EW, undated letter from between June 1861 to August 1861. "Why are the men so sluggish?...": Ibid. "Noble boys!...": LM to EW, August 12, 1862. Now, Lucy wanted to refuse...: LM to EW, September 15, 1862.

CHAPTER 50

172 "Georgie, I can't feel willing to have you go...": FG to GG, August 12, 1862. "inclined to think he shall go...": Merrill, 106. His father's hope was...: Ibid., 107.

CHAPTER 51

173 He was in "one of his most delightful...": Stevenson, 372. "enjoyable throughout...": Ibid., 372. Whittier also suggested...: Ibid., 374. "oppressed and suffering people...": Ibid., 67. "I shall certainly take his advice...": Ibid., 372.

174 In the end, they claimed...: Ibid., 381.

CHAPTER 52

175 As soon as Union troops started freeing...: Scheips, 419, 423. While Lewis's father had once written...: *Douglass' Monthly*, July 1861. In late summer 1862, Lewis...: McPherson, 396. Pomeroy proposed a new...: Scheips, 423; McPherson, 396.

176 Pomeroy asked Lewis's father…: Douglas, 73. "Day after day freshens…": Lewis Douglass to Amelia Loguen, June 14, 1862. Douglass was also sure to tell the senator…: Bernier, 16–17. Lewis decided he would leave…: Ibid.

CHAPTER 53

178 *The Liberator* printed the full text…: *The Liberator*, September 26, 1862. Ellen's mother thought it…: EW to Susan B. Anthony, September 18, 1862. "slave-hunting in the Free States…": Quoted in Smith, 3.

178 "O! That proclamation! Is it not worth living for… ": LM to EW, October 1, 1862. "Dick was quiet…": Ibid.

CHAPTER 54

181 Draftees could hire a substitute…: Mayer, 533. "Some 300 [white men] were drafted today…": GG diary, October 15, 1862.

CHAPTER 55

182 He said his goodbyes to his family…: Bernier, 16–17. "nothing [would] arise…": Lewis Douglass to Amelia Loguen, December 8, 1861. When Lewis arrived in Philadelphia…: Lewis Douglass to Amelia Loguen, November 20, 1862. The Central American Colonization Scheme Abandoned…: *The Liberator*, September 5, 1862.

183 "the colonization expedition": *New-York Daily Tribune*, October 16, 1862. Lewis didn't know what to do…: Lewis Douglass to Amelia Loguen, November 20, 1862. "wise ending to a singularly foolish beginning…": Quoted in McPherson, 397.

CHAPTER 56

184 Charlotte "was astonished, stupefied…": Stevenson, 382.

185 She was nervous that…: Ibid., 383. Being on the water calmed… Ibid., 385. She stepped into a boat rowed…: Ibid., 389. Then the men began to sing "Roll, Jordan, Roll…": *The Liberator*, December 12, 1862. "For to hear when Jordan roll…": Allen.

186 "Ah! It was good to be able to sing that here…": Stevenson, 390. They couldn't make it all the way…: Charlotte Forten writes that the plantation is "Oaklands," but the Oaks was where Towne was staying and the name of the home on the plantation that had belonged to the Pope family. The next morning, everything…: Stevenson, 391. The house

was dilapidated, Charlotte thought…: *The Liberator*, December 12, 1862

187 Here in South Carolina, Charlotte saw…: Long, 43. That would never be as real…: Stevenson, 399–400.

188 "Had we not other causes…": *The Liberator*, December 19, 1862. General Rufus Saxton had declared it…: *The Liberator*, December 26, 1862. As soon as Charlotte heard Higginson's name… *The Liberator*, December 19, 1862. "the happiest, the most jubilant…": Stevenson, 407. Charlotte received a package…: Ibid.

CHAPTER 57

189 Lucy's father had been speaking…: "Negro Songs," *Dwight's Journal of Music* 21, no. 9 (August 9, 1862), LM, "Songs of the Port Royal 'Contrabands,'" *Dwight's Journal of Music* 22, no. 6 (November 8, 1862).

CHAPTER 58

193 Since she was young…: Stevenson., 117. Seeing the happiness of this… Ibid., 140.

194 Charlotte, Ellen Murray, and Laura Towne…: Charlotte writes that they gathered at the school in her journal and the church in her article about the occasion. I can't determine which is correct, so I stuck with the church since that was what she published. "It was very pleasant to see…": Charlotte Forten, "New-Year's Day on the Islands of South Carolina, 1863," *The Atlantic*, 254. "O, none in all the world…": Ibid., 254. Charlotte loved her voice…: Stevenson, 425. "to her heart's content…": Forten, "New-Year's Day," 253.

PART 5

195 "There must come liberty and there must come peace": Lucy Stone quoted in *The Liberator*, June 16, 1854.

CHAPTER 59

197 New Year's Day 1863 would be "the most glorious day…": Stevenson, 428.

198 First, the ruins of the old British fort…: Forten, "New-Year's Day," 253. Dr. Rogers was a close friend…: Smith, Black Soldiers in Blue, 317. "How delighted I was to see him…": Stevenson, 429.

199 After the speeches, Charlotte joined…: Ibid., 428–34. For as long as she could remember, those words…: Ibid. She knew that the government…: Forten, "New-Year's Day," 257.

CHAPTER 60

200　Despite the chill in Boston…: WGjr diary, January 1, 1863. As the Garrisons entered…: Mayer, 545. Famous New England writers: Blight, 382. A pro-slavery mob almost killed…: Mayer, 122; Alonso, 47. Lobgesang…: Felix Mendelssohn: Lobgesang (Song of Praise), A Symphony-Cantata, Op. 52.

201　The proclamation was not perfect…: Egerton, 63. "It has been a most magnificent day…": GG diary, January 1, 1863.

CHAPTER 61

203　Dick was struck in the left cheek…: Lucy quotes this in her February 10, 1863, letter to EW.

204　Lucy wanted to cry….: New-York Daily Tribune, January 3, 1863. Actual totals of Union casualties would reach almost thirteen thousand, among a total of about twenty-five thousand deaths on both sides, according to the National Battlefield Trust. "Death is the last Professor…": LM to EW, January 21, 1862 (Lucy copied portions of Hough's letter in her message to Ellen).

205　"Womanhood is as good as manhood anyway…": LM to EW, February 10, 1863.

CHAPTER 62

206　She saw Black children…: Charlotte Forten, "Life on the Sea Islands," The Atlantic, May 1864, 587.

207　"I am glad I saw her—very glad…": Stevenson, 442–43.

CHAPTER 63

208　On January 26, 1863, Secretary…: Douglas, 71. George Luther Stearns…: Ibid., 72. "the same wages, the same rations…": McGlone, 167; Douglass' Monthly, March 1863.

209　"Manhood requires you…": Frederick Douglass, "Why Should a Colored Man Enlist?" Douglass' Monthly, April 1863. This was the chance to "wipe out…": Douglass' Monthly, March 1863. "The Syracuse men," Lewis told Amelia…: Lewis Douglass to Amelia Loguen, March 31, 1863.

CHAPTER 64

213　"5 ft 9 inches Brown complexion…": Bernier, 124. Finally, Lewis had to "promise…": Lewis Douglass to Amelia

Loguen, April 8, 1863. His pants were a light blue…: Ibid. As a sergeant major…: Douglas, 74.

214　But his building was not yet…: Lewis Douglass to Amelia Loguen, April 8, 1863. "immediately punished, by chaining…": Ibid.

CHAPTER 65

215　They'd rented a hall in central Boston…: Alonso, 201–202. Their old teacher Theodore Weld…: Ellen's letter to her mother about the party doesn't mention George's presence, but his diary mentions the party, and he did like to dance. I think his absence in the letter is more about Ellen's lack of interest in George. The last time Lucy…: LM to EW, November 11, 1861; The Liberator, November 8, 1861. Ellen thought she could tell…: EW diary, October 1859, SC; Alonso, 202.

216　Lucy and Ellen stayed…: GG diary, March 20, 1863. They visited friends…: WGjr diary, March 1863. Lucy played and…: Charters, 151; WGjr diary, March 19, 1863.

CHAPTER 66

217　Norwood Hallowell walked into the Garrison home…: (Norwood was also nicknamed "Pen" by his family, but George, Lucy, and their friends and family all refer to him as Norwood) Egerton, 42. He had injured his arm…: WGjr diary, January 1, 1863. George had immense respect…: GG diary, April 20, 1863. George even donated…: GG diary, March 20, 1863. More Black men wanted…: GG diary, May 7, 1863.

218　By May 11, George…: GG diary, May 11, 1863; WGjr diary, May 11, 1863. When his father returned…: WGjr diary, May 16, 1863; GG diary, May 18, 1863. But as much as his father hated…: WLG to GG, June 11, 1863. This was not about an adventure…: GG to Mr. Goodrich, July 1, 1863. George's mother was more concerned…: WLG to GG, June 11, 1863.

219　On June 1, George spent…: GG diary, June 1, 1863. She wrote that she heard…: FG to GG, June 6, 1863. Other family friends gave him presents…: Goodrich to GG, July 1, 1863.

CHAPTER 67

220　By early May 1863…: Lewis Douglass to Amelia Loguen, May 9, 1863. On May 18, 1863…: Lewis Douglass to Amelia Loguen, May 20, 1863.

221　Now that they were in the army…: Emilio, 27. "We are fighting a battle…": Ibid., 29. Lewis thought of the "inexpressible…": Lewis Douglass to Amelia Loguen, May 20, 1863.

222　When the governor spoke to the regiment…: Lewis Douglass to Amelia Loguen, April 15, 1863. It took them almost four hours…: Emilio, 33. Sometimes, it could be nice to have such a prominent father…: Blight, 399.

CHAPTER 68

226　Wendell believed hiring a substitute…: WLG to GG, July 30, 1863. George knew that his brothers…: Henry Mayer estimates that 60 percent of draftees in 1863 paid the fee. George also heard that the draft…: GG diary, July 13, 1863.

227　The rioters murdered eleven…: Egerton, 118–119; Mayer, 553. The police and the military managed…: WGjr diary, July 14, 1863. The band still played…: Mayer, 554. "We feared no attack…": GG to HG, August 3, 1863. The parade paused at the statehouse…: WGjr diary, July 14, 1863, SC; Noah Trudeau, 36–37. George saw his mother and father…: GG diary, July 21, 1863.

228　Even though George went to Dix Place…: WGjr diary, July 18, 1863; WLG to GG, August 6, 1863. As they approached the wharf…: Trudeau, 36–37. The rumors were already rampant… FG to GG, July 30, 1863. "nothing but praise to give you…": WLG to GG, Aug. 6, 1863.

CHAPTER 69

229　Lewis slogged through sand…: Blight, 400–401; Clinton Cox, 66; Emilio, 64–68. The bombs going off…: Emilio, 70–71. They kept moving forward…: Ibid., 72.

230　"Now I want you to prove yourselves as men…": Quoted in Trudeau, 81. And as the hail hit, men fell…: Lewis Douglass to Amelia Loguen, July 20, 1863. They collapsed like stalks…: Quoted in Trudeau, 83. Men ran out of the way…: Lewis Douglass to Amelia Loguen, July 20, 1863. They lost formation…: Trudeau, 82. Lewis yelled for the men to press on…: Blight, 400. Something struck Lewis…: Quoted in Trudeau, 83. One moment he was surround…: Lewis Douglass to Amelia Loguen, July 20, 1863. Around Lewis was a sea of bodies…: Trudeau, 86.

231　"Remember if I die I die…": Lewis Douglass to Amelia Loguen, July 20, 1863.

CHAPTER 70

235　One jacket was so torn up…: Stevenson, 495. "Brave fellows!…": Ibid., 497.

235　"I take my good Dr.'s advice…": Ibid., 499.

CHAPTER 71

240　Wendell Garrison's letter lay…: LM to WLG, September 4, 1863. Lucy had even spoken to Wendell's sister…: FG to GG, August 6, 1863. "Forgive this hard, unsatisfactory letter…": LM to WLG, September 4, 1863. Or like Ellen's brother…: EW to LM, August 21, 1863.

CHAPTER 72

242　"The whole regiment goes bathing every morning…": GG to WLG, August 23, 1863.

243　"not got a constitution strong…": GG to WGjr., September 1, 1863. They would learn to keep cool…: GG to WGjr, September 1, 1863. This fatigue duty was only…: GG diary, August 3, 1863. "They enlisted with the…": GG to HG, September 6, 1863. The work was hard, and seemingly…: GG to WGjr, September 1, 1863; GG to HG, September 6, 1863.

CHAPTER 73

244　Lewis arrived at the hospital… Douglas, 80; Egerton, 157–58. In his letters since the Battle of Fort Wagner… Lewis Douglass to Amelia Loguen, July 20, 1863. Lewis could scarcely admit how sick…: Bryan Greene, "America's First Black Physician Sought to Heal a Nation's Persistent Illness," *Smithsonian Magazine*, February 26, 2021. Those two symptoms were not…: Jabir, 71. "spontaneous gangrene…": Egerton, 157–58.

245　Lewis's father rushed…: Douglas, 80. Lewis's father also pressed…: Blight, 409.

CHAPTER 74

246　To get a box from home…: GG to WLG, November 26, 1863. Inside, he found cranberry jelly…: WLG to GG, September 18, 1863. George learned that Wendell…: WeG to GG, October 21, 1863. Their father printed parts…: WGjr, to GG, September 18, 1863. Thirty-two men had died…: GG diary, September 1863; Trudeau, 43.

247　The troops felt this was…: Egerton, 208. George finally did receive pay…: GG to WGjr, December 10, 1863. George's brother Frank thought…: Francis Garrison to GG, September 27, 1863. "There was hardly a bakers dozen…": GG to WGjr, December 10, 1863. "but admire their unanimity in refusing…": Ibid.

CHAPTER 75

248 He could sit in the quiet library…: Lewis Douglas to Amelia Loguen, May 9, 1863. This was the place where their family…: Blight, 421; Fought, 190. Like their father, Nathan…: Fought thinks he may have run away in 1858, but she is not clear on this detail of Sprague's life. Rosetta had always thought…: Sprague Douglass, 95.

249 In the parlor, the reverend led…: Douglas, 86; Minutes of the Universalist General Convention, 1880, 28. "for we cannot speak to a colored girl in this city…": Lewis Douglass to Amelia Loguen, January 31, 1864. "love, obey, cherish and protect each other…": Ibid.

CHAPTER 76

250 Charlotte returned to South Carolina in October 1863…: Stevenson, xxxvii.

CHAPTER 77

251 Over the winter, George…: GG diary, February 6, 1864. Shy George was very surprised…: GG to WGjr, February 10, 1864. Tubman had been on Folly…: GG diary, February 6, 1864.

252 She wanted to return to the North, but…: GG to WGjr, February 10, 1864. She learned where the Confederate troops…: Egerton, 99, 190; Sterling, 260. In one particularly daring raid…: Sterling, 258–60.

CHAPTER 78

253 The audience on the first morning…": *The Liberator*, May 20, 1864. "Mr. Garrison was right…": LM to EW, May 27, 1864.

254 Even Wendell Garrison admitted…: WeG to GG, May 22, 1864. "Wendell developed into…": LM to EW, May 27, 1864. He had resolved…: GG to LM, date unknown. "We have come to the decision…": LM to EW, June 26, 1864.

255 Christian Recorder—APRIL 23, 1864…: Reprinted in Trudeau, 112. Weekly Anglo-African—APRIL 30, 1864…: Ibid., 83— 84. Christian Recorder—MAY 24, 1864…: Ibid., 146–47. Probably Corporal John H. B. Payne.

CHAPTER 79

256 During the spring of 1864…: GG to

WLG, May 1, 1864. On June 1, 1864, George's commanding officer…: GG diary, May 19, 1864, and June 1, 1864. In fact, it was a great relief…: GG to HG, June 7, 1864.

257 "Shoot him!": GG to HG, March 29, 1864. "Please use your influence…": GG to WLG, May 1, 1864. George's father said that he had private…: GG diary, May 12, 1864. George knew that the bill…: WLG to GG, June 21, 1864. "full justice will be done…": Hopefully, the equal pay…: GG to WGjr, June 14, 1864. "[I] hope it will do some good…": GG diary, July 24, 1864.

CHAPTER 80

258 Lewis and his employer worked on Hilton Head…: Lewis Douglass to Amelia Loguen, May 20, 1863; Egerton, 242. Lewis sold food and goods…: Giselle White-Perry. In Mitchelville, the freed people…: Lewis Douglass to Amelia Loguen, September 28, 1864. Every night, Lewis could hear…: Byrd, 15–30. Every night, Lewis…: Lewis Douglass to Amelia Loguen, September 28, 1864. Lewis found he could share…: Quoted in Bernier, 471.

CHAPTER 81

263 "There are autumn strains…": LM to GG, September 1, 1864. Lucy kept up a correspondence with Laura Towne…: LM to GG, September 4, 1864. Towne could do what…: LM to GG, November 2, 1864.

264 On the evening of September 17, 1864…: WGjr to GG, September 25, 1864. They decorated the parlor…: FG to GG, October 9, 1864; GG to GG, September 17, 1864.

CHAPTER 82

266 A regimental doctor who…: GG diary, October 4, 1864. George would have liked…: GG to Francis Garrison, September 9, 1864. George's men had their own…: GG diary, September 29, 1864; October 5, 1864.

267 Five days later, the men…: Trudeau, 150–52. They adopted resolutions during the ceremony…: Ibid., 154. It was time for him and his siblings…: GG to GG, October 2, 1865. His sister, Fanny, wrote…: FG to GG, August 21, 1865. George hoped that their father…: GG to GG, August 12, 1865.

CHAPTER 83

269 "There must be tremendous…": GG diary, November 7, 1864. He hoped that President Lincoln…: GG diary, September 15, 1864;

WLG to GG, November 8, 1864.On November 16, George received...: GG diary, November 16, 1864. George thought the news...: GG to WLG and HG, November 2, 1864; GG to WGjr, November 21 1864. He was expecting Confederate...: GG to WLG, November 11, 1864. Soon, George could be back...: GG to WGjr, November 21, 1864.

270 He could listen to his father...: WGjr to GG, November 20, 1864.On November 27, 1864, George...: GG to WLG and HG, December 3, 1864. Then they had no choice...: GG diary, November 30, 1864; GG to FG, December 11, 1864.

271 "It was a perfect massacre...": GG to WLG and HG, December 3, 1864. "Everything here is dull...": GG diary, December 20, 1864. On December 23, George...: GG diary, December 23, 1864.

CHAPTER 84

272 A rainy day wouldn't dampen Lucy's mood...: M. Du Pays, "Letters from New York, XXIII," *The Liberator*, December 23, 1864 [M. Du Pays was a pen name of Wendell Garrison]. Lucy's father had been traveling: Brown, 69–70; Cohen, 305. When the Freed-men's Association realized...: WeG to GG, December 25, 1864; The Pennsylvania Freedmen's Bulletin (February 1865). Lucy walked with them...: LM to EW, December 15, 1864. The Association modeled the schools...: "Letters from New York, XXIII," *The Liberator*, December 23, 1864.

273 They visited five of the Freedmen's Association schools...: Ibid. Lucy's father had also...: WeG to GG, December 25, 1864. Wendell told Lucy...: WeG to LM, September 4, 1864. "The moment is critical...": WeG to GG, December 25, 1864. At one point in Washington, Wendell...: LM to EW, December 15, 1864. When the December 15 issue of the Independent...: "The Freedmen and Their Friends," *Independent* 16, no. 837, December 15, 1864.

CHAPTER 85

277 George and the 55th Massachusetts marched...: GG diary, February 20, 1865. On the evening of February 21...: GG to WGjr, March 1, 1865. The men of the 55th were overjoyed...: GG diary, February 21, 1865. As they paused on one street...: Ibid. The men of the 55th responded...: GG to FG, March 15, 1865. Rebel soldiers and overseers...: GG diary, March 7, 1865; April 8, 1865.

279 "The end of this most accursed...": GG diary, April 13, 1865; GG diary, April 14, 1865. George's father was, of course...: GG diary, April 15–16, 1865.

280 Before returning to Boston...: GG to [Unknown first name] Drew, April 25, 1865. George and his father began the day...: GG diary, April 18, 1865. George stood outside...: GG diary, April 22, 1865.

PART 6

283 "Are we who are alive spared for some purpose?": EW to LM, August 21, 1863.

CHAPTER 86

285 Lewis wrote to his sweetheart...: Lewis Douglass to Amelia Loguen, March 26, 1865.

286 On Monday, June 5, 1865... Lewis H. Douglass to Frederick Douglass, June 9, 1865. His father once wrote a public letter...: Frederick Douglass, "To my Old Master," Thomas Auld." Lewis and his siblings had gone to school...: In Baltimore, Maryland, the Oblate Sisters opened a Catholic school for Black children in the late 1820s and there were other private and home-based schools (not unlike the one Charlotte Forten's aunt ran in Philadelphia) among free Blacks in the state. See Joseph Browne, " 'To Bring out the Intellect of the Race': An African American Freedmen's Bureau Agent in Maryland," *Maryland Historical Magazine*, Winter 2009; "Oblate Sisters of Baltimore," https://oblatesisters.com/history (accessed August 20, 2024).

287 "The white people will do any...": "Mr. Frederick Douglass," *The Sun*, June 15, 1865, 2. Lewis was proving to his father...: Frederick Douglass, "The Annotated Frederick Douglass," *The Atlantic*, November 13, 2023. Lewis worked the rest...: Lewis Douglass to Amelia Loguen, January 7, 1866. The convention's goal was...: "MARYLAND: Convention of Colored Persons," *The New York Times*, December 30, 1865.

288 "This I conceive to be... ": Lewis Douglass to Amelia Loguen, January 7, 1866.

CHAPTER 87

289 Charlotte had not been well since she...: Alonso, 115. Dr. Lewis had advertised...: John Greenleaf Whittier to Theodore Dwight Weld, July 28, 1865, reprinted in *The Letters of John Greenleaf Whittier*. Young women were weak...: Dio Lewis, Catalogue and circular

of Dr. Dio Lewis's Family School for Young Ladies, Lexington, Mass., 1865. Whittier asked Theodore...: John Greenleaf Whittier to Theodore Dwight Weld, July 28, 1865, reprinted in *The Letters of John Greenleaf Whittier.*

290 Charlotte yet again faced...: *The Biography of Dio Lewis*, 110. "To take her at all would...": John Greenleaf Whittier to Annie Fields, September 13, 1865, reprinted in *The Letters of John Greenleaf Whittier*. In October 1865, Charlotte...: Stevenson, 49.They would not deny...: "New England Branch Freedmen's Union Commission," September 1, 1866, Duke University Libraries Digital Repository, https://repository.duke.edu/dc/broadsides/bdsma20801 (accessed August 22, 2024). In Maryland, it was hard for white teachers...: "Report of the Teachers' Committee," *The Freedmen's Record* IV no. 4 (April 1868).

CHAPTER 88

292 George also returned to help...: Alonso, 220. George's mother worried about...: Ibid., 237.

CHAPTER 89

294 "I think I should start to hear you...": Ellen Wright Garrison to Lucy McKim Garrison, December 1865. The day had been sunny and warm...: Lucy McKim Garrison to Helen [Garrison?], December 1, 1865. In their first months of marriage...: "About Us," *The Nation*, https://www.thenation.com/about-us-and-contact/ (accessed August 23, 2024). Lucy helped Wendell...: Charters, 186–87.

295 By the fall of 1866, Lucy was pregnant...: Ibid., 172. Wendell met with Allen...: Allen, xxxvii.

296 On May 4, 1867, Lucy gave birth...: WeG to HG, June 23, 1867, quoted in Charters, 204. "We welcome the volume before us...": Quoted in Charters, 216.

CHAPTER 90

297 "We are very glad that...": Quoted in Charters, 220. The first time she'd heard...: Quoted in Barnes, 243. Now, from a chilly Boston...: Quoted in Charters, 220–221. Even without Dio Lewis's school...: Stevenson, xxxviii; John Greenleaf Whittier to Charles Sumner, September 10, 1870, reprinted in *The Letters of John Greenleaf Whittier*; Greenridge, 198.

298 Her people were now free in Charleston...: Greenridge, 225.

CHAPTER 91

301 In January 1866...: Bernier, 17. "general instruction in the common...": Quoted in Bernier, 18.

CHAPTER 92

303 In August 1868...: Alonso, 238. The fire could not have come...: Ibid., 244–45. George had planned on being...: Association of Officers of the 55th Massachusetts Volunteer Infantry Records, 1864–1904; MHS (Box 1, Folder 14, Circulars, 1867–1880, Image 8).

CHAPTER 93

305 Throughout his life, Lewis Douglass...: Bernier, 21–23. By the time her daughter, Katherine...: Charters, 240.

306 Lucy's health continued to get worse...: Charters, 245. In 1878, Charlotte began a courtship...: Grimké, Francis J. Francis didn't believe that...: Greenridge, 279. Charlotte continued to write poems...: Stevenson, xxxix–xl. George had also been keeping newspaper clippings...: GG to Capt. [Charles C.] Soule, March 27, 1895.

307 George and Annie Anthony finally...: Alonso, 307.

309 This percentage increased...: Brown, Lois A., 45. In *Slavery by Another Name*...: Blackmon, 67. Black men were arrested and sentenced...: ACLU report, https://www.aclu.org/news/human-rights/captive-labor-exploitation-of-incarcerated-workers.

310 Americans are being forced to work for nearly...: Brown, Clair H. And while slave patrollers...: Lepore.

PHOTO CREDITS

p. 3: Library of Congress, Prints and Photographs Division

p. 19: Boston Public Library, Rare Books Department

p. 28: Library of Congress, Prints and Photographs Division

p. 41: Library of Congress, Geography and Map Division

p. 44: Garrison Family Papers, Smith College Special Collections

p. 48: Garrison Family Papers, Smith College Special Collections

p. 56: Garrison Family Papers, Smith College Special Collections

p. 61: Library of Congress, Prints and Photographs Division

p.62: Garrison family papers, Massachusetts Historical Society

p. 68: Garrison Family Papers, Smith College Special Collections

p. 75: Library Company of Philadelphia, Annie Woods Webb Papers

p. 88: Garrison Family Papers, Smith College Special Collections

p. 91: Garrison family papers, Massachusetts Historical Society

p. 120: Garrison Family Papers, Smith College Special Collections

p. 135: Library of Congress, Prints and Photographs Division

p. 139: Garrison Family Papers, Smith College Special Collections

p. 154: Garrison Family Papers, Smith College Special Collections

p. 164: Library of Congress, Prints and Photographs Division

p. 168: Massachusetts Historical Society

p. 178: Library of Congress, Prints and Photographs Division

p. 191: Garrison Family Papers, Smith College Special Collections

p. 202: Garrison Family Papers, Smith College Special Collections

p. 210: Massachusetts Historical Society

p. 214: Museum of African American History, Boston and Nantucket

p. 219: Garrison Family Papers, Smith College Special Collections

p. 241: Garrison Family Papers, Smith College Special Collections

p. 265: Garrison Family Papers, Smith College Special Collections

p. 293: Garrison Family Papers, Smith College Special Collections

p. 296: Garrison Family Papers, Smith College Special Collections

p. 298: Library Company of Philadelphia, Annie Woods Webb Papers

p. 300: National Park Service (FRDO 4552)

INDEX

Black veterans, pension discrimination against, 304
Bloomer, Amelia, 87
Boston, Massachusetts, 16, *19*, 77, 84, 116, 173, 202, 222, 224, 303
    55th Massachusetts Regiment in, 226–28
    abolitionists in, 99
    Charlotte Forten in, 21–25, 169, 289–90, 297–98
    draft riot started in, 227
    George Garrison in, 14–16, 26–28, 30–32, 40–41, 45–47, 114–16, 145–46, 148, 172, 181, 200–201, 217–22, 226–28, 242, 292–93
    Lucy McKim in, 215–16
Boston Daily Evening Transcript, 16
Boston Evening Transcript, 46, 133, 219, 268
Boston Female Anti-Slavery Society, 54
Boston Journal, 159, 278
Boston Lancers, 27
Boston Library, 298
Boston Music Hall, 54, 200, 275
    Grand Jubilee Concert, *202*
Boston Vigilance Committee, 16, 22, 26–27
Brazil, 311
Breckenridge, John C., 132
Brisbane, William Henry, 198
Brontë, Charlotte, 79
Brooklyn Daily Eagle, *299*
Brooks, Preston, 77, 130
Brown, Anna, 119
Brown, Ellen, 119
Brown, Henry "Box," *4*, 5–7, 73
Brown, John, 35, 81, 82–83, 95–96, 112, 126, 127, 153, 208, 209, 222, 278
    arrest of, 111
    body of, 117, 118
    burial of, 119
    death of, 104, 115–16, 125
    Douglass and, 97
    execution of, 115–16
    Frederick Douglass and, 97, 104, 106
    in Harpers Ferry, Virginia, 103–4, 133
    in jail, 113, 114
    in Kansas, 110
    in Rochester, New York, 97
    trial of, 112, 114–15
Brown, Mary, 112–13, 117, 118, 119
Brown, Oliver, 119
Brown, Sarah, 119
Brown, Watson, 119
Buchanan, James, *44*, 46, 53, 59
Burns, Anthony, 16, 17–20, 21–25, 26–28, *28*, 29, 34, 51, 69, 98, 99, 116, 153, 310
Butman, Asa, 16
Byberry, Pennsylvania, 67, 121

Camp Meigs, 209, 213–14, 217, *219*, 220–21, 222, 242, 266

Camp Saxton, 295
Canada, 12, 13, 54, 107, 111, 115, 116, 207, 278
Cassey, Henry, 155
Central American Colonization Scheme, 175–76, 182, 183, 259
Charleston, South Carolina, 118, 145, 185, 229, 266, 290, 298
    assault on, 232, 233, 236–37, 238, 239, 270
    march toward, 277–80
    rebel evacuation of, 276
Charleston Hotel, 279–80
Charles Town, (West) Virginia, 115, 115n7, 117, 118
Chase, Beverly, 149, 156, 170–71, 204, 241
Chase, Dick, 149, 156, 170–71, 178, 179, 203–4, 215, 241, 254
    death of, 254
Chase, Edith, 204
Chicago, Illinois, 65, 129
Child, Lydia Maria, 56
Chiriquí, Panama, 175–76, 182, 183, 259
citizenship, Black Americans and, 59–60, 141, 168, 291
Citizens Policing Project, 308, 309
the *City Belle*, 65
Civil War, 1, 145–94, 157, 159, 197–281. *See also specific locations*
    beginning of, 145–46, 146, 147–48, 149, 152–53, *154*
    contrabands and, 157
    death of Dick Chase in, 203–4
    deaths in, 203–5, 241
    draft and, 226–27
    drawing to close, 269–70, 276, 277–80, 281
    first general engagement of, 151
    injuries in, 230–31, 241
    in the press, 146, 151, 157, 158, 159, 211, 212, 233, 255
    war effort, 170–71, 173–74, 179
Cole, John, 161
colonization, 175–76, 182, 183, 259
Colorado, 301
Colored Orphan Asylum, 227
Commission in Boston, 298
Concord, Massachusetts, 116, 172
Confederacy, 137, 152, 167, 252
Confederate Army, 214, 243, 245, 252, 270, 298
contrabands, 157, 159, 160, 192, 252. *See also* freed people
Convention of Radical Political Abolitionists, 34, 35, 81
cotton, 161, 310

Dangerfield, Daniel, 99
Darien, Georgia, 225
Davis, Jefferson, 152
Dayton, Wm. L., 38
Declaration of Independence, 28, 83
the *Delaware*, 280